Migration Between Nations

From refugees fleeing wars or natural disasters to economic migrants pursuing better paid jobs abroad, international migration is an inescapable part of the modern world. *Migration Between Nations: A Global Introduction* provides a succinct and accessible overview of the varied types of migrants who cross national boundaries.

Drawing upon a wide-ranging selection of case studies and the latest research findings, migration patterns and recent trends throughout the world are surveyed and summarized, with particular attention to movement from the global south to the global north. In a highly inter-disciplinary analysis, the social, cultural and economic integration of migrants and of their offspring in their new homelands are also explored. Employing approaches from a number of disciplines, the methods and techniques that researchers use to study various aspects of migration and integration are also explained.

Migration Between Nations: A Global Introduction will be essential reading for students in a wide range of disciplines in the humanities and social sciences, including sociology, anthropology, ethnic studies, geography, global studies, history, and political science.

Mark Abrahamson is Emeritus Professor of Sociology at the University of Connecticut, USA. His former positions include Executive Director of the Roper Center for Public Opinion Research; Program Director at the National Science Foundation; and Professor of Sociology at Syracuse University, USA. He is the author of more than 20 books and monographs, and numerous research articles in major social science journals. Among his recent books are *Globalizing Cities: A Brief Introduction* (Routledge, 2019); *Studying Cities and City Life: An Introduction to Methods of Research* (Routledge, 2016); *Urban Sociology: A Global Introduction* (Cambridge University Press, 2014), and *Classical Theory and Modern Studies: Introduction to Sociological Theory* (Pearson, 2010).

Migration Between Nations
A Global Introduction

Mark Abrahamson

LONDON AND NEW YORK

First published 2023
by Routledge
4 Park Square, Milton Park, Abingdon, Oxon OX14 4RN

and by Routledge
605 Third Avenue, New York, NY 10158

Routledge is an imprint of the Taylor & Francis Group, an Informa business

© 2023 Mark Abrahamson

The right of Mark Abrahamson to be identified as author of this work has been asserted by them in accordance with sections 77 and 78 of the Copyright, Designs and Patents Act 1988.

All rights reserved. No part of this book may be reprinted or reproduced or utilised in any form or by any electronic, mechanical, or other means, now known or hereafter invented, including photocopying and recording, or in any information storage or retrieval system, without permission in writing from the publishers.

Trademark notice: Product or corporate names may be trademarks or registered trademarks, and are used only for identification and explanation without intent to infringe.

British Library Cataloguing-in-Publication Data
A catalogue record for this book is available from the British Library

ISBN: 978-0-367-74541-7 (hbk)
ISBN: 978-0-367-74542-4 (pbk)
ISBN: 978-1-003-15840-0 (ebk)

DOI: 10.4324/9781003158400

Typeset in Bembo
by MPS Limited, Dehradun

Contents

List of Figures ix
List of Tables x
List of Boxes xi
Preface xii

1 Globalization and Migration 1

Globalization 1
   Globalization and Migration 2
Types of Migrants 4
   Migrant Workers 4
   High-Skill Workers 6
   Transnational Professionals 7
   Low-Skill Workers 8
   Refugees 8
   Trafficked Migrants 11
   Exiles 12
   Foreign Students 14
   Family Migration 15
   Marriage Migration 16
Tourism and Migration 19
   International Tourism 19
   Immigrant Immersion Tourism 20
   Medical Tourism 21
Notes 22

2 The Economic Driver 26

Macro Perspectives 26
   From Push Pull to Neoclassical Macro 27
   Leaving Venezuela 28
Micro Perspectives 29
   Neoclassical Micro Theory 29
Aspirations Versus Capability 31

        Aspirations and the Inverted U 32
    New Economics of Labor Migration STET 34
        Meso Analysis 34
        Household Risk Avoidance 34
        Relative Deprivation 34
        Conclusions 35
    Actual Economic Returns 35
    The Welfare Magnet Thesis 37
    Migrant Selectivity 38
        Methodological Issues 39
        Socioeconomic Status Selectivity 40
        Socioeconomic Selectivity and Downward Mobility 43
        Personality Selectivity 44
    Notes 46

3 Environmental Drivers: Climate Change and Natural Disasters   48
    The Status of Environmental Migrants 49
    Methodological Issues 51
        Measuring the Environmental Event 51
        Measuring Migration as a Response 52
        Conclusion 53
    The Empirical Research 53
        In the Global South 54
        In the Global North 58
        Conclusion 60
    Proximate Drivers 61
        Economic 61
        Types of Entrapment 63
        Civil Conflict 64
    Adaptation 65
    Notes 67

4 Connections Between Origins and Destinations   70
    Cultural and Linguistic Distance 70
        Culture and Its Measurement 70
        Language as Culture 71
        Language and Its Measurement 72
        Cultural Distance and Migration 73
        Linguistic Distance and Migration 74
    Chain Migration 75
        Migration Chains as Stimuli 77
        The Chain Multiplier 78
        Cumulative Causation 78
        Family as Compensation 80

Stepwise Migration 80
  Transnational Families 82
      Men Left Behind 82
      Women Left Behind 84
  Remittances 85
  Return Migration 87
      Aspirations and Plans 87
      Generational Differences 89
      Drivers of Return 90
  Reintegration 91
  Notes 92

5 **Undocumented Migrants**   95
  Estimating Undocumented Populations 96
  Undocumented Migrants in Leading Destination Nations 98
      The U.S. 99
      Germany 100
      Australia 101
  Surreptitious Border Crossing 103
      Unaccompanied Minors From Central America 104
      Smugglers 105
      Distinguishing Between Smuggling and Trafficking 107
      Trafficking 108
      Sexual Exploitation 109
      Sex Workers 111
      Agency? 111
  Visa Overstays 111
      Enforcement and Detention 112
  Deportation 114
  Notes 115

6 **The Social Integration of Migrants and Their Offspring**   118
  Conceptualizing Integration 118
  Dimensions of Integration 120
      Socioeconomic Standing 120
      The "Immigrant Optimism Paradox" 122
      Place Effects 124
      Gender and Motive 125
      Race, Skin Tone and Gender: The New Immigrant Survey 126
      Time and Place Generalizations 127
  Spatial Integration 128
      The Chicago School 128
      New Immigration Patterns 128
  Intermarriage 131

       Marriage Markets 132
       Linguistic and Cultural Proximity 132
       Marital Dissolution 134
       Marital Opportunities 135
       Education and Gender 136
       Asian Americans 137
Assimilability as a Criterion 138
Transnationalism 140
Notes 141

7 Migrant Settlements   144

Refugee Camps 144
Ghettos 146
       Summary 149
       Ghettos in European Cities 149
       Dispersal Policies 150
Enclaves 151
       Leave or Stay? 153
       Tourism 154
       Summary 155
       Becoming Cross-National 155
Ethnoburbs 156
       Los Angeles and Monterey Park 158
       Cross-National Enterprises 158
Comparing Settlement Types 159
Notes 160

8 Immigrants' Contributions and Natives' Perceptions   162

Misperceptions About Immigrants 162
       Fear of Crime 163
       Crime in Sanctuary Cities 165
Welfare Benefits 166
Economic Impact: Low-Skill Workers 167
Economic Impact: High-Skill Workers 168
Community Effects 170
To Change Misconceptions 171
Perceptions of Size 171
Changing Attitudes 173
Notes 174

Glossary   176
Index   179

Figures

1.1 The Voluntary–Forced Migration Continuum 9
4.1 Linguistic Similarity Scoring 72

Tables

1.1	Global Refugees	9
1.2	International Tourism	20
5.1	Estimates of the Undocumented Migrant Population in the U.S. 2010–2019	99
5.2	Smugglers' Routes and Fees	106
6.1	Education Across Generations	122
6.2	Native-Immigrant Dissimilarity Indexes for Selected European Countries	130
8.1	Foreign Students in Graduate Programs	169

Boxes

1.1	Micronesian Migrants in a U.S. Meatpacking Plant	5
1.2	Syrian Refugees in Turkey	10
1.3	Student Hostesses in Koreatown	15
1.4	Danish Wives and Cuban Husbands	18
1.5	Somali Medical Tourists From Britain	22
2.1	Leaving Children Behind in Venezuela	28
2.2	Remittances and Household Risk Avoidance	30
2.3	The Real Cost of a Big Mac to McDonald's Workers	36
2.4	New Zealand's Migration Lottery	42
2.5	Status Loss for Positively Selected Migrants	43
3.1	Trying to Obtain Refugee Rights in Bosnia	50
3.2	The Effects of Hurricanes in Guatemala	57
3.3	Leaving the Gulf of Guinea	61
3.4	A Missouri Town Adapts to the Loss of Geese	66
4.1	Chain Migration From Bangladesh to Italy	75
4.2	Chain Migration of Mexican Gay Men	76
4.3	Stepwise Migration of Multinational Maids	81
4.4	Husbands Left Behind in Ghana	83
4.5	Conflict Over Remittances in Nepal	86
4.6	Deciding Whether to Return to Liberia	88
5.1	Churning Among Jobs in New York	100
5.2	Undocumented Workers in Australia	102
5.3	Unaccompanied Minors in U.S. Detention	104
5.4	Trafficking Afghan Women for Forced Marriages in Pakistan	110
5.5	An Overstayer's Detention in Japan	113
6.1	Educational Frustration and Suicide in South Korea	123
6.2	The Index of Dissimilarity	130
6.3	Asian American-White Intermarriage	137
6.4	Palestinian Women in Iceland	139
7.1	Treating Patients in a Greece Refugee Camp	145
7.2	Grocery Stores in Toronto's Chinese Enclave	152
7.3	Diversity in Melbourne's Suburbs	157
8.1	Consequences of Criminal Convictions for Noncitizens	164
8.2	Refugees in Small Cities	170
8.3	The U.S.'s Fact-Free Immigration Policy	172
8.4	Egyptian Soccer Player in Liverpool Changes Attitudes	174

Preface

There has been an outpouring of research on migration during the past couple of decades, and it has resulted in many specialized books and the emergence of journals that prominently feature research on migration. The growth in this literature provided the impetus to write this book. I thought that students would benefit from a relatively small book that provided an overview of the important issues associated with migration, and that is the book I have attempted to write. It is intended to both provide a survey of trends and an analysis of patterns.

The first organizational decision I made was to focus solely upon migration across nations. More people move within than between nations, of course, and much of the migration within nations is temporary and involves relatively short distances. The dynamics of internal migration are often different and I wanted to keep the focus upon moves that involve crossing national borders.

I have assumed that there are substantial similarities among the leading immigration destination nations of the global north with respect to migration patterns. I further assumed that the results of studies conducted in different destination nations could be conjoined in working toward generalizations about many aspects of migrants' travel trajectories and adjustments. In addition, I wanted to try to generalize about migration throughout the world rather than between any two specific nations; hence the subtitle of the book, *A Global Introduction*.

I have tried consistently to minimize jargon, and present the material in the most straightforward and readable way possible. I recognize that it is important, at the same time, to introduce students to major concepts in the literature, and I have endeavored to do so, including a Glossary at the back of the book that I hope will prove to be very useful. In every chapter, the reader will also encounter boxed materials which illustrate and clarify major themes in the text. I hope they will be read as integral parts of the book. (A listing of all the boxed material follows the table of contents.)

The editorial staff that I have worked with at Routledge have been extremely helpful and supportive. I want explicitly to thank Rebecca Brennan, the editor who helped to oversee this project from its inception, and Chris Ford for helping me to improve the looks and form of this book.

1 Globalization and Migration

Moving across most of the nations in the world, one finds the same products (e.g. cell phones) and the same corporations (e.g. H&M). There is also great similarity in people's ideas and values (e.g. the desirability of travel) and in fads and fashions (from jeans to popular music). Within these almost interchangeable nations, the people of the world are also very much in motion: as tourists, foreign study students, transferred executives, refugees and so on. And they are moving across national boundaries, sometimes effortlessly and sometimes with great difficulty, but they are in motion; and inter-governmental agreements and cross-national agencies have followed the movement of people and products.

It is the increased interconnection among economies, cultures and governments of the world that is at the core of globalization. While our focus in this book is specifically upon migration, it is important to begin the discussion by placing current patterns of migration into a broader global context. This entails recognizing that migration – along with trade, finance, culture and international government – are all interconnected and collectively comprise the key components of globalization.[1]

Globalization

Over time there have been dramatic increases in the amount of economic activity that has crossed national boundaries. The amount of world trade grew larger and became an increasingly important part of the economies of the world's nations. The flow of investments across nations also rose, especially involving firms in one nation purchasing firms (from restaurants to manufacturing plants) in other nations. Global supply chains expanded as more nations became involved in the integrated, inter-nation manufacturing, distribution and sale of the component parts of products, from computers to automobiles.[2]

Transnational corporations (TNCs), also referred to as multinational corporations (MNCs), have played an especially important role in globalization.[3] They are defined as enterprises that have facilities in at least one country other than the one in which they are headquartered. Some definitions also stipulate that at least one-quarter of a firm's revenue must be obtained outside of the nation in which it is headquartered. That criterion is designed to exclude firms, located near national borders, that incidentally sell a few products in the neighboring nation. Because there are few such firms, most definitions of TNCs do not include this requirement. In fact, the larger TNCs actually tend to have principal offices in many nations and over one-half of their revenue is typically derived from foreign locales. And they have huge global workforces. TNCs currently employ slightly over one-fourth of the world's labor force. According to recent figures, Wal-Mart, for example, had over two million

DOI: 10.4324/9781003158400-1

employees, with 750,000 working outside of its U.S. home. To illustrate further, Siemens, the German-based electronics company, employed over 400,000 people, with approximately 70% working outside of Germany.[4] By transferring managers and executives across disparate locations, TNCs move people, along with their products, around the entire world.

The growth of TNCs, along with all forms of global economic activity, fluctuated during the first two decades of the 21st century as a global recession, between 2007 and 2009, depressed economic activity. By 2016 global economic activity again began to increase, more slowly than in the preceding century, though by 2019 the pace of economic globalization had substantially increased.[5] But then the COVID-19 pandemic struck the world, primarily in 2020, depressing every nation's economy, closing national borders both to people and capital flows, and disrupting global supply chains.

As this is written, at the onset of 2021, some forecasters predict that the globalization of economies will be set back for the foreseeable future. However, there is more evidence to suggest that the long-term trend toward increasing globalization will continue, after the interruption. This prediction is based upon the resilience that globalization has shown in the face of setbacks in the past. For example, many forms of cross-national activity – from trade agreements to the confederation of governments – have in recent decades been unpopular as nationalism has been emphasized in many state elections. Some multi-nation trade agreements have been nullified as a result, but they have almost always been replaced by new agreements. Some cross-nation governing arrangements have lost members; but even where that has happened, strong cross-nation ties have remained. To illustrate, in the years after Britain voted in 2016 to leave the European Union (E.U.), there was actually a substantial increase in cross-border investments among the remaining Eurozone nations, and even an increase in British investment in Europe.[6]

Furthermore, when confronted by a common threat – such as Russia's invasion of Ukraine in 2022 – the E.U. and Britain closely aligned their activities to each other's. Their coordination and cooperation was so intense that one British daily newspaper ran the headline, "U.K. back in Brussels."[7] (Brussels is the headquarters of the EU.)

Finally, we note that the same cultural industries involving television shows, recorded music, and so on, span the globe, generating similar clothing preferences and slang expressions, similar ways of interacting and viewing relationships, careers, families, and so on. While a pandemic or government action can halt the global tour of a concert or close local venues of global theme parks, any such pause is very likely to be temporary. Meanwhile, the mass media and the Internet continue to promote shared values and ways of life across the entire world. Zachary Karabell has concluded that with respect to globalization, including correspondingly high rates of migration, "the sheer scale of what has been created over the past several decades ... will preclude a lasting reversal."[8]

Globalization and Migration

As we have noted, increased migration is an integral component of globalization. To further clarify their connection, consider how marriages have changed. In the past, in most nations, marriages were typically negotiated by people in a local market; how local varied, from villages to cities, but it was usually a geographically quite constrained area. With greater global connectedness of all sorts, more people are selecting marriage partners from across substantial distances, and from different nations. The couples in some cases meet without assistance, through an online site or while one of the future partners is traveling abroad. Many other marriages are arranged through international marriage brokers, or by extended families whose members live in different parts of the world. In many nations, migration for marriage or family reunification now rivals jobs as a reason for requesting visas.

To illustrate further, note how increased migration has impacted higher education. For students, greater global connectivity means more information about educational opportunities in other nations. Students have the same impersonal sources of information that have long been available, in books, newspapers and so on; but they are also increasingly able to access personal information directly. Few people of typical student age do not know someone who has lived and studied in a foreign place. From the accounts of returning students, as well as educational marketing campaigns, collective ideas concerning what it means to study in another nation have been formed, and people all over the world find it increasingly easy to imagine themselves as foreign students.[9] As we will describe later in this chapter, student enrollment in foreign programs has steadily increased in recent decades.

The United Nations defines international migrants as people who change the country in which they have usually resided. It includes all people who moved to a different nation and remained for at least three months, regardless of their reason for moving. Therefore, it combines a few groups that are sometimes treated separately: refugees, people transferred to a job in another country, students in foreign study degree programs, etc. UN statistics also distinguish between short-term and long-term migrations, defining short-term as moves which last for at least three months but less than one year. In other words, if people return to their origin nation in less than three months, they are not considered to have been global migrants. Long-term is defined as a change in nation of residence that lasts for one year or longer. These are UN recommendations and while many nations follow them, all do not.[10]

The UN figures provide the most complete data set, but they are dependent upon raw data compiled separately by individual nations whose practices and criteria vary. For example, many nations count the number of people who enter but make no effort to count emigration or out-flow, that is the number of former residents who exit the nation. And among those nations that do try to count emigres, some depend upon inferences, relying upon indicators such as non-renewal of insurance, withdrawal of a residence permit, etc. Finally, record keeping in some nations does not carefully distinguish between migrants, as defined by the UN, and such non-migrants as tourists and people attending a business meeting.[11] In consequence, small differences among nations in their "official" migration rates should not be given much weight.

With the above caveats in mind, let us turn to the data. Combining short and long lengths of stay and focusing upon the total number of migrants shows a clear, unbroken trend in which the number of people designated as migrants has increased each decade over the past 50 years. The raw numbers increased from 84 million migrants in 1970 (which was then 2.3% of the world's population) to 272 million in 2019 (then comprising 3.5% of the world's population). In 2019, the latest figures available at this writing, according to the UN figures about three-fourths of all migrants were between the ages of 20 and 64 (i.e. peak labor force participation age). Males comprised 52% of the migrant population and females 48%.[12]

With respect to the number of in-migrants, the U.S., home to approximately 50 million migrants in 2019, was the leading destination nation, by a substantial margin. The U.S. was followed by Germany, Saudi Arabia and the Russian Federation, in that order, but each of them was home to fewer than 20 million migrants. The U.S. was so far ahead of any other nation with respect to in-migration that it is not likely the difference was an artifact of measurement. However, one should be cautious in inferring any ranking among the three nations that followed the U.S. because the differences among them are small.

As a proportion of its total population, the United Arab Emirates (UAE) had the largest migrant body. (It held that place since 2000.) In UAE and most of the other Gulf nations, migrants comprised an absolute majority of the population. Asia has, for many years, been the region with the largest migration out-flow, and the specific nation with the largest emigration in 2020 was India. It was substantially ahead of a second grouping of nations – including Mexico, China and the Russian Federation – that followed it in emigration.[13] To connect the nation with the largest migration out-flow (India) to the nation with the largest proportion of in-migrants (UAE), we can note that by the spring of 2020 there were approximately three and one-half million Indian emigres working in the UAE as construction laborers, waiting tables, cleaning homes, etc. And the Indian emigres comprised roughly 30% of the UAE's total population.[14]

We should note that all of the migration statistics presented by the UN are, unless otherwise noted, based upon the migrants who are counted by government officials as they exit and/or enter. Those migrants that cross national borders surreptitiously – via human smugglers, traffickers or the like – or whose legal status changes while they are in a foreign nation are generally referred to as "undocumented." They are also sometimes referred to as migrants in "irregular status." The UN, the European Parliament, the Associated Press and other media outlets all avoid the term "illegal" because of its negative connotations.[15] Undocumented migrants will be discussed throughout this book, but in detail in Chapter 5.

Types of Migrants

Our attention turns now to a discussion of the major categories of people who migrate. The typologies, most of which follow United Nations designations, are based primarily upon what appear to be the main reasons people emigrate, for example, for a job, to unify a family, etc. However, it is important to recognize that many of these reasons overlap. Thus, refugees – migrants who are forced by threats to flee their home country – are often seeking work, as well; but they are not counted twice in estimating the total number of migrants. Most of the categories of migrant workers introduced in this section will be further discussed in the chapters that follow.

Migrant Workers

The International Labour Organization (ILO), a specialized agency of the UN, defines migrant workers as people who have emigrated from their country of citizenship and are currently employed in their new nation – or unemployed but seeking employment. The United Nations Statistics Division further clarifies that they are foreigners admitted to a country for work-related purposes and that both their length of stay and type of employment are usually restricted. Some UN data also include the accompanying families in their tabulations of the size of the migrant worker category, but the statistics presented here will follow the narrower definition of the ILO.

Approximately 60% of the world's international migrant population consists of migrant workers because searching for employment is one of the major reasons that people cross national borders. ILO classifies the movement of emigres in relation to their country of citizenship. So, for example, a person who was born in Germany, and was working in Germany, but did not hold German citizenship would be counted by ILO as a migrant worker. On the other hand, a French citizen returning to France after working abroad would not be considered a migrant worker.[16]

According to the ILO delineation, in 2017 (the latest figures available) there were 164 million migrant workers. Europe (with 32% of the total) and North America (23%) were the regions with the largest numbers of foreign workers followed by the Arab States (14%) and Asia (13%). Migrant workers comprised less than 20% of every region's total labor force except in the Arab States where they comprised 41% of the total. The age, sex and other demographic characteristics of migrant workers followed distributions very similar to those of all migrants. Specifically, about 90% of the migrant workers were between the ages of 25 and 64, prime labor force ages, and they were 42% female and 58% male.

The types of employment that are taken by migrant workers are highly diverse, but they can be divided into two very different categories. First, there is a high skill-high wage grouping which includes such positions as: managers and executives, lawyers and accountants, scientists and engineers. Second, there is a low skill-low wage category which includes jobs such as: restaurant and hotel kitchen staff and maids, domestic workers, farm and construction laborers.

In recent years most of the nations considered most desirable by would-be migrant workers have made it more difficult for foreign workers to enter. Visas or work permits are severely limited and in many cases largely confined to people with advanced degrees and demonstrable skills. As a result, workers in the low-skilled category typically have very limited opportunities and that makes them vulnerable to being exploited. A more-or-less typical example is provided by the situation of migrant workers from Micronesia who have moved to small towns in the U.S. to take jobs in meat packing plants. Their situation is described in Box 1.1.

Box 1.1   Micronesian Migrants in a U.S. Meatpacking Plant

Micronesia encompasses a cluster of small islands in the Pacific Ocean, between Hawaii and the Philippines. The 112,000 people living on the islands are generally poor, working at service jobs in the tourist industry, subsistence farming and fishing. Good-paying jobs are hard to find. In 2018, a recruiter for a U.S. pork processing plant offered people jobs paying $15.95 an hour; ten times what they were earning in Micronesia. Plus the offer included free transportation and free meals. Hundreds happily accepted and made the 7,000-mile journey across the ocean and then through the cornfields of Western Iowa. Two days later they arrived, many with little more than their shorts and flip-flops.[17]

The plane rides were long, the airport guide that was promised when they changed planes never arrived, and most lacked money to buy food or water during their journey. Tired, hungry and confused when they finally arrived in the town where the plant was located, they met with the recruiter who began by collecting their passports in order to limit their mobility within the country. He told them that if they became ill or missed their shifts they would be deported, and he then explained that their first $1800 in earnings would be docked in order to repay their plane tickets that were supposed to be free. They were placed in a hotel, and the next morning they were crowded into the company's shuttle that took them between the hotel and the pork plant where they worked 10-hour shifts.[18]

An anthropologist's fieldwork conducted in an almost identical meatpacking plant, a few miles down the road, provided a detailed description of the harsh conditions under which migrants worked in meat packing companies. Some of them were assigned to a hot, humid and smelly "kill room" where they slaughtered and cut up the hogs. Others picked up the trash and shoveled the meat that fell as the hogs bodies moved down the line on which they were being butchered. Some carried heavy hog parts to the downstairs cooler that was so cold there was often ice on the floor.[19]

To make matters worse, the Micronesian migrants did not like living in the hotel that was initially free but then required $1500 a month for a small space with three occupants. Lacking passports, however, they had no ID with which to cash a check and pay the security deposit that would have been required for an apartment in town. It did not take long for many of the migrants to become disillusioned and unhappy, and wish they could just return to Micronesia. "How can I go back?" one of the migrants asked. "I'm stuck. I don't have money."[20]

Government officials in Iowa, the U.S. state in which the meat packing plant was located, kept promising to look into the abuses alleged by the Micronesian workers. Corporate officials also said they would investigate the allegations, but most of the migrants complained that no one ever came to interview them or to inspect their working and living conditions.[21]

Migrant workers in various industries, in nations across the world, very often find that basic rights are absent from the workplace. Interrupted employment is also commonplace because migrant workers tend to be the first casualties of economic downturns. For example, when in 2020 the COVID-19 virus forced store, farm and factory closings around the world, in just one day in April: 30,000 migrant workers were sent out of Thailand and crossed the border to return back to Myanmar; 15,000 migrant laborers left Iran and returned across the border to Afghanistan, etc.[22]

High-Skill Workers

For workers in the high-skill category, such as scientists and engineers (S&E), it is usually easier to obtain work visas and to move between nations. In fact, in those nations that have a great deal of employment in high-skill occupations, such as the U.S., Canada and Western Europe, the foreign-born have come to comprise a large percentage of the workforce in these occupational categories, even though they are a small percentage of the migrant labor force. In the U.S., for example, in 2015, about 30% of all workers in S&E were foreign-born; and among all those holding doctorates, the foreign-born percentage was about 45%. Just between 1993 and 2015 all of the foreign-born percentages presented above nearly doubled.[23]

In any given year there are thousands of managers, executives and professionals employed by TNCs that are transferred to an office in a nation other than the one in which they are currently employed, though precise data are lacking. In most instances, the relocation is technically voluntary, though refusal to accept a relocation assignment is likely in most firms to have adverse effects upon future career mobility.

In some organizations, inter-nation transfers are almost part of the job descriptions of high-level staff. United Nation's agencies, for example, tend to have mandatory rotation schedules so that employees can anticipate the timing of future transfers and their probable locations. In one large sample of UN employees, over one-quarter were found to have been relocated more than ten times in their careers, and over 80% had been relocated more than five times. By contrast, for the employees of nongovernmental TNCs, such as global banks, three or four lifetime transfers seem more typical.[24] The timing and location of transfers in the private sector also tend to be less predictable. Decisions effecting large groups of employees are usually made in the headquarters of TNCs, but local conditions often modify how these decisions are actually implemented.[25] In addition, the timing and location of transfers are difficult to anticipate in the private sector because relocation decisions depend, at least partially, upon happenstance: whether local business is increasing or decreasing, whether there is executive turnover in one of the corporate offices, etc.

There are limited descriptive data concerning the intra-firm, cross-national labor pool other than the fact that it tends very disproportionately to involve high-level positions. Some information can be gleaned from a yearly survey conducted by KPMG. Their sample includes hundreds of organizations that volunteer to participate in a web-based survey. Whether its results can be generalized to a larger population is unknown, though the sample is very over-represented by U.S. firms; in most years they comprised nearly one-half of the total KPMG sample while their share of the world's TNCs is estimated at just under 40%.[26] According to the most recent survey, conducted in 2018, the U.S. and the UK were both the leading origin and destination locations for inter-nation transfers. The largest proportion of relocation assignments (46%) was long-term, i.e. between one and five years in length. An additional 19% of the transfers were permanent and 16% were short-term, less than one year in duration.[27]

Transnational Professionals

There are also large groups of diverse professionals – lawyers, accountants, public health experts, software engineers and so on – who move frequently across national borders but do not typically remain as employees of any one TNC. In that sense they resemble the traditional "free professionals," such as autonomous physicians and lawyers, who historically were not employees of any organization. The contemporary transnational professionals may be licensed within one nation and may be members of a nation-based professional association, but their expertise is applicable across national boundaries rather than confined to any "home" nation. For example, a group of University of Chicago-trained economists went on to transform the economies of Chile, Brazil and Mexico.[28]

To be a transnational professional requires that one possess specific knowledge and skills (e.g. language facility) and master a body of applicable knowledge (e.g. how to combat infectious diseases). The identities of these professionals are usually tied to their expertise and not to a corporation or a nation. Detailed observations of and interviews with one group of transnational professionals, international start-up entrepreneurs, reported that they did not think the term migrant applied to them because their specialties did not have a territorial locus. They saw themselves as "global people" who worked out of the leading global cities and moved rapidly between places and projects.[29]

Low-Skill Workers

Several studies conducted in a number of nations have reported that lower-level positions in TNCs, unlike those at the higher level, are typically filled from a local labor pool rather than from transfers.[30] The janitors, temporary office help and other local hires often receive very low wages and work under very difficult conditions. The situation faced by women in the ranks of low-level TNC employees tends to be still worse. Especially in developing areas of Asia, Africa and Latin America, the female employees are usually paid even less than men, are more likely to be laid off, and have almost no opportunity to experience upward mobility.[31]

The major exception to a firm's local hiring of low-level employees occurs when TNCs outsource positions to subcontractors who recruit migrant workers (often described as "posted" workers) from low-wage nations. The length of the relocation assignments for these employees varies greatly, from as little as about three months to as long as several years. Wages and working conditions for such workers are typically very poor. For example, firms in Germany have hired subcontractors to recruit workers from Poland and Romania. These posted workers are paid low wages and frequently work under conditions that violate German and European Union standards, but the subcontractors are typically able to evade detection. These migrant workers fall into the cracks between the importing and exporting nations, and subcontractors benefit from the ambiguity surrounding which nation has enforcement responsibility.[32]

Refugees

Refugees are legally defined as migrants who have been forced to flee from the nation in which they were residing. The most complete data on forced migration is assembled every year by the United Nations High Commissioner for Refugees (UNCHR), often referred to simply as the UN Refugee Agency.[33] Headquartered in Geneva, Switzerland, its objective is to provide a variety of services to displaced people who the agency puts into one of two categories based upon where they move: "Internally Displaced Persons" (IDP) flee an immediate threat, but do not cross a border, remaining elsewhere within the same nation. "Refugees" are similarly in peril and flee, but they cross a national border. In any given year the number of IDPs tends to far exceed the number of refugees. In 2018, for example, a total of 13.6 million people were *newly displaced*. Of that total, 10.8 million were classified as IDPs. Our interest in this book, however, is in the refugees.

A coercive circumstance is involved in the official definition of both groups, that is, UNCHR considers them as having a "well founded" fear that forced them to flee their homes in order to escape persecution, war or violence. Agencies can confront a degree of ambiguity in inferring whether people have been forced, though. In some instances virtually everyone would agree that for a group of people to have remained in place they would almost surely have faced death or imprisonment, hence it is reasonable to conclude they were forced to leave. On the other hand, what if the people who flee the country are part of a group confronted with the possibility of restricted opportunities, loss of income, or greater prejudice? Could they have stayed under those conditions?

Deciding whether any group of people should be designated as forced to flee, based upon the circumstances they faced, and therefore be considered refugees, has to be made on a case by case basis, and can involve uncertainties.

Deciding whether a group of migrants are refugees has important political and legal implications. The 1951 Refugee Convention Act, administered by UNCHR, grants certain rights and protections to migrants designated as refugees in the 145 nations that are signatories of the Act. In addition, many nations utilized refugee criteria in bureaucratically processing people's requests to enter. Looking primarily at migrants' external circumstances, officials make these consequential labeling decisions. To social scientists, who tend to pay more attention to the perceptions of migrants, themselves, a rigid forced-voluntary dichotomy often makes little sense. From extensive interviews with migrants, many analysts have concluded that it is not possible to describe most people's decision to migrate as simply voluntary *or* forced. Empirically, it often appears to involve a mixture of both.[34] This conceptualization is illustrated in Figure 1.1.

Where along the above continuum should a line be drawn officially to identify migrants who were forced, and therefore are entitled to refugee status? Anywhere above the 50-50 point? At 75-25? Only if the migration is entirely forced? If we are to proceed based upon migrants' self-reported experiences and attitudes, it is not clear where along the continuum illustrated in figure one a cut-off should be imposed. However, because the most comprehensive data on refugees is compiled by UNCHR, a complete statistical description of refugees requires following their imposed dichotomy, but the reader should bear in mind the reservations noted above. (The voluntariness of migration decisions is further discussed in later chapters.)

Between 1995 and 2010 there were yearly fluctuations in the number of refugees, as designated by UNCHR, but the annual variations were very small, and there was no overall trend. After 2010, however, there was a dramatic global increase in the *total number* of people considered to be refugees, from approximately 10 million in 2010 to over 20 million by 2018.[35] At the time that number was projected to continue to increase, though the effects of possible pandemics in the future are difficult to estimate.

In both 2017 and 2018, nearly 70% of the world's refugees came from the same five nations. They are displayed in Table 1.1 which also shows the number of refugees from

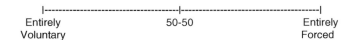

Figure 1.1 The Voluntary-Forced Migration Continuum.

Table 1.1 Global Refugees

Country of Origin	Number (in millions)	Leading Destination Nations
Syria	6.7	Turkey, Lebanon
Afghanistan	2.7	Pakistan, Iran
South Sudan	2.3	Sudan, Uganda
Myanmar	1.1	Bangladesh, Malaysia
Somalia	0.95	Ethiopia, Kenya

which each nation was the country of origin and the two countries that became the leading destination nations for refugees from that country of origin. See the figures in Table 1.1.

Turkey, by virtue of the large influx from Syria, had the largest refugee population in 2018. Of a total of 3.7 million refugees, 98% were from Syria. Turkey hosted the largest number of refugees every year between 2014 and 2018, due largely to the Syrian influx. Pakistan was home to the second largest refugee population, the majority having come from Afghanistan.

The exodus from Syria was due to a civil war in which Syrian army forces, with Russian assistance, attacked rebel-held lands, bombing and burning homes, schools, stores and hospitals. Millions of Syrians fled their homes and headed northwest to cross the border into Turkey, but in 2019 Turkey closed its border to block additional Syrian refugees from entering. This resulted in hundreds of thousands of Syrian families remaining as IDPs in northwest Syria, across the border from Turkey, living in flimsy tents or packed together under stadiums.[36] Initially, conditions were generally better for the Syrians who entered Turkey before the border was closed, as described in the following case study in Box 1.2.

Box 1.2   Syrian Refugees in Turkey

As the conflict among warring factions within Syria began to escalate (in 2012), Syrians in large numbers began to seek refuge across the border in Turkey. They were initially welcomed, for the most part, and the Turkish government built camps which provided sanitary conditions and pre-fabricated housing. Only about one-half of the earliest refugees required these accommodations. The rest either found apartments or had friends or relatives with whom they could live. As the exodus out of Syria continued, the vast majority of refugees moved to Turkey's major cities. The largest concentration was in Istanbul which in 2019 had an estimated one million Syrian residents (some registered and some not.) Three other large Turkish cities, located near the Syrian border, each had nearly one-half million Syrian refugees. In all of these cities, most of the refugees lacked work permits which forced them to seek employment in the "informal economy," as maids, street vendors, etc. The informal economy is defined by an absence of official records. Workers in the informal economy are usually paid in cash, off the books, but are paid poorly.[37] As a result, almost two-thirds of Syrian refugees lived at or below the poverty line.[38]

Providing schools, hospitals and administrative services to support the growing refugee population became increasingly expensive, and public sentiment toward the Syrians became less welcoming. The refugees reported becoming targets of xenophobic hostility and employment discrimination. Particularly in Istanbul, the situation of the Syrians became critical by the summer of 2019 as Turkish authorities conducted widespread identity checks in Syrian neighborhoods and then removed an estimated 100,000 unregistered Syrians. Some were sent to refugee camps outside Istanbul and – although the government denied it – agencies reported that many were deported back across the Syrian border into an active war zone.[39]

The problems faced by Syrian refugees in Turkey were further exacerbated by an agreement between Turkey and the European Union (EU). The EU agreed to provide some financial assistance to help resettle the Syrian refugees but insisted in return that the majority of Syrians that crossed through Turkey to reach other EU nations would have to be returned to Turkey. Along with migrants from other nations, many Syrian refugees used Turkey as a first stop, then traveled to Greece, and some continued across the Balkans to Europe, and Germany in particular. This series of moves describes "stepwise migration" in which there are intermediate stops before migrants reach a final destination.[40] Turkey feared being further overwhelmed by migrants and offered to pay to airlift refugees to other nations willing to take them in, but as of this writing (in mid-2020) could find few nations that were willing to take in Syrian refugees.

As this book was going into production there was also a huge movement of refugees who gathered whatever belongings they could carry and walked, ran, jumped on trains in order to escape from Ukraine following Russia's invasion in 2022. In just the first two weeks following the invasion, it was estimated that about two million people, mostly women and children, fled from the country. Over one-half of them crossed the border into Poland.[41] What lied ahead for them, as this was written, was unclear.

Trafficked Migrants

A second type of forced migrant involves people who are trafficked. In this case, it is not widespread turmoil that prompts a large segment of the population to flee, but a specific group that tricks or forces selected people to migrate. The International Organization for Migration (IOM) defines trafficking as entailing the recruitment and transfer of people that relies upon threat, abduction or fraud to control people for the purpose of exploiting them. If any coercion or deception is involved, then even if the person consents to the move it is still considered to be trafficking. Not all trafficking involves crossing national boundaries. In fact, over one-half of the victims do not leave their nation. Our interest is in the estimated 42% who are trafficked across national boundaries.[42] (The IOM is an inter-government agency affiliated with the U.N. that compiles migration statistics and provides a variety of services to migrant communities.[43])

There is a clear connection between refugees and trafficking because people who are desperate to escape from war or persecution are in a vulnerable situation. They may be easily fooled into making an unwise migration decision and/or in the turmoil that is causing people to flee, institutional safeguards that could protect people in normal times may be weakened. A clear example of the connection between refugees and trafficking is provided by the consequences of the civil war in Syria, described in the preceding case study. It resulted in both an increased number of Syrian refugees and an increase in the number of Syrians who were trafficked.[44]

Data on both the perpetrators and victims of trafficking are necessarily incomplete because they rely primarily upon information obtained when people are caught, and all types of trafficking may not be equally likely to result in detention. If some types of trafficking have higher arrest rates than others, then the overall picture would be skewed.

Field workers can sometimes add estimates to adjust the figures, but data on human trafficking remain reliant mostly on apprehensions.

According to the latest report on trafficking compiled by IOM in 2016, females, including both women and girls, comprised about three-quarters of the victims. Compulsory sexual activity was frequently the criminal objective as they were coerced into sexual slavery or prostitution, and sometimes into forced (underage) marriages. The percentage of males who were trafficked, though still well below that of females, increased steadily after 2006. The males were trafficked mostly to be used for forced labor. The children, both male and female, comprised just over one-fourth of all of those who were trafficked. Many were sold or given over by their families or relatives. What then happened to the young victims varied; some were forced to become beggars, others were conscripted into militias and became child soldiers, others were re-sold.[45] (Trafficking is further discussed in Chapter 5.)

Exiles

There is little consistency in how the term "exile" is utilized in the migration literature. It is not clear exactly what makes an exile different from other types of migrants (e.g. refugees). In some cases, the terms refugee or migrant are used to describe *the people* who have left their native countries, voluntarily or not; and exile (or "in exile") describes *their separation* from that native country. In other words, exile then refers to a separation and is not used as a label for people. However, in some analyses the term exile is applied to anyone who is separated from any larger entity to which that person could be regarded as a member. To illustrate how broadly the term has been applied, Allyson Hobbs has analyzed the experiences of fair-skinned black people in the U.S. – "racially ambiguous individuals" based upon their skin color – who at some point in their lives passed themselves off as white. Her case studies covered a roughly 70-year period from the late 19th to the mid-20th century when being white in the U.S. was especially tied to multiple advantages.

Some of the black people whose lives Hobbs studied looked white but chose never to try to pass for white because of their strong racial identity and commitment to the black community. Those who did choose to pass, according to Hobbs, probably experienced some loss of self. Rejecting one's racial identity and the community associated with it was voluntarily to place oneself into what she termed "exile" because of all the impediments that they would have faced if they had chosen at some point to cross back over the color line.[46]

Undocumented Mexican immigrants in the U.S. have similarly been described as attempting to pass, in this case as mainstream U.S. citizens. Toward that end, dozens of undocumented migrants that Angela Garcia interviewed told her that they tried to avoid certain kinds of haircuts, dressed like professional people and practiced walking down street hurriedly, as though they were late for a meeting. They monitored their use of slang expressions and worked on eliminating their accents. Passing became part of who they were and this consuming effort to mask their unauthorized status separated them from the ethnic group of which they would otherwise be part. The pressures of passing made them into exiles.[47]

As most typically used in the migration literature, however, the blacks who passed as white and undocumented immigrants who passed as citizens would probably not be described as exiles. They may have fit the term with respect to being separated from some larger group, but the separation was self-induced. Exiles, on the other hand, like refugees, usually feel pushed away by external circumstances, and express regret over their separation from a group with which they continue to identify. For example, there was a large group of Russian emigres, branded as radicals, who moved to London early in the 20th century because of fear of imprisonment. They actively followed news of events leading up to the Russian revolution and sent financial contributions to the revolutionaries.[48]

The term expatriate, or expat, is almost synonymous to the term exile when the latter is used to describe a category of people rather than the fact of their separation. To be specific, the term expatriate is used similarly to exiles to describe someone living in a country other than the one in which the person was born or raised. However, a continuing commitment to their former country is implied by the fact that expatriates, by definition, typically retain citizenship in their country of origin.[49]

The continuing commitment to a former place of residence implies another characteristic of exiles, namely, a disinclination to assimilate. It is common for groups described as exiles to exhibit this attitude. To illustrate, many of the older Cubans in Miami, who left Cuba in the 1980s, continued to insist, more than 25 years later, that they were exiles which to them meant they were not going to try to integrate in Miami because they planned to return to Cuba one day. The younger Cubans laughed and said, "Move on," knowing that very few of them were ever going back.[50]

The Cuban experience in Miami raises the question of how long members of a group must express a commitment to return some day for the group to be considered exiles. Among some Jews, for example, Israel is regarded as the homeland, and those living anywhere else are deemed to be exiles, living in diaspora. Some contemporary Jewish enclaves in Finland, Iran, Tunisia, and elsewhere have survived for hundreds of years by limiting their contacts with the non-Jewish world around them and continuing to observe ancient religious traditions. Many view themselves as living in diaspora, hence in exile, but over hundreds of years very few members of these communities have emigrated to Israel and very few plan to do so in the future.[51]

One additional dimension that is sometimes employed to distinguish exiles from other types of migrants or refugees concerns their relatively high socioeconomic status in the countries from which they emigrated. Some of the early waves of Cuban migrants, for example, were comprised largely of wealthy business owners, successful professionals, and their families. Most of the later cohorts were predominantly unskilled and poorer. The term exile (or expatriate) has, in this case, been utilized to describe the earlier Cuban migrants, but not the later ones.[52]

In sum, when the term exile is applied to people or groups it tends to distinguish them from other migrants by their continuing commitment to their country of origin, and their expressed wish to return, if certain conditions are met. In some cases, it is also used to differentiate exiles based upon differences in socioeconomic status in their countries of origin. Thus, migrants are assumed generally to have been poor, and to have migrated in search of economic opportunities, while exiles were economically secure and left in search of political, religious or other freedoms. However, the term is not used consistently in the migration literature, and UNCHR utilizes the term more as a verb than a noun. Specifically, refugees who are separated from their country of origin, but not resettled to a third country or integrated into the destination nation are defined as being "in exile." When the term appears later in this book its exact usage will be specified.

Foreign Students

Included within the broad category of people who travel to another nation in order to pursue some form of study are very diverse groups. At one extreme are short-term, non-degree students focusing upon a very specific area of inquiry: language acquisition, painting techniques, or the like. Many do not meet the UN's minimum length of stay criterion (i.e. three months) to qualify as migrants. At the other end of the continuum are students enrolled in multi-year, formal degree programs. And there are a large number of courses of study that fall between the extremes. Because of this heterogeneity, it can be difficult to estimate the total number of people who travel to another nation for educational purposes, and the estimates offered by different organizations can vary substantially.

Following UN figures again (UNESCO, in particular) the most inclusive category is an "internationally mobile student" and this category includes anyone who enters a nation different from her or his country of origin in order to participate in educational activities. A sub-category, termed "foreign student" is reserved for non-citizens enrolled in degree courses. Most analyses, ours included, focus upon these two groups.[53]

Study abroad or exchange students are further differentiated and subsumed under the term, "credit-mobile students." While these credit-mobile students are receiving some form of instruction while in another country, they remain enrolled in institutions located in their home countries. Most statistics on international students, including UNESCO's, do not include those in the credit-mobile category in part because these programs, usually of several months duration, do not typically require visas; and visa statistics are important in compiling all of the student estimates.

UNESCO figures indicate that the number of internationally mobile students – that is, the most inclusive student category – increased almost every year between 2000 and 2017, from two million to well over five million. The U.S. and U.K. have, by a large amount, been the historically most favored destinations for these foreign students. More recently their dominance as destinations has declined, though not disappeared, as Canada, Australia and China have become more popular destinations.[54]

For many of the internationally mobile students, living and studying in a foreign nation is a very meaningful experience which many have described by emphasizing how different it is from the experience of tourists. The disparity begins from the time foreign study students arrive in the city or town in which their school is located. Most of the students are relatively immobile, except for brief forays. Tourists, by contrast, tend to keep moving to new destinations, not staying in one place for very long. As a result, tourists do not ordinarily become particularly familiar with or comfortable in any locale while many foreign students come to feel at home in their extended campus surroundings and develop a sense of belonging.[55]

In addition, foreign students – that is, students in degree programs – often feel that their study abroad experience will become a credential in their future search for employment. Given the strong tendency for the nations that attract the most foreign students to also be the nations with the strongest labor markets, many of these students may be able to pursue careers with firms in the nations in which they studied, or with foreign firms that are connected to that nation. Tourism, on the other hand, rarely leads to any type of employment.

Data concerning how often foreign students choose to remain as migrant workers in the nation in which they studied abroad are very sketchy. There have been a number of small studies conducted among limited types of students enrolled at specific universities. None provide an overall picture, but from these studies we can tentatively infer that family ties and perceptions of career opportunities appear to be the major variables influencing students' plans to remain or to return home.[56] (Whether or not they will be able to obtain a work permit or appropriate visa is a separate issue.)

As we have noted, statistics on foreign study students are based largely upon visa records, and are therefore subject to some distortion by occasional abuses of student visa applications in a number of nations. One example is described in Box 1.3.

Box 1.3 Student Hostesses in Koreatown

There has been a practice for young women in South Korea to use student visas to emigrate to the U.S. when their actual goal is not primarily educational but to obtain work as a hostess or escort in bars and nightclubs in the Korean enclave in Los Angeles (known locally as, "Koreatown"). These young women find immediate and well-paying employment entertaining, and serving as companions to, local Korean businessmen. Though the women are paid, their relationships with the businessmen are more social than sexual.

Brokers in Seoul work with potential recruits to Koreatown's entertainment establishments to prepare the documents the women will need to convince officials in the U.S. embassy of their serious intention to pursue an academic program. To complete their documentation, the same brokers also make the necessary administrative arrangements with Los Angeles area schools. Once in Los Angeles, the women spend most of their time working as hostesses or escorts. Their employers in the entertainment establishments hire security personnel to provide notice of any impending raid by customs officials.[57]

All of these women are indentured workers, required to work to repay the brokers who arranged all the details of their emigration. Nevertheless, employment in Koreatown's entertainment establishments is attractive to many young Korean women because its high wages permit them to regularly remit funds to their families in South Korea. Working in Los Angeles also enables them to improve their English language skills enough later to obtain other forms of employment which could qualify them for permanent residency in the U.S. And some of the women do manage to earn degrees while working in Koreatown and then move into higher skilled positions in the U.S. or South Korea.

Family Migration

The most complete data on migration driven by family ties are available for the 37 nations that are members of the Organisation for Economic Cooperation and Development (OECD). It is a voluntary organization that includes, but is not limited to, most of the economically most advanced nations. The Asian nations that are the largest exporters of migrants are not members, and only some of Latin America's leading export nations are members (Colombia and Mexico). However, most of the nations that are the leading destinations of migrants are included, including: Australia, Canada, France, U.S., U.K.

None of the Gulf States are members, but it will be recalled that they have large in-migration relative to their population size, but fewer in-migrants in total than the leading destination nations that are in OECD. It is important to bear in mind the limitations of the OECD data sets, but they provide the most complete picture of family migration.

In 2017, around two million new migrants moved to OECD nations for family reasons, comprising 40% of all permanent migration to these nations. These figures fluctuated only slightly from year to year between 2011 and 2017. The U.S. received the largest number of family in-migrants, followed at a distance by Canada, Australia and France, in that order. The largest migration for family category is termed, Family Reunification. It involves a person, most often a spouse, seeking to enter a nation to join a family member with prior citizenship or legal status in that nation. In all of the OECD nations a legal spouse is always eligible for family reunification, a registered partner is eligible in most of the nations, and a fiancé is not usually eligible. A dependent child is eligible for family reunification in every nation, but married adult children and grandchildren, and other adult relatives, are eligible in about one-half of the nations.[58]

As noted, the U.S. has for a number of years been the largest recipient of family migrants. Its family reunification policies have been relatively liberal, permitting citizens to sponsor a parent, sibling, and adult married child in addition to a spouse/partner and dependent child. This has resulted in what analysts have termed an "immigration multiplier." In the U.S., in recent years, the average immigrant multiplier has been 3.45 meaning the average new immigrant later sponsored almost three and one-half additional migrant family members.[59]

The movement of members of an extended family to re-connect with a family member who previously emigrated is one example of "chain migration." It is defined as entailing a stream of migrants from within the same country of origin moving to the same location in the same destination nation. The chain can involve members of a family, or friends, or people who lived in the same village, or a combination of all of them.[60] Chain migration is further discussed in Chapter 4.

Marriage Migration

Marriage migration, as the name implies, involves one spouse moving to the country of residence of the second spouse when that second spouse is a citizen or legal resident of the destination country. It is more common for the woman to move than the man, and the most common direction, regardless of who moves, is from the "Global South" to the "Global North." Most, but not all, of the nations in the south lie south of Latitude 30 degrees south, but the terms are not primarily employed for geographic referents. The nations considered south (mostly in parts of Africa, Asia and Latin America) are poorer and politically less stable than those of the north (which are mostly in Europe and North America). In many cases, the differences emanate from an earlier time when nations in the global south were colonies of those in the global north. Essentially the same groupings of nations were previously labeled as more or less developed, or first world and third world. The World Bank, an independent agency of the UN, considers the north-south brackets less invidious, and therefore preferable, and this terminology has been widely followed in recent years.[61]

How couples from different nations get together in the first place varies. One alternative involves formal assistance, meaning that the couple had help from someone expected to play the matchmaker role by virtue of a kin relationship or because they were paid for their services. Historically, within many nations, parents or other family members played this mediating role. Across nations today, first and second-generation immigrants often look to their homelands to find spouses for themselves or for their offspring, and they are more likely to rely upon family ties and friendships rather than marital agencies. Some of the marriages that result are clearly arranged, that is, it was parents or guardians of the couple that made the major decisions concerning who will marry who. Sometimes their decisions are final, and sometimes the couple involved has veto power over parents' choices. In other cases, the external trappings of arranged spouse selection follow the culturally prescribed form, but the couple involved are actually the ones that steer the relationship to a large degree.[62]

Another form of cross-national assisted mate selection involves mail-order brides, a practice that goes back to at least the early 17th century when contracts were drawn for women to travel from England to the Virginia colony in North America. Arranging for a mail-order bride has continued in many nations, though in recent decades it has typically involved betrothed women leaving global south nations to move to prospective husbands in global north nations. These arrangements, well into the 20th century, were often transacted through largely unregulated international marriage agencies. Some of them have remained in operation, but in recent years, the Internet has greatly facilitated mail-order bride arrangements, and it has also led to an expansion of lifestyle choices; for example, there are now sites offering same-sex male-order grooms.[63]

Many marriages that cross national boundaries are, of course, negotiated only by the couple involved, and they are based upon many of the same factors that propel marriages among people within the same nation: sexual attraction, compatibility, common interests, etc. However, marriages that entail migration of one of the spouses are also sometimes transacted for other reasons, and these other objectives may be primary (to either spouse) or coexist in addition to the "usual" reasons. When facilitating one of the spouse's ability to emigrate is an important motive for marrying, the migration literature terms these "marriages of convenience." In many of the nations considered to be the most desirable destinations for a migrant, mostly located in the global north, marriage to a person who is already a citizen of that nation is one of the best ways for a migrant to legally enter.

All of the OECD nations make some effort to assess the "genuineness" or "authenticity" of marriage migration requests by examining various documents and/or interviewing applicants. When entry for a spouse is requested in Finland, for example, immigration officials try to determine whether it is a "good" marriage (permit to be offered) or one which was either forced or arranged primarily for migration purposes (no permit). Looking for indicators to guide their subjective conclusions, the officials examine how much time the couple has spent together, whether they previously shared the same address, if they speak the same language, etc.[64]

Overall, as we have noted, marital out-migration is more common for brides than grooms and this gender disparity has been especially pronounced in a number of Asian nations. How women fare in these marriages has been widely studied, but with less than consistent findings. To begin, it is not clear the degree to which the emigrating women are enticed by better living conditions and more opportunities, or whether desperation is the primary motive. In addition, many studies have contended that when female marriage migrants move from global south nations in Asia (Afghanistan, Cambodia, Laos, etc.) to marriage partners in Europe and North America, they are in vulnerable and powerless positions. On the other hand, a few studies have argued that these women have been able over time to maneuver themselves into positions offering a degree of autonomy and mobility.[65] These issues are further examined in Chapter 4.

The female to male surplus of marital out-migrants in Asia has resulted in local "bride drains" which have implications for the communities they have left, and the women who have remained, in particular. To be specific, the bride drain has in the affected nations resulted in lower rates of marriage, due to the scarcity of potential brides, and it has also led to changes in the relative status of men and women. In Viet Nam, for example, large numbers of women have left poor villages to marry men in the global north, frequently in Western Europe. They have then been able, via remittances, to help support their parents. That is a highly desired practice in Vietnamese families that has traditionally been associated more with sons than daughters. It has increased the perceived value of daughters and more generally raised the relative status of women. Supply and demand have further enhanced the role of women in these communities because the out-migration of female brides has led to the relative scarcity of women remaining in the local marriage market.[66]

In some nations, particularly in Latin America, it has become increasingly common for the gender roles involved in marriage migration to have reversed. In Costa Rica, Cuba and elsewhere in the region, female tourists from the U.S. and Western Europe have been involved in what has been termed, "sex tourism" or "romance tourism."[67] According to some ethnographers who have studied the issue, the image of the virile Latin male has been attractive to a number of Western women, and they have considered a sexual dalliance with a local man to be part of their Latin American tourist experience. They did not, at the onset, imagine it turning into an enduring relationship. For the Latin men, however, a more permanent relationship with a woman from a wealthier nation was desirable because it offered the possibility of upward mobility by increasing their chances of emigrating to a nation with greater economic opportunities.[68] In these cases emigration continues to be from the global south to the global north, but it is males in the global south who are moving.

Box 1.4, which follows, describes the marriage migration of Cuban men who have linked up with women tourists who traveled from Denmark to spend time in Cuba with the possibility of romance with the locals on their minds.

Box 1.4 Danish Wives and Cuban Husbands

Between 2000 and 2016 Denmark issued about 350 family reunification migration permits to persons from Cuba. These permits enable a Cuban spouse legally to enter and take up residence in Denmark. In 2016 about two-thirds of all the Cubans in Denmark entered with this type of permit. All of the couples had met in Cuba while the Danish partner was either vacationing or enrolled in a short-term foreign study program. Most of the Danish visitors were female and white, and their socioeconomic status almost always exceeded that of their future Cuban husbands, most of whom were either black or mulatto. For most of the women, marriage was totally unanticipated because it grew out of what they initially viewed as likely to be a "fling:" a short-term romantic or sexual relationship without any future commitments.[69]

For most of the Cuban men, marriage to a woman from Denmark offered the promise of upward mobility because the labor market in Denmark was much stronger than Cuba's. One Cuban man who after an affair with a Danish visitor eventually married her, and then emigrated to Denmark with her, told Nadine Fernandez, "I felt like I had won a scholarship."[70] However, adjusting to life and marriage in Denmark was typically difficult for the Cuban men. The gendered division of labor they grew up with in Cuba and learned to expect was strongly patriarchal while Denmark's was much more egalitarian. The men reported feeling frustrated and unhappy. Similar results have been reported in a wide range of other nations: When the groom has migrated to the bride's place of residence, it has tended to result in high rates of desertion and domestic violence.[71] A large percentage of all marriages in Denmark tend to be unstable, according to Fernandez, and about one-half of all of them end up in divorce. However, among Cuban-Danish couples, most of whom barely knew each other before marriage, the rate is even higher.[72]

If a marriage that involved an emigre is terminated, the emigre's ability to remain in Denmark can be jeopardized. While the official position of the state is to be vigilant in monitoring the dissolution of what it suspects may have been marriages of convenience, pro-forma divorces often escape bureaucrats' notice. In addition, some of the Cuban men in Fernandez' sample remained in Denmark 10 years after a divorce from their Danish wife by continuously seeking temporary residence and work visas. When the marriage resulted in children, the offspring were automatically granted Danish citizenship by virtue of being born to a Danish mother, and the Cuban fathers were then permitted to remain in Denmark, without any further action on their part.

Tourism and Migration

Most of the traveling done by tourists does not meet the U.N.'s minimum length of stay criterion to be considered migration. Tourism is nevertheless discussed here because of the numerous connections between tourism and migration. We begin by noting that a large percentage of international tourism involves travel to the same cities and nations that we have previously seen to be the leading global migration origins or destinations. That is not coincidental because a good deal of tourism involves emigres returning to visit their former homelands. Similarly, people often visit a place as a tourist, become familiar with it, and later decide to move there as a permanent resident. We will consider some examples later in this chapter. Finally, migrant enclaves have often become major tourist attractions in the cities in which they are located. (These enclaves are discussed in Chapter 7.)

International Tourism

Accurate information on the number of international tourists is difficult to obtain for a variety of reasons. The first problem is definitional. The World Tourism Organization (WTO), a special UN agency, presents as an ideal definition: The number of people who travel to a country other than the one in which they usually reside, and stay for a period exceeding one day, but less than 12 months. Also part of the definition is the requirement that the main purpose of the travel cannot entail remunerated activity. The focus is solely upon inbound travel and WTO counts the number of arrivals and not the number

20 *Globalization and Migration*

Table 1.2 International Tourism

City	Foreign Visitors (in millions)
Bangkok	22.78
Paris	19.10
London	19.09
Dubai	15.93
Singapore	14.67

of different people who arrive in a place, so people who travel to a different foreign country more than once (and stay for at least one day) are counted as tourists each time.[73]

Data meeting the WTO requirements, as described above, are not available for all nations. Some countries count all visitors, including those who stay for less than a full day; visitors on a part-day excursion from a cruise ship, for example. The data are also assembled by different sources in different nations, including: immigration officials, tourism accommodation establishments, police, and so on. The criteria they employ in counting tourists vary somewhat, so one must be cautious in comparing specific nations.

Regardless of how it has been measured, however, the number of international tourists has been shown to increase almost every year since the mid-1990s. It has dipped only slightly during global recessions. To be specific, in 1996 there were fewer than 600 million international (inbound) tourists. In 2007 the number increased to 911 million and by 2018 it reached approximately 1.4 billion.[74] The global increase, and the size of the increase experienced by specific nations both correlated strongly with rates of migration. To be specific, high rates of emigration are associated with increased tourism because people who emigrate are especially likely later to return to their country of origin as tourists. In addition, nations with high rates of tourism tend to attract large numbers of in-migrants seeking employment in travel, tourism and hospitality industries.[75]

The five cities that attracted the greatest number of overnight international visitors in 2018 are presented in Table 1.2. In recent decades, the yearly fluctuations in the rankings of the leading cities tend to be small. Note that these figures do not count the number of foreign visitors who exit from a plane or ship unless they spend at least one night in the city. Otherwise the rankings would be overly influenced by the degree to which cities served as international transfer points. In addition, as explained above, small differences among cities should be interpreted with caution. The global figures, compiled at the end of 2018, are presented in Table 1.2.

The city that benefited the most financially from global tourism was Dubai, with annual tourist revenue above $31 billion (U.S.).[76] It is, of course, the principal city in UAE, previously identified as the nation in which migrants comprised the largest share of the total population, though its exotic resorts, malls and museums attract millions of tourists with no prior connection to Dubai.

Immigrant Immersion Tourism

Every year thousands of people sign up for international travel that is designed to provide the tourist with an in-depth cultural experience. Some of the programs are designed to facilitate learning a language or how to cook native dishes, but of interest to us are those trips in which observing and meeting with migrants is a major objective. These trips are organized by churches, colleges, immigrant aid organizations, etc., and they can ordinarily last for as little as one week or for as long as one year.

The most complete assessment of a migrant immersion tour is probably Gary Adler's analysis of BorderLinks, an organization that brings church or college groups to the U.S. Mexican border where they meet with customs officials and spend time interacting with Mexican migrants hoping to settle in the U.S. but living in immigration shelters or border towns on the Mexican side of the wall separating them from the U.S. The immersion experience is designed to generate understanding and sympathy for the migrants and it seems to be successful in this regard. Most participants described their experience as transformative. However, Adler found it difficult to decide whether the immersion produced any long-lasting changes among participants or made them more inclined to act on behalf of the migrants. The problem, he concluded, was that participants were given little background information about the political and social conditions that led to their migration and border settlements. So, they felt saddened but were not mobilized to act on behalf of the migrants.[77]

Medical Tourism

Every year thousands of people travel across national boundaries in search of some type of medical care that they believe is better than what is available in their home country. Their length of stay abroad can be as brief as a few days and can be one-time event, or it may involve recurrent visits, and in some cases lead to a permanent move. This variation has made it difficult to find the best way to label medical-related travel. The earliest analyses usually described it as "medical tourism," so that is how it is being referred to here. However, tourism usually implies leisurely and entirely voluntary travel for pleasure. The international search for medical assistance, by contrast, is more likely to entail stress and it is not as fully voluntary as most tourism. At the same time, many people seeking foreign medical assistance combine the medical consultation or treatment with sightseeing, adding a conventional tourist dimension to their travel.[78]

Some medical travel might also be best viewed as a "quest" or a "pilgrimage." In response to a pessimistic medical prognosis in their home country, a number of people search for a foreign alternative and are willing to travel a great distance in order to access an experimental treatment they believe may help to alleviate their problem. A variety of medical issues can lead to this type of travel: debilitating symptoms that are not given a medical diagnoses, infertility, illnesses viewed as fatal in their home country but not everywhere, etc. It is the faith and hope that desperate people place in a distant alternative that suggests viewing their travel as resembling a pilgrimage.

Medical travel can be the idiosyncratic preference of an individual or it can be tied to a cultural pattern in which visits to distant family and friends are expected to occur periodically in conjunction with travel to seek medical assistance. Somali patients who travel from the UK, described in the following case study (in Box 1.5), illustrate how medical tourism can be part of this type of cultural pattern.

> **Box 1.5   Somali Medical Tourists From Britain**
>
> During the last half of the 20th century, there were several waves of migrants from Somali who moved to neighboring African countries, to North America and to Western Europe. Some of the Somali expat concentrations became very large; for example, in 2020 there were a total of over 100,000 Somalis living in major cities in the UK. Large numbers also emigrated to Germany and the Netherlands. Many of the Somalis living abroad maintained ties with Somali emigres living in other nations, and these ties shaped the destinations they chose when they sought outside medical care. Through these ties, they obtained information about what medical treatments might be available in these other nations, though they also received information via targeted advertising. For example, commercials for German clinics and doctors regularly appeared on Somali television channels available via satellite in the UK.[79]
>
> Among members of the Somali community in the UK, and specifically in Manchester and Camden, Britain's National Health Service (NHS) was generally viewed unfavorably. Many felt that in the health care system available to them, medical staff did not give them adequate attention. They felt that doctors and nurses asked too few questions about their ailments and were too quick simply to dispense a prescription in order to get rid of them. They were told to return in a month or two if they did not feel better as they were hurried out the door.
>
> Within the UK, the alternative to the NHS was a doctor in the private sector, but it was a very expensive alternative. With help from the local Somali communities, the Somalis living in the UK could get health care in Germany or the Netherlands more cheaply than from UK facilities that were outside of the NHS. In addition, the travel to these other nations enabled them to re-establish connections with family and friends from whom they had been separated, as well as giving them an opportunity to do some sightseeing. Somalis in Germany and the Netherlands not only provided Somali travelers from the UK with information about local medical facilities but also provided help with room and board and medical costs when needed.

Finally, in some instances, what began as medical tourism has led people permanently to move to a different nation. In Cuenca, Ecuador, for example, there are hundreds of retirees from the U.S. who initially traveled to Ecuador to take advantage of that nation's inexpensive and easily accessed health services. Most of them wound up buying homes and settling in a "gringo" enclave where they remained largely because they believed they could not afford comparable health care in the U.S.[80]

Notes

1. See, for example, Jeffrey D. Sachs, *The Age of Globalization*. Columbia University, 2020.
2. For a review of economic globalization in the late 20th century, see Chapter Three and Appendix C in, Angus Maddison, *The World Economy*. OECD, 2006.

3 For further discussion of TNCs, see Grazia Ietto-Gillies, *Transnational Corporations and International Production*. Edward Elgar, 2019.
4 Employment and revenue figures from, UN Conference on Trade and Development, *World Investment Report*. 2012, and Organization for Economic Development and Cooperation, *Multinational enterprises in the global economy*. May, 2018.
5 International Monetary Fund, *World Economic Outlook*. July, 2019.
6 Zachary Karabell, "The End of Globalization?" *The Wall Street Journal*, March 21–22, 2020.
7 Stephen Castle, "How Russia's Invasion is Helping." *The New York Times*, March 5, 2022, p A10.
8 Ibid, p C2.
9 Andrea Kolbel, "Imaginative geographies of international student mobility." *Social and Cultural Geography*, 21, 2020.
10 United Nations, *World Migration Report*, 2020. (See especially chapter two.)
11 Ibid.
12 UN, *World Migration Report* 2020. See especially chapter two.
13 Ibid.
14 Worldometer, *United Arab Emirates Population*. May, 2020.
15 For these and other definitions, see International Organization for Migration, *Migration Data Portal 2020*.
16 Ibid.
17 Due to a historic tie to the U.S., the Micronesians were allowed to work in the U.S. without visas or green cards. For further description of the Micronesian economy, see the Asian Development Bank, *Report on the Federated States of Micronesia*, December 1, 2018.
18 Jack Healy, "Crossing an Ocean to Butcher Hogs, and then Set Adrift." *The New York Times*, October 14, 2019, p A14.
19 A vivid ethnographic account of migrants' work in an Iowa meatpacking plant is provided by, Deborah Fink, *Cutting into the Meatpacking Line*. University of North Carolina, 2020.
20 Healy, op.cit., p A14.
21 Ibid.
22 Hannah Beech, "In a World of Migrant Workers, A World of Risk." *The New York Times*, April 11, 2020, p A4.
23 National Science Foundation, *S&E Indicators 2018*, chapter three. In 2015 the U.S. government issued about 600,000 visas for high-skilled workers, over half on J-1B visas that are issued for up to three years, with the possibility of an extension to six years.
24 Transfers within UN agencies and global banks are examined in, Ranji Devadson, "The Golden Handcuffs?" *Journal of Ethnic and Migration Studies*, 43, 2017.
25 See the discussion of how General Motors decisions made in the U.S. were implemented in Australia, in, Stephen Clibborn, "The politics of employment relations in a multinational corporation during crisis." *Economic and Industrial Democracy*, 2019.
26 OECD, *Multinational Enterprises in the Global Economy*. May, 2018.
27 KPMG, *Global Assignment Policies and Practices Survey*. KPMG, 2020.
28 For further discussion, see Brooke Harrington and Leonard Seabrooke, "Transnational Professionals." *Annual Review of Sociology*, 46, 2020.
29 Katrin Sontag, "Mobile Entrepreneurs." Budrich UniPress, 2018.
30 See, for example, Marisa F.F. Tavares, "Across establishments, within firms." *Journal for Labour Market Research*, 54, 2017.
31 The Women's International League for Peace and Freedom has produced a number of papers, available online, describing women's roles in TNCs. See, for example, "Transnational Companies and their Impact on Women's Human Rights." 11 June, 2014.
32 For further discussion, see Ines Wagner, *Workers Without Borders*. Cornell University, 2018.
33 For more information about the agency, see: http://www.unchr.org
34 See Marta B. Erdal and Ceri Oeppen, "Forced to leave?" *Journal of Ethnic and Migration Studies*, 44, 2018.
35 UNCHR, *Global Report 2018*. See also Figure 1 in, Serdar Kaya and Phil Orchard, "Prospects of Return." *Journal of Immigration and Refugee Studies*, 18, 2020.
36 "800,000 Syrians on the Run, With Nowhere Left to Go." *The New York Times*, February 17, 2020, p A6.

37 See Jacques Charmes, "The Informal Economy," In Erika Kramer-Mbula and Sacha Wunch-Vincent (Eds), *The Informal Economy in Developing Nations*. Cambridge University, 2016.
38 Omer Karasaapan, "Turkey's Syrian Refugees – the welcome fades." *Brookings Future Development*, October 25, 2019.
39 Izza Leghtas, "Insecure Future." *Refugees International Field Report*, September, 2019.
40 See Anju Mary Paul, "Stepwise International Migration." *American Journal of Sociology*, 116. 2011.
41 Michael Schwirtz, et al., "Desperation Grows for Trapped Civilians." *The New York Times*, March 8, 2022, p A1.
42 For further descriptions, see IOM, *Traffickers and Trafficking*. UN, 2014.
43 For further discussion, see Fabian Georgi and Suzanne Schatral, "Toward a Critical Theory of Migration Control." In Martin Geiger and Antoine Pecoud (Eds), *International Organizations and the Politics of Migration*. Routledge, 2017.
44 UNODC, *Global Report on Trafficking in Persons 2016*.
45 Ibid. See also IOM, *Human Trafficking Global Database*, 2017.
46 Allyson Hobbs, *A Chosen Exile*. Harvard University, 2016.
47 Angela S. Garcia, *Legal Passing*. University of California, 2019.
48 Lynne A. Hartnett, "Relief and Revolution." *Journal of Ethnic and Migration Studies*, 45, 2019.
49 World Tourist Organization, *op.cit.*, p 12.
50 Public Broadcasting System, "Saving Elian." *Frontline*, 2001.
51 Annika Henroth-Rothstein, *Exile*. Bombardier Books, 2020.
52 See, for example, Chris B. Current, *Questioning the Cuban Exile Model*. LFB Scholarly, 2010.
53 These terms are described in, UNESCO, *Facts and Figures, Mobility in Higher Education*, 2015.
54 UNESCO, *Internationally Mobile Students*, 2019.
55 Laura Prazeras, "At home in the city." *Social and Cultural Geography*, 19, 2018.
56 See, for example, the study of STEM students at UC-Santa Barbara, reported by, X. Han, et al., "Will they stay or will they go?" *PLoS One*, 10, 2015.
57 Carolyn Choi, "Moonlighting in the nightlife." *Sexualities*, 20, 2017.
58 For more information about OECD and family migration data, see OECD, *International Migration Outlook*, 2017, and OECD, *Migration Data Portal*, 2019. See also, Kate Hooper and Brian Salant, "It's Relative." *Migration Policy Institute*, April, 2018.
59 Jessica Vaughan, "Immigration Multipliers." Center for Immigration Studies, September, 2001
60 See Alisdair Rogers, et al., *A Dictionary of Human Geography*. Oxford University, 2013.
61 For a discussion of these terms, see Thomas H. Eriksen, "What's wrong with the global North and the global South?" *Global South Studies Center*, 1, 2015.
62 For further discussion, see Caroline B. Brettell, "Marriage and migration." *Annual Review of Anthropology*, 2017.
63 For a history of mail-order brides, see Marcia Zug, *Buying a Bride*. New York University, 2016.
64 Saara Pellander, "An acceptable marriage." *Journal of Family Issues*, 36, 2015.
65 See the review of studies in, Wei-Jun Jean Yeung and Zheng Mu, "Migration and marriage in Asian contexts." *Journal of Ethnic and Migration Studies*, 45, 2019.
66 Daniele Belanger and Guillaume Haemmerli, "We no longer fear brides from afar." *Asian and Pacific Migration Journal*, 28, 2019.
67 For a discussion of sex tourism, especially from the female perspective, see Jacqueline S. Taylor, "Female sex tourism." *Feminist Review*, 109, 2006.
68 For further discussion of sex and mobility in Cuba, see Carrie Hamilton, *Sex and Revolution in Cuba*. University of North Carolina, 2012.
69 Nadine T. Fernandez, "Tourist brides and migrant grooms." *Journal of Ethnic and Migration Studies*, 45, 2019.
70 Ibid, p 3146.
71 See the discussion in Brettell, op.cit.
72 Fernandez, op.cit.
73 World Tourism Organization, *Yearbook of Tourism Statistics*, 2020.
74 Ibid.
75 The criteria are presented and explained in, World Tourism Organization, *Tourism and Migration*, 2009.

76 Ibid.
77 Gary J. Adler, *Empathy beyond U.S. Borders*. Cambridge University, 2019.
78 For further discussion see Meghann Ormond and Dian Sulianti, "More than medical tourism." *Current Issues in Tourism*, 20, 2017.
79 Neil Lunt, "The United Kingdom's Somali population as medical nomads." *Journal of Ethnic and Migration Studies*, 10, 2019.
80 Matthew Hayes, *Gringolandia*. University of Minnesota, 2018.

2 The Economic Driver

The drivers of international migration are the forces – both external to people (e.g. collapse of an economy) and internal (e.g. desiring lifestyle freedom) – that provide the impetus to, or shape people's desires to, move. They can also be defined as the variables that correlate with, and thereby help to explain, rates and patterns of migration. These drivers can in some cases independently influence migration, but multiple drivers are often involved, especially when a migration is widespread.

In terms of the number of people who are led to migrate across national boundaries, the economic driver has historically been especially important. To be more specific, the variable that has usually been singled out as most crucial is economic disparity which entails the differences in labor force remuneration between nations. The greater that difference, the more migration is expected to occur from the poorer to the wealthier nation.

Macro Perspectives

The earliest theories that attempted to explain how the economies of nations impacted migration between them were cast in macro terms. Precisely what macro entails varies somewhat among social science disciplines, but it almost invariably pertains to large-scale structures and processes. In Sociology, for example, macro ordinarily encompasses the analysis of an entire society or variables that characterize a society, such as its demographic structure or system of government; or it can entail processes of social change that transform a society, such as industrialization or modernization's impact upon gender roles. In Economics, to illustrate further, macro involves aggregate activities of the entire economy, such as overall productivity (e.g. GDP) or levels of unemployment; or changes in these aggregate phenomena that have economy-wide effects.[1]

The early theories, stemming from the 19th century, described macro drivers as "determinants" of migration, implying an automatic, or reflexive, connection between them and people's movement. If one nation's economy declined while another's improved, large numbers of people were simply expected to move from the deteriorating economy to the one that was doing better. Little attention was paid to how people experienced the events that were occurring or how they decided upon a course of action. In effect, agency – people's ability to formulate a course of action independently of structural constraints – was either dismissed or ignored. This tendency is characteristic of most macro theories because they are trying to explain aggregates or large in scale processes. As a result, they tend to be very abstract, and explaining precisely how macro phenomena shape people's actions can be problematic.

DOI: 10.4324/9781003158400-2

From Push Pull to Neoclassical Macro

The contemporary emphasis upon economic drivers and economic disparities between nations has as its primary predecessor the push-pull theory, and it is probably the oldest theory of migration that is still discussed today. It was first presented, in systematic form, by the geographer Ernest Ravenstein in the late 19th century. In a series of papers analyzing census documents from a sample of nations, he concluded that most migration was due to economic conditions that produced a spatial dis-equilibrium. Stated abstractly, he proposed that movement between two places was a function of their masses (i.e. population size) and the distance between them. This formulation was intended to parallel Newton's second law of motion. More concretely, he reported that it was the difference between the limited opportunities of poor agricultural areas ("push") and the more attractive possibilities offered by industrial cities ("pull") that accounted for most of the migration he observed in the late 19th century. The moves in his sample largely involved short distances and most moves were within nation rather than international. However, he concluded that the push-pull model operated similarly for migration both within and between nations, except for the tendency for international migrants to involve a higher excess of males to females.[2]

Over the years, while the push-pull theory was able to explain some patterns of migration, many analysts considered it to have fundamental flaws. The theory's harshest critics contended that it was a static model that simply listed differences between places and then regarded the differences as "automatically" generating a flow of people between them in order to attain a balance or equilibrium. Migration, they argue, is better conceptualized as a more dynamic process because there are all sorts of contingencies that arise between a migrant's origin and a destination and the push-pull theory does not capture these dynamics.[3]

Many migration analysts nevertheless continue to rely upon some of the basic assumptions of the push-pull model, but without referring to it as push-pull theory, and no longer try to parallel Newton's Laws of Motion. For example, Nicholas Van Hear and colleagues state that, despite the criticisms, they continue to find the theory useful in explaining empirically observed patterns of migration. In particular, they see merit in the theory's basic idea that external material conditions – i.e. macro structural forces, such as fluctuations in the economic institution – shape migration process "by making certain decisions, routes or destinations more likely."[4] In this pared down form it is a more conventional macro economic theory and it has a lot of supporting empirical evidence.

Illustrative of contemporary research that relies upon such a macro model is a recent global study conducted by the World Bank (WB). The investigators computed mean (i.e. average) wages in a sample of 88 nations from the global north and south, and then calculated wage differentials between each pair of nations. The wage differentials were variable one. The WB researchers also obtained data on the number of emigrants moving between each pair of nations in their sample. That was variable two. In their analysis they found a strong positive relationship between these two variables: the greater the difference in mean wages between any two nations, the greater the emigration from the lower to the higher wage nation. Because average wages in the U.S. were higher than in Canada, for example, even though both were high-wage nations, more people emigrated from Slovenia (a lower-wage country) to the U.S. than to Canada. Overall, WB found that a difference of $2,000 between an origin and destination nation made an emigrant 10% more likely to choose that destination nation. Finally, separate analyses of economic migrants and refugees showed that economic differences between nations played a similar role in the migration decisions of each group.[5]

Leaving Venezuela

Venezuela presents an interesting nation in which to study the migration effects of a macro economic driver because, to date, the largest emigration ever in the Americas has involved the recent movement out of Venezuela. In 2013, the nation entered a recessionary period that grew dramatically worse in (and after) 2015 when the nation's oil production declined along with the price of oil. Prior to 2013, Venezuela was the wealthiest country in Latin America, due primarily to oil revenue, and had a surplus of in- to out-migration. In 2013 there was also a change in government and a more autocratic regime took power, and was widely accused of corruption and incompetence. Oil revenue continued to decline, unemployment and under-employment increased and it became almost impossible for many people to buy food, medicine, and other basic necessities.[6]

Between 2016 and 2020, an estimated five to six million Venezuelans left the country in search of jobs. From among nearby nations, Venezuelans emigrated to those with the best economies. Columbia, with whom Venezuela shares hundreds of miles of common border, is the closest nation, it has the highest income levels of Venezuela's immediate neighbors, and it has received, by far, the most Venezuelan emigrants. Just how powerful the economic driver has been is illustrated by the thousands of Venezuelan parents who left their children to emigrate to Colombia in hopes of finding work. See the discussion in Box 2.1.

Box 2.1   Leaving Children Behind in Venezuela

By 2020, after years of a deteriorating economic situation, most people fortunate enough to find any job in Venezuela could not earn enough to feed themselves, let alone their children. In desperation, they emigrated to Colombia, and to Chile, Peru, and elsewhere in hopes of finding work. Many parents left their children behind, either because they feared that the trip would be too difficult or too dangerous for their children or because they could not afford to take them along. An estimated one million children were left with grandparents, other relatives, or in the care of older siblings, children themselves.[7]

Especially because many of the households were headed by single mothers, the departure of the sole parent was usually extremely difficult for the children left behind. As Aura Fernandez, a single mother, waited in front of her home for the bus that would be the start of her trip to Colombia, her eight-year-old son promised he would not cry, her 10-year-old daughter hid in the kitchen, and her 12-year-old son hauled her suitcase into the yard. She felt torn, but her children were eating only one small meal a day, and she saw no alternatives in Venezuela. She left her children under the supervision of her parents, and set out along with thousands of other desperate Venezuelans. In Colombia, she found a job as a housekeeper that paid better than any job she could find in Venezuela, and every two weeks she sent as much money home as she could to her parents.[8]

> How long migrating parents will ultimately be separated from their children is often indefinite. Aura Fernandez, for example, returned home at Christmas but found the children were still only eating one meal a day so she returned to Colombia. To illustrate further: Ysabel Abad Rojas left three children under her parents' oversight when she went to Colombia in search of work, but she had little success. Penniless and frantic, she was easily recruited by drug gangs to smuggle cocaine out of Colombia, but she was apprehended before she could cross the border, and jailed in Colombia. As this is written, she is awaiting a likely sentence of 8 to 15 years.[9]

At the same time that we recognize the impact of macro economic drivers, consider the fact that despite economic adversity within a nation and economic disparities between nations, everyone does not leave lower-wage nations. In fact, more people usually remain in a lower-wage nation than migrate to a higher-wage nation. Macro theories are framed at a level of analysis that is necessarily removed from the actions of concrete individuals. Therefore, macro drivers do not enable analysts to explain what accounts for the differences among people because they do not explicate the processes that intervene between macro events and people's actions. In other words, there is no clarification of *how* the macro event leads to concrete behavior (e.g. moving).[10] Questions of this type were instrumental in leading migration theorists to develop a micro level theory.

Micro Perspectives

Micro refers most fundamentally to small-in-scale analyses. In sociology it entails the study of individuals and small groups, usually in face-to-face interaction. Micro economics focuses upon decision-making by individuals and organizations, for example, how they analyze supply and demand in setting prices. In geography, to illustrate further, micro analyses examine relations between people and places in small spaces, such as a neighborhood or a business office.[11]

Cutting across social science disciplines, micro analyses consistently emphasize the deliberate actions of individuals within a perspective that assumes that macro structures and processes may be influential, but are not deterministic. Agency is correspondingly stressed. Finally, most of these theories assume that micro phenomena are the building blocks of larger entities so that over the long run analysts can work inductively from explanations of the local and specific to the more general and abstract.

Neoclassical Micro Theory

During the 1960s and 1970s, there were a number of journal articles that pushed migration theory toward more consideration of individuals' cost-benefit assessments in reaching the decision to migrate. The most basic migration postulate in the micro perspective is that workers will continue to move as long as the marginal benefits exceed the marginal costs, that is, as long as the incremental increase in benefits received by migrants is greater than the incremental increase in their costs.

A notable contribution to the development of the micro perspective was a paper by economist Michael Todaro which presented a behavioral model, focusing upon the process through which people go in choosing either to remain or leave. While he primarily discussed intra-urban moves, his theory was equally applicable to inter-nation moves. He proposed that individuals' decisions were based upon a rational calculation of the net economic benefit that a move could entail. To migrate obviously entails costs from the actual expense of moving to lost wages in the transition. People will not undertake the costs of moving unless they think the eventual return will be worth it. The relevant considerations are the size of the income differential between origin and destination, plus the individuals' calculation of the probability of finding employment in the destination that would be sufficient to compensate for the costs of relocating.[12]

The development of models that could explain how individuals calculate rewards and costs has remained a central concern of contemporary micro theorists. For example, a major factor in determining net benefits is what Clemons and associates refer to as the "place premium." It is the increase in wages that is due to the place, itself, rather than the training or skill of people in its labor force. To illustrate, in the U.S. compared to a large sample of low-wage nations, there is an average place premium in purchasing power of $13,600. (Purchasing power adjusts wages to reflect the costs of commodities in different nations. See the explanation in Box 2.2.) The cost of moving includes diverse expenses, such as travel fees, visa requirements and so on. So, the theoretical expectation would be that workers would continue to leave low-wage nations and migrate to the U.S. as long as the costs of the move were less than $13,600.[13]

Box 2.2 Remittances and Household Risk Avoidance

For households facing economic adversity, particularly in less wealthy nations with limited safety nets, it is often considered the best strategy for one member of the household to migrate to another nation whose employment opportunities may be better. Household members can then more easily pool resources to cover the cost of one of them traveling to another country rather than the entire household. For example, in an impoverished Guatemalan village, the father of one young man sold his last four goats for $2,000 to pay for the cost of his son's migration.[27]

The individual who leaves is usually expected to send money back to the people left behind. These remittances are often of critical importance to the household, and the individual who migrates usually feels a strong obligation to keep sending money, even if economic conditions deteriorate in the destination nation. The following examples involve migrants who left households behind in Mexico and moved to the United States. In the summer of 2020, a Covid virus outbreak slowed the U.S. economy, and good-paying jobs became harder for migrants to get. They nevertheless felt great pressure to keep sending money home.

Elias Bruno found work for a construction company in Florida that enabled him to send remittances that helped to support five people in his household who remained in Mexico. When there were fewer construction projects because of the economic slowdown, he began to station himself outside a hardware store waiting for a homeowner or another contractor to come by and hire him on a daily basis. "You have to make every sacrifice to feed your family," he said.[28] Despite the problems he has faced in finding enough work, he still continued to send them at least $200 every month.

> Rafael Romero found a job working for a company in Maryland that both finished and patched the asphalt in stores' parking lots. He was earning $1400 per week until many businesses were closed by the epidemic, and no longer spent money on their parking lots. During the good times, he was able to send $600 per month to help support his extended family: his parents, children and siblings. When a lot of the work disappeared, he was only able to remit $300 per month so he left his temporary home and traveled 250 miles to Virginia, where he heard there were more better-paying jobs. "We aren't going to let down our families who depend upon us," he said.[29]

In addition to placing an emphasis upon individual assessments, Todaro broadened the narrow economic focus, recognizing that the potential costs people consider include the difficulty of adjusting to a new labor market and leaving family and friends. Writing at the same time as Todaro, sociologist Everett Lee further elaborated on the number of "intervening obstacles." Here he noted other impediments to migration such as immigration restrictions and lack of transportation. Noting such barriers has remained an important part of contemporary research. For example, the previously introduced World Bank (WB) study concluded that "economic costs and benefits remain critical determinants of migration decisions ..."[14] However, WB analysts stated that costs include not only physical distance between origins and intended destinations but social-cultural differences between origins and intended destinations. Specifically, inter-nation differences in language and culture acted as barriers to, and cost of, emigration much the same as the physical distance between them.

Another important insight in the development of the micro perspective came from Lee emphasizing that people have imperfect knowledge of the difference between origin and potential destinations. They may make inaccurate assumptions, especially concerning job availability in the potential destination and the likely reception given to newcomers. Even if unrealistic, however, these perceptions influence the decision of whether or not to migrate. Further, these perceptions systematically vary among individuals so that macro differences among places are not the automatic migration driver. In other words, to understand how people reach the decision to migrate requires a micro-level analysis. For example, older individuals may be less likely to migrate because their greater familiarity with their place of residence may lead them to over-value it.[15]

Aspirations Versus Capability

There is also the matter of wanting to migrate as opposed to being able to migrate, and the tendency for macro theories not to distinguish between them. Large in scale economic downturns may make people wish that they could move elsewhere, but their ability to do so is a separate matter and the distinction is most likely to arise in an individual-level analysis. For example, Mexicans who live in rural areas are more likely than their urban counterparts to want to migrate to another country because they perceive their current opportunities as more limited. However, urban residents who want to leave typically face fewer obstacles – because they tend to have more resources and more access to transportation – and are therefore more likely to migrate than similarly inclined people in non-urban regions of the country. Across both types of areas, the desire to migrate correlates strongly with migration, but the correlation is stronger in urban than rural areas. Stated differently, the rural areas of Mexico contain more involuntary non-migrants.[16]

According to a Gallup World Poll Survey conducted in 140 nations between 2010 and 2015, more than 20% of the surveyed respondents expressed a desire to migrate to a different nation. However, no large, multinational sample contained that large a proportion of people who actually migrated. We noted in Chapter 1, for example, that around 2015 about 3% of the world's population was estimated to consist of international migrants. Such large differences between desires to move and actual moves have led the European Commission's research group to warn forecasters that, "a wish to migrate is not a reliable enough indicator ... about future migration."[17]

The macro drivers clearly impact people's aspirations to move, but for many reasons the relationship between aspiration and behavior is contingent rather than automatic. In selecting a course of action in reaction to the same set of forces, variations occur because people confront different sets of obligations. For example, family ties inhibit some people from moving, but not others. In addition, some people can better afford the typical costs of migration and have differential access to the necessary modes of transportation. Furthermore, individuals and groups often differ in how the "same" situation is perceived, and as a result they choose different courses of action. For example, members of different religious groups may diverge in whether they see a political change as so threatening to them as to suggest a need for members of the faith to emigrate.

Aspirations and the Inverted U

At the same time that the neoclassical theories helped to explain patterns of migration, studies often reported some discrepancies between the theory and their data. In some places, the observed rate of migration was less than would have been expected given the amount of inequality between countries. In other cases, a higher than expected rate of mobility has been observed to continue despite declining disparities between nations.[18] One reason for the discrepancies between the theory and data lies in the relationship between amount of wealth in country of origin and the magnitude of differences in wealth between countries.

As adjusted per capita annual incomes in a nation increase to somewhere between $6,000 and $8,000 (studies differ), there is a corresponding step for step increase in that nation's rate of emigration. This relationship is presumably due to the fact that as a nation's wealth increases, more people have the resources that can enable them to migrate. This strong positive relationship between income and emigration is linear, that is, it can be plotted on a straight line because as income increases there are proportional increases in emigration. However, as the wealth of nations increases above $6–$8 thousand dollars per capita, emigration levels off and then declines. So, if an analysis includes a wide range of nations, and not just the poor ones, the relationship between income and emigration is better captured by an inverted U rather than a straight line.

The classic theory of the inverted U was presented in 1971 by geographer Wilbur Zelinsky and is usually referred to as the "mobility transition theory." He proposed that societies go through a series of developmental stages (i.e. become more modern) primarily determined by their wealth and fertility, and that these stages are associated with different emigration patterns. At the lowest end of the development hierarchy, nations are very poor and have very high birth rates. People in these societies tend to give little thought to emigrating, but in any case few could afford to move. As a nation moves toward a more middle stage of development, more people are aware of alternatives and more people have the requisite means to leave. Emigration rates increase; but as nations' wealth and modernity continue to increase toward a higher stage, people's incentive to move is reduced by greater opportunities at home. Rates of emigration are again low.[19]

One of the most thorough assessments of the mobility transition or inverted U theory was reported by economist Michael Clemens. Extrapolating from a dozen or more studies, he concluded that within the low-income category, a nation's rising income is strongly associated with increased emigration, almost without exception, until nations reach the mid-stage turning point. Emigration levels off at this point and then among high-income nations it falls (but not below that of the poorest nations). The inverted U pattern, Clemens concluded, is "unmistakable." The policy implication is also clear: If a wealthy destination nation (e.g. U.S.) wished to discourage emigration from the poorest nations, providing economic aid to those nations would, at least in the short run, be counter-productive.[20]

Digging deeper into the inverted U, Dao and associates say its shape can be best understood by distinguishing between the effects of ability and aspiration to move. They propose that ability continues to rise across all income stages and would, by itself, result in a continuation of the linear relationship between income and emigration. Aspirations, by contrast, level off as income increases, and then decline, and thereby account for the inverted U. A few studies may provide some support for their contention, but as they note, it can be difficult empirically (if not conceptually) to separate capability and aspiration.[21]

Further insight into how aspirations to emigrate are influenced comes from studies of young people in a number of nations. Of most relevance to us is the research that has been conducted in nations, or regions within nations, that are experiencing economic difficulties, but would not be placed into the lowest income levels. Many rural areas in eastern Germany fit this description. There is consensus among studies in finding that the primary impetus for young people in these places to emigrate would be to improve their economic positions. However, the decision to move is not made in a vacuum. Few people think about moving and make decisions in isolation. They are typically enmeshed in friendship and family networks in which economic conditions are socially defined as making emigration desirable and logical or unwise and unnecessary.[22]

It would not be surprising if there were a relationship between relative economic conditions and the nature of people's shared definitions of their economic situation. In that case, somewhat better local economic conditions would likely be paired with more hopeful local social-cultural views and they would conjointly restrain emigration.

In sum, the micro neoclassical economic model brought agency into the migration model, stressing the importance of individual differences in the evaluation of the costs and benefits of moving or staying. Aggregate migration flows between nations – the macro variable – are then seen as the cumulation of individual cost-benefit decisions.[23] However, by the mid-1980s, many economically-oriented migration analysts believed that micro perspectives had been taken too far, and that important macro considerations were being overlooked, and they concluded that both the neoclassical micro and macro models should be replaced by a new economics of labor migration (NELM).

New Economics of Labor Migration

NELM was initially presented not only as a synthesis of the neoclassical macro and micro perspectives but also as a new way to study migration, different from either of the two previous approaches. Among its major innovations was a change in focal point, from a micro emphasis upon individuals to an emphasis upon the household, or family, as the decision-making unit. (In most instances, households overlap closely with either nuclear or extended families, but focusing upon households enables analysts to deal with a broader range of possible living arrangements.) It was in the household unit, according to Stark and Bloom, that decision were made concerning whether all, some or none of the members of the household should migrate.[24]

Meso Analysis

In emphasizing the role of the household, NELM brought the meso level into the analysis. It is an intermediate level between the macro and the micro. Two types of studies can be placed into this category: (1) studies of specific groups or organizations that focus upon the ties among members. Following this approach, analysts frequently attempt to view the way relationships form an interlocking network. Or (2) studies that attempt to bridge the macro and micro, showing for example how individual cost-benefit analyses are translated into aggregate patterns.[25]

Household Risk Avoidance

According to Stark and Bloom and other NELM advocates, in addition to wanting to maximize their combined income, households consider risk mitigation a crucial criterion in evaluating the stay versus go alternative. In less wealthy nations, which are the major origins of economically-driven migration, there are a very limited number of ways in which people can hedge their bets. Unlike wealthier nations, they usually have neither government nor company offered insurance against a variety of adverse circumstances that people could confront: crop failures, loss of employment, etc. As a result, households in less wealthy nations often agree that one member of the household should leave to find employment in another nation. Further, the travel and relocation costs will be a lot less for one person than for the entire household. And if it does not work out for the migrant, he or she will have a place to return, and all of the household's accounts will not have been placed in a single basket. On the other hand, if the migrant is successful, she or he can send remittances back to the household members who remained behind (see Box 2.2). Then, depending upon the relative success of the migrant in finding good employment, those initially left behind may move to join the migrant. It is, therefore, the household (rather than any individual) that is seeking to maximize income and minimize risk.[26]

Relative Deprivation

NELM also proposed, unlike its immediate predecessors, that fluctuations in migration would not necessarily correlate highly with inter-nation changes in economic disparity. Even if a nation's economic standing declined, increased out-migration might not occur if leaving the country was not congruent with households' concern with minimizing risk.

And even if a nation's economy improved and disparity with other nations decreased, how the household was faring in comparison to others in the community or nation could also serve as a driver. This introduced the long-standing sociological concept of "relative deprivation" into the migration picture. This concept was formulated in studies of soldiers in World War II which found that their dissatisfaction was related more to differences in treatment, by rank, than to the absolute amount of deprivation they were experiencing. So soldiers expressed more dissatisfaction back at the base where some people were living in better conditions than others, and less dissatisfaction at the battlefields where everyone was in the same miserable boat. The investigators concluded that how satisfied people were with their situation depended largely upon how they saw themselves faring in comparison to others. Feelings of deprivation, in other words, are based on an assessment of one's relative position.[30] In any society, at any given time, some segments are likely to do better than others. For those households that see themselves lagging behind, relative deprivation can be an incentive to migrate, even if their nation's overall economy is improving.

Conclusions

Although NELM broke new ground, it has not been free from criticism. Particularly relevant are the issues raised by economist Alexandre Abreu. While he approved of NELM's substituting households for individuals as the focal unit, he felt that in following NELM analysts were still placing too much emphasis upon economic motivations, and correspondingly, paying too little attention to within-household dynamics. How, for example, do households reach decisions concerning who among them should migrate? How do gender and age affect these decisions? More interdisciplinary analyses were needed to answer these questions. Finally, Abreu argued that NELM under-appreciated how structural constraints affect migration decisions. In effect, NELM was criticized for too closely following its micro predecessor rather than balancing it with a macro perspective.[31]

Many of the criticisms offered by Abreu and others are currently being addressed in contemporary studies. For example, there is a growing literature on household decision-making dynamics in relation to migration, and it involves diverse contributions not only from economists but from sociologists, geographers, anthropologists and others.[32] And the macro approach, as we have noted with contemporary examples, continues to have adherents who are able to demonstrate that a macro perspective can explain large-scale migrations.

Actual Economic Returns

While not every migrant seeking better economic opportunities in another nation actually finds them, there are a number of studies that report moving to a wealthier country is typically associated with personal economic gain. To illustrate, a group of economists compared the wages (adjusted for differences in purchasing power between nations) of people who migrated to the U.S. to the wages of those who remained in the same low-wage nations as the ones the migrants left. In an effort to control, or at least minimize, differences between those who moved and those who were stationary, the entire sample consisted of men, 35 to 39 years of age, with high school education or less. On average, the economists found that the emigrants' adjusted earnings in the U.S. were about five times greater than the earnings of similarly aged and educated men from the same nations (mostly in the global south) who did not migrate – a substantial place premium.[33]

Other research suggests that moving to a higher-income nation, even on a part-year basis can yield a sizeable economic return. New Zealand, for example, brings in a large group of seasonal migrants from low-income nations who return every year to work on farms during planting and harvesting periods. Sampling from within these low-wealth nations, Gibson and McKenzie compared the incomes of households with such seasonal workers to those without. They found, over a two-year period, that incomes of the households with a seasonal migrant increased by over 30% relative to the households without a migrant. From interviews, they also found that people's subjective feelings of economic well-being were considerably higher in the households that contained a seasonal migrant.[34]

In sum, research suggests that those who emigrate from a low-income to a high-income nation can expect earnings substantially higher than that of their contemporaries who remain behind; but the cost of living also tends to be higher in high-income nations. Will the benefits be as great as they appear? If migrants manage to earn five times more, for example, will their purchasing power be similarly enhanced? An interesting way to answer this question is presented in Box 2.3 which examines earnings and purchasing power of McDonald's workers in different nations.

Box 2.3 The Real Cost of a Big Mac to McDonald's Workers

A "real" wage rate, according to economists, is calculated by dividing wages by the price of various products and services. The resultant figure indicates how much an hour of work, by an average paid worker, can buy. The best known of these calculations is Purchasing Price Parity (PPP) and it is often used to compare how much the same basket of commonly purchased goods costs workers in different nations in terms of hours of work. So, if the average worker in Nation A can purchase that basket of goods with earnings from 30 minutes of work and it takes a worker in Nation B one hour to buy a comparable basket, then the effective purchasing power (i.e. the real wage rate) in Nation A is twice that of Nation B.[35]

One problem with the basket of goods often used in comparing nations' PPP is that there are inter-nation differences in what goods and services are commonly purchased. Potatoes are more important in some nation's food baskets than rice in others; people in some nations regularly go to movie theaters, while people in other nations rarely attend. Comparability can, therefore, only be approximated. Economist Orley Ashenfelter decided to substitute a Big Mac for the basket of goods. It is widely consumed sandwich all over the world, rich nations and poor, north and south, and it is as close as one can find to an identical product wherever it is sold. And to compute PPP in each nation, he focused upon the wages paid to the average McDonald's crew member.[36]

In wealthier nations, McDonald's workers could purchase a lot more burgers with each hour's work than workers in poorer nations. Given the local cost of a Big Mac, and the wages of local McDonald's employees, one hour of work was enough to purchase almost three Big Macs in Japan; almost two and one-half in the U.S. and a little over two in Canada. In the economically less well-off nations, by contrast, McDonald's workers could afford to buy much less. For example, overall in a large group of Latin American nations (Argentina, Costa Rica, Ecuador, etc.) it took almost three hours for a crew member to buy a single Big Mac. In other words, McDonald's workers in Japan had nearly nine times more purchasing power than workers in the Latin nations (i.e. 3 per hour versus 1/3 per hour). Generalizing from the McDonald's data, Ashenflelter concluded that, "there are extraordinarily large differences in the effective wage rates received by workers doing the same work and using the same sets of skills in the rich and poor countries."[37]

The Welfare Magnet Thesis

Given the acknowledged importance of economic drivers to global migration, some analysts have raised the question of whether generous welfare benefits operate like good-paying jobs as a magnet for emigration. The welfare magnet theory proposes that some migrants who would otherwise remain at home may decide to migrate in order to obtain more generous benefits abroad; and then if the job market in the destination country does not turn out well, sizeable welfare outlays may discourage return migration. This theory was originally presented by George Borjas, and he provided support for the theory by examining where immigrants clustered in the U.S.[38]

The major cost of migrating to the U.S. from another country, Borjas argued, is getting to the U.S. To then decide to settle in a state with generous welfare benefits rather than a closer-to-the-border state with limited benefits entails a very small marginal cost. To demonstrate that migrants would choose to put down roots in generous states, he examined the distribution of migrants, by state, and ranked states on the size of the welfare benefits they offered. He found that there was more clustering of immigrants in states that offered the highest benefits, and this finding seemed consistent with his theory.

A number of studies followed, examining the welfare magnet theory in different groups of nations and reporting inconsistent results. Overall, they have found only conditional support for the welfare magnet theory. The welfare expenditures of nations have sometimes been shown to be positively related to the size of migrant inflows, especially for migrants from the global south, though the magnitude of the effect has generally been small. Many of these studies have also been criticized for their lack of statistical controls, raising the possibility that it is not welfare benefits that are the attraction, but some other variable that happens to be associated with those benefits. For example, nations with generous benefits tend to be wealthier, and these nations usually offer more jobs with good wages. So, perhaps it was the high wages and not the welfare benefits that drew the migrants. Particularly relevant is an analysis by sociologist Aaron Ponce who found that when he held constant other economic variables that are usually associated with a nation's in-migration rate, the overall effects of welfare benefits on migration were markedly reduced. His data suggested that the high cost of living and high taxes that were associated with generous welfare benefits might discourage economically motivated in-migration from all but the poorest nations.[39]

Some of the inconsistency in findings may also be due to differences in the types of welfare benefits that were examined in the different studies. For example, if the migrant pool has many families with young children, then the size of the old-age benefits a nation offers may be of little interest. To focus more specifically upon the possible attractiveness of different types of welfare, De Jong and associates studied migration patterns within 25 European nations; that is, people who left one of the European nations to settle in another European nation. This sample, they state, provides a "natural laboratory" in which to isolate the effects of welfare because these nations differ from each other in the welfare domains that they prioritize; and entry policies are irrelevant because of free movement within the EU.[40]

They examined migration between European nations that occurred between 2002 and 2008, focusing upon the relationship between a nation's yearly welfare expenditures, the type of welfare emphasized, and the number of in-migrants the nation attracted in the following year. They found that when a nation offered generous family benefits, it attracted large numbers of young families with children while generous old-age benefits attracted large numbers of the oldest migrants. However, a government's spending on unemployment benefits not only failed to attract people of working age, it actually had a negative effect.

Finding for young families and the oldest migrants are consistent with the welfare magnet theory and may need no additional explanation. The finding on unemployment benefits is inconsistent with the theory, and the investigators speculated on why this relationship would be negative. They suggest two possibilities: (1) perhaps younger adults are less interested in unemployment benefits because they have not worked long enough to qualify for generous unemployment assistance and/or (2) perhaps higher unemployment expenditures imply labor market problems which discourage would-be migrants of working age. The investigators left the unanswered questions for future studies to resolve. We can nevertheless conclude that the welfare magnet theory receives the most support when the generosity of a nation's welfare benefits corresponds with certain demographic characteristics of migrants. Under these conditions, welfare benefits can operate like an economic driver of migration.

Migrant Selectivity

While studies consistently report that moving from a low-income to a high-income nation, even on a part-time basis, results in economic gains, attributing a precise causal effect to such emigration has been hampered by methodological concerns. What especially confounds analyses of migration's economic returns is the possibility that in any samples of nations being compared there were systematic differences between those people who emigrated and those who remained behind. If those who opted to leave were either better or less educated or either more or less motivated, for example, then any observed differences between the outcomes of migrants and non-migrants could be due to pre-existing differences. This introduces the issue of selectivity, and in recent years it has been one of the most studied issues in the migration literature.

It is very difficult to specify exactly when research interest in selectivity began, but there are a couple of early publications that warrant mention. One of the earliest systematic studies of differences between migrants and non-migrants from the same area was reported by Carle Zimmerman, a rural sociologist. Around 1920 he studied young people from farm families in the state of Minnesota, some of whom moved to nearby towns and cities, and some of whom remained in their rural areas. He was interested in how the movers and the stayers differed from each other and he calculated the differences between them in age, gender, family wealth, and so on. While Zimmerman did not examine international migration and did not identify his research question as one of selectivity, he clearly helped to introduce the issue into the migration literature.[41]

Methodological Issues

Some years after Zimmerman's work, there was a stream of methodological publications that were not specifically directed to migration that nevertheless helped later to focus attention upon selectivity in migration. Of particular importance, Social Psychologists Cook and Campbell published a book in 1979 that examined a variety of interpretive issues in non-experimental research (that is, studies that lack the controls typically found in an experimental design). They noted that any time two groups are being compared on the effects of an event or experience it is possible that the people who happen to be in one of the groups will have had, prior to the research, an experience that people in the other group has not had. It can then be very difficult to separate the effects of that prior experience from the effects of the variable being studied. This problem, they concluded, besets all types of non-experimental research, but they did not assign a label to the problem.[42] A few years later, sociologist Stanley Lieberson expanded upon Cook and Campbell's work, further clarifying the need to separate the impact of an experience or event from effects that were better attributed to a prior selective sorting process. He explicitly identified this methodological issue as a selectivity problem.[43]

One model against which Lieberson, Campbell and Cook, and others were comparing most social science research was a laboratory experiment on rats conducted by an animal behaviorist. The subjects (e.g. rats) are specially bred to eliminate genetic differences, and they are kept under highly controlled conditions to eliminate the possibility of differences in their experiences prior to an experiment. Then the subjects are differentially exposed to some condition in a single experiment which enables an investigator to infer that any differences observed among the animals are due to the variables the investigator manipulated in the experiment. When humans are the subjects in research, the same degree of pre-experiment control is obviously impossible. The alternative for social scientists is to randomly assign subjects to experimental and control groups. In principle that will eliminate any systematic differences between those in each group. Any observed differences can then be attributed only to the variable being studied.

However, almost all migration studies follow a non-experimental design, and are therefore vulnerable to a selectivity problem because the past experiences of people are not randomly controlled. The people who happen to move or to remain behind may, prior to the time the research began, have differed from each other in ways that can confound efforts to interpret any differences that are later observed between them.

Some migration studies have designed special procedures to examine selectivity with respect to specific variables, such as education, income, physical health, etc. A number of studies have also followed a method initially described by Cynthia Feliciano. To measure educational selectivity, she constructed an index that compared the educational level of groups of migrants to the overall educational level of their origin country's population. To be more specific, she compared the migrants to their birth cohort in their origin country in order to eliminate the effect of changes that may have occurred in the origin country after the migrant's cohort completed their education.[44] This procedure has been widely followed in selectivity studies focusing upon both education and income.

If, on the other hand, there are substantial regional differences in the population within the origin nation, Feliciano later suggested that the most appropriate group to compare to the migrants might not be the entire country's population, but the population in the migrants' region of origin, assuming that most of the migrants came from the same region. The objective, of course, is to identify the most equivalent non-migrant group in the home country in order to minimize pre-existing differences.[45]

Socioeconomic Status Selectivity

Socioeconomic status usually refers to the standing of a person relative to others in a community or society. As its name implies, it involves a ranked hierarchy that combines people's social and economic attributes. It is most typically measured by level of education and the prestige of one's occupation. Other variables, such as lifestyle, wealth or place of residence, are also sometimes utilized as measures of socioeconomic status; but particularly when combined, education and occupation correlate highly with many other variables, including income.[46]

Depending upon the data that are available, some studies rely upon a single indicator, for example, education. Others rely upon a combination of variables, with education and occupation the most commonly utilized. Because all of the socioeconomic indicators tend to be inter-related. the use of different measures usually produces similar results. (At some times and places, immutable characteristics, such race and ethnicity can also be involved in determining socioeconomic standing.)

A number of studies, such as Feliciano's noted above, have found that emigrants are positively selected on education and other indicators of socioeconomic status compared to homestayers. Particularly if they are living in a low-income nation with limited employment opportunities, people with more education and skills may feel trapped, and be more inclined to emigrate as a result. However, there are also studies that report a negative association between migration and education.[47] Especially if educational requirements are increasing in the home nation, less educated people may find it difficult to find work, and may decide to emigrate in response.

Most of the studies on educational or income selectivity have examined a single ethnic group's international movement from one origin to one destination, so it is likely that different findings are at least in part a function of variations among migrant streams. For example, Mexican migrants to the U.S. have tended to be less educated (hypo-selected) than their non-migrant counterparts while Nigerian migrants to the U.S. have been much more educated (hyper-selected) than non-migrant Nigerians. In addition, compared to the U.S. population, Mexicans are under-educated while Nigerians are over-educated.[48] (There are also substantial selectivity effects on the second generation which are discussed in Chapter 4.)

Some insight into why there are differences in socioeconomic selectivity among emigrant groups comes from a study of asylum seekers from five different nations. All applied to Germany for asylum between 2013 and 2016, claiming that they faced threats to their lives at home, though actual threat levels varied among their countries of origin. Lucas Guichard was able to obtain data on the would-be migrants level of education at the time they applied, and this enabled him to examine self-selection patterns. He found that asylum seekers fleeing Iraq and Syria were positively selected. Migrants trying to leave Albania and Servia, by contrast, tended to be negatively selected on education while there was no apparent self-selection for asylum seekers from Afghanistan.[49]

A number of different conditions were apparently responsible for the variations in self-selections. For example, Guichard reported that Serbians seemed able to take advantage of a large network of Serbians who previously migrated to Germany. Their assistance reduced migration costs which enabled people with fewer economic resources, due to limited education, to migrate. The result was a pattern of negative socioeconomic self-selection for the Serbs. To illustrate further, the asylum seekers from Iraq and Syria had a longer distance to travel and faced higher transportation costs. This placed more of a premium on financial resources, hence migrants from these nations tended to positively self-select on education.

Even among migrants from the same nation there appear to be differing selectivity effects across time, or among earlier and later migrant streams referred to by demographers as "developmental stages." Across a number of origin and destination nations there are often three fairly distinct migrating stages:

1 A pioneer stage in which migrants tend to be younger and unmarried, with fewer familial or employment attachments that could restrain their emigration. They also tend to come from families with well above average financial resources to finance the emigration. The pioneers have been described as the innovative risk takers who pave the way for later waves.
2 A take-off or early adopter stage in which people benefit from the experience of the pioneers and as information spreads across social networks, there is an increase in the number of people who migrate and selectivity is reduced. Differences between those who stay and those who leave become smaller both with respect to socioeconomic characteristics and attitudinal variables.

    An interesting example of the first two stages is provided by a migration stream from Governador Valaderes, Brazil, to Boston. Its first stage began when a small group of entrepreneurial women left their community and found that they were able to support themselves by cleaning the homes of suburban Boston families. They were successful in attracting more clients and slowly established home cleaning services. They then began to recruit a larger group of women from their community of origin. The pioneers helped the women in the next wave to make travel arrangements and helped to place them into positions as domestic cleaners.[50]
3 A late adopter stage in which most of the people inclined to emigrate have already left so the number continuing to leave is markedly reduced, and those who do leave in this stage may either be representative of their nation or hypo-selected on socioeconomic variables.[51]

The initially slow increase in the rate of emigration followed by a more rapid rate of increase has been described by Douglas Massey and others as the theory of "cumulative causation." The theory initially emphasized how the impetus to emigrate diffuses within a community and becomes a self-sustaining process. Later research led to a modification in which the rapid increase was expected to level off at some point as the destination nation becomes saturated with more emigres than it can support and the outflow results in better opportunities in the origin nation for those who remain.[52] (The theory of cumulative causation is discussed at length in Chapter 3.)

In sum, with respect to socioeconomic status specific groups of migrants tend with some consistency to be either hypo- or hyper-selected making it essential explicitly to take selectivity effects into account when examining migrants' outcomes. It is often very difficult, however, totally to control for possible selectivity effects because the migration statistics that are available often lack some of the requisite data.

Further, even when more data are available, the statistical manipulations often provide less control than the control that would be built into an experiment. Fortunately, a New Zealand migration lottery offered a serendipitous opportunity to conduct a natural experiment in which the effects of selectivity could be largely controlled. To be specific, each year for several years, New Zealand let a quota of 250 people from Tonga permanently migrate. The Kingdom of Tonga comprises a series of Polynesian islands, 1500 air miles from New Zealand. It is an extremely poor nation in which many people make bare subsistence living from fishing or farming.[53] Winning New Zealand's lottery enables Tonga residents to move from a very low to a high-wage nation, and because the drawing is random, one can safely assume that there are no systematic differences between winners (who get to move) and losers (who remain behind). The results of the study are summarized in Box 2.4.

Box 2.4   New Zealand's Migration Lottery

Thousands of Tongans applied to New Zealand's migration program each year and 250 were randomly selected annually. Based upon the typical size of the applicant pool, one's chances of being chosen were about one in ten. Once people were selected they were given six months to find a full-time job in New Zealand, after which they could file a final residence application. Spouses and unmarried children could accompany the lottery winner meaning it was usually a nuclear family that migrated; but the total number of family members who were going to move counted against the 250-person quota.

Over a period of three years, John Gibson and associates found that the typical lottery winner was 33 years old at the time of the application, two-thirds were married, and 84% of the winners eventually migrated to New Zealand. A few were later unreachable, leaving the investigators with a sample of 194 migrating households from whom they were able to obtain information. The investigators were also able to go back to the Tongan villages and obtain information about 143 lottery losers.

The baseline data showed that the two groups – (1) winners who emigrated and (2) those who applied but were not chosen – had very similar incomes in Tonga prior to the lottery. This further reinforced the assumption that the two groups were essentially the same, separated only by a random event, winning the lottery, and therefore self-selection differences among migrants would be eliminated because all had entered the lottery, wishing to emigrate.

After their first year in New Zealand the migrants' adjusted wages were more than two and one-half times greater than those who remained involuntarily in Tonga because they lost in the lottery; and this difference between the two groups only increased across time. After 10 years the migrants earned, on average, about three times more than those who remained in Tonga. The investigators concluded that it was difficult to imagine any other way, besides migrating to a high-wage nation, for people in low-income nations to comparably increase their wages.[54]

Socioeconomic Selectivity and Downward Mobility

The data previously reviewed in this chapter indicated that migration often resulted in substantial economic gains. However, most of the relevant studies did not attempt to measure or control socioeconomic selectivity effects. Several recent studies now suggest that upward mobility may be problematic for positively selected migrants, especially if they are moving to an economically advanced nation with stricter labor force regulations than those found in their country of origin. Under these conditions, for many migrants, positive selectivity on socioeconomic status can mean downward mobility.

Engzell and Ichou examined upward and downward mobility in a large and representative sample of immigrants to 18 European countries. They came from over 100 diverse nations. For each person in their sample, they measured selectivity by comparing the person's level of education to the average education of people of their gender and birth cohort in their country of origin. The investigators also obtained data on the immigrants' current income and occupation. Comparing immigrants' status in their countries of origin to their status in their destination nation provided the investigators with a measure of upward or downward mobility for each of their respondents.[55]

From the analysis, the researchers found that migration resulted in a loss of status for many of their positively selected migrants Most of those in this category were people who left managerial and professional positions in their home countries and found they could not duplicate these positions in their new nations. Several examples are discussed in Case Study 2–3 at the end of this section.

From questionnaires, the investigators found that many of those who left privileged positions in their homelands that they were unable to duplicate were disappointed in their new nations. How much better they had fared in their countries of origin continued to shape their perception and evaluations. Specifically, they saw themselves as worse off financially than they had been and they were less optimistic about the future than other immigrants who were currently in the same socioeconomic position but had not experienced downward mobility.[56] Some examples are presented in Box 2.5.

Box 2.5   Status Loss for Positively Selected Migrants

The post-migration experiences of a few migrants to the U.S., all of whom left economically less advanced nations, illustrate how downward mobility can be commonplace for those who, socioeconomically, are positively selected migrants.[57]

Julio Godoy emigrated from Guatemala in 2013 after spending the previous 25 years in high-level, very well-paying managerial positions at several large banks. He expected to find a good position in banking in the U.S. as soon as he improved his English skills so he devoted himself to studying English, but he progressed slowly and when his savings ran out he was forced to take a job cleaning airplanes. He spent years working 60 hours per week at the airport which left him little time to study. His English hardly improved, leaving him stuck in what he described as a vicious cycle.

Aeksandra Dino had a Master's Degree and worked as a psychologist in her native Albania before migrating to the U.S. in 2015. Potential U.S. employers would not offer her a comparable position so she finally took a job slicing meat in a deli.

> Several years later she was still hoping to duplicate the position she held in Albania, but without success. In the meanwhile, she volunteered at a local community center, counseling homeless people.
>
> Rafel AlHiali had a medical degree and nine years of experience in his native Iraq before he migrated to the U.S. in 2012. Lacking a medical residency program in the U.S. he was not permitted to practice in the U.S. He tried for years to be accepted into a medical residency, but was denied admission because he lacked clinical experience in the U.S. He eventually took a position as a part-time medical interpreter for Iraqi patients, and kept hoping he would again be able to practice medicine.

Personality Selectivity

From a psychological perspective, it has been proposed that emigrants may be positively selected on some personality traits as well as according to socio-economic attributes. Given external circumstances that provide opportunities to emigrate, those members of a community that possess a "migrant personality" will presumably be the ones most likely to move. The traits most frequently assumed to be the components of the migrant personality include high motivation to achieve and a willingness to take risks. These inferences have sometimes been suggested by results that seemed, to investigators, to be anomalous; for example, when the aspirations of migrants were found to exceed those of native-born, even when socioeconomic status was held constant. (With regard to educational aspirations, this anomaly has been described as an "immigrant optimism paradox." Because most of the research focuses upon the children of migrants, i.e. the second generation, this research is discussed in Chapter 4.)

In other studies, the personality traits assumed to characterize migrants have been inferred from their behavior, but direct measures have been lacking. Pioneer migrants, for example, take a chance when they move to unchartered places where they will be largely alone as newcomers. This has led some migration analysts to see the migrants as adventurous and infer that they must be more inclined than most to take risks.[58]

When migrant's personalities have been directly examined it has typically involved reliance upon questionnaires. These are paper and pencil assessments that relay upon how people see themselves rather than clinical evaluations designed to produce professional personality profiles. A few of the studies have reported some personality differences between movers and stayers, but the samples were not adequate to support any strong conclusions. To illustrate, a group of analysts studied one-half dozen personality traits in a sample of Poles living in the Netherlands and compared those results to a sample of Poles who remained in Poland. On most of the measured traits, the two groups were mostly alike, but there appeared to be significant differences with respect to interpersonal attachment styles and assertiveness.[59]

However, the Netherlands study relied upon a sample of convenience that is not known to generate representative samples. Specifically, the investigators chose people they happed to find at schools and churches, without any systematic selection procedure. Despite the fact that they had a suspect sample, that they examined only one group of migrants in a single country, and the fact that movers and stayers were not significantly different from each other on most of the measured personality traits, they concluded that their finding provided support for inferring that there was a migrant personality.

To illustrate further, Bhai and Dramski worked from a representative national survey to create a sub-sample of respondents who had migrated to the U.S. and compared this sub-sample to those respondents who were born and remained in the U.S. This yielded better sub-samples than the study of Poles described above, but the data were still confined to a single destination nation. Their results again showed that movers and stayers were alike on many of the personality traits measured, but as predicted, they found that people who had emigrated to the U.S. answered the personality self-perception questions in a way that indicated they were more open to new experiences than those born in the U.S.[60] They concluded that their findings showed that immigrants had a distinct set of character skills even though this might seem a little too strong an assertion given their results.

As of this writing, it appears that the most complete assessment of personality traits in relation to migration was probably the study reported by a team of sociologists led by Javier Polavieja. Their research involved samples of recent migrants to Europe from nine different nations. Their questionnaire contained indicators of: desires for wealth, the importance of success, adventurousness and risk-taking. These indicators correlated very highly with each other and were combined into an index which the authors described as a measure of achievement-related motivational orientations (ARMOs). They then compared the scores of recent migrants to samples of their non-migrant co-nationals. They found some partial and limited support for the migrant personality thesis, but for the most part their findings for various immigrant groups were not consistent. For example, there were generally positive signs of ARMO selectivity for Andrean males and for both Brazilian males and females who migrated to Portugal. However, there was generally negative selectivity for Moroccan females, for both Romanian males and females who migrated to Spain, and for Polish migrants in Scandanavia. And for several groups who had migrated to different nations, there was no indication of positive or negative selectivity. Overall, the authors concluded, motivational selectivity does not follow any clear pattern.[61]

Soysal and Cebolla-Boada proposed that many studies may not find much evidence of migrants' personality selectivity because the samples analyzed typically contain large number of less skilled and less educated people. For them, economic motivations may simply overwhelm any differences in personality. To see whether sampling has unduly affected these findings, the investigators selected a more homogenously skilled and educated sample consisting entirely of Chinese students who were pursuing undergraduate or graduate degrees. One group remained in China and another group migrated to colleges in Germany and the U.K.

All of the students filled out questionnaires which asked their self-perceptions on four attributes thought to be characteristic of a migrants' personality: creative, independence, risk-taking and orientation to achievement. When the personality self-appraisals of the students who migrated were compared to those who remained in China, the results showed no differences. The students who left China to study displayed a degree of positive socioeconomic selectivity (as indicated by their fathers' education and occupation), but evidence of personality selectivity was totally absent.[62]

In sum, the research we have reviewed has reported only very limited support for the existence of a migrant personality that would selectively predispose some people to emigrate. However, this line of research has been particularly hampered by measurement and sampling problems compared to studies of socioeconomic selectivity.

Notes

1 For further discussion of the macro approach to migration, see the "Introduction" in Caroline B. Brettell and James F. Hollifield (Eds), *Migration Theory*. Routledge, 2015.
2 Ernest Ravenstein, "The laws of migration." *Journal of the Statistical Society*, 48, 1885.
3 See, for example, Hein de Haas, "The Determinants of International Migration." Working Paper 32, *International Migration Institute*, University of Oxford, April, 2011.
4 Nicholas Van Hear, Oliver Bakewell and Katy Long, "Push-pull plus." *Journal of Ethnic and Migration Studies*, 44, 2018.
5 The World Bank, *Moving for Prosperity*. July, 2018.
6 Javier Corrales, *Venezuela's Transition to Authoritarianism*. Brookings Institution, 2020.
7 Tom Phillips and Clavel Rangel, "A million children left behind." *The Guardian*, February 20, 2020.
8 Julie Turkewitz, "You Grow Up Fast." *The New York Times*, March 25, 2020.
9 Phillips and Rangel, op.cit.
10 For further discussion, see Peter Hedstrom and Petri Ylikoski, "Causal mechanisms in the social sciences." *Annual Review of Sociology*, 36, 2010.
11 See, for example, Christopher C. Liu and Matt Marx, "Micro-geography." *Industry and Innovation*, 27, 2020.
12 Michael P. Todaro, "A model of labor migration and urban unemployment." *American Economic Review*, 59, 1969.
13 Michael Clemens, Claudio Montenegro and Lant Pritchett, "Bounding the Price Equivalent of Migration Barriers." *Center for Global Development*, Working Paper 428, June, 2016.
14 The World Bank, *Moving for Prosperity*. July, 2018, p 85.
15 Everett Lee, "A theory of migration." *Demography*, 3, 1966.
16 Mathew J. Creighton, "The role of aspirations in domestic and international migration." *The Social Science Journal*, 50, 2013. For a review of the aspiration-mobility literature, see Jergen Carling and Kerilyn Schewel, "Revisiting aspiration and ability in international migration." *Journal of Ethnic and Migration Studies*, 44, 2018.
17 S. Migali, et al., *International Migration Drivers*. European Union, 2018, p. 7. Also see this volume for further discussion of the Gallup Poll.
18 Ann-Maria Eurenius, "A family affair." *Population Studies*, 24, 2020.
19 Wilbur Zelinsky, "The hypothesis of the mobility transition." *Geographical Review*, 61, 1971.
20 Michael A. Clemens, "Does Development Reduce Migration?" IZA Working Paper 8592, October, 2014.
21 T.H. Dao, et al., "Migration and Development." *Institut de Recherches Economiques et Sociales de l'Universite catholique de Louvain*. Discussion Paper 2016–29.
22 For a review of these studies, see Frank Meyer, "Navigating aspirations and expectations." *Journal of Ethnic and Migration Studies*, 44, 2018.
23 See the summary in, Douglas S. Massey, et al., "Theories of international migration." *Population and Development Review*, 19, 1993.
24 Oded Stark and David E. Bloom, "The new economics of labor migration." *American Economic Review*, 75, 1985.
25 For further discussion, see Sandro Serpa and Carlos M. Ferriera, "Macro, meso and micro levels of social analysis." *International Journal of Social Science Studies*, 7, 2019.
26 For further discussion, see Massey, op.cit.
27 *The New York Times Magazine Climate Issue*, July 26, 2020.
28 Miriam Jordan, "Immigrants Keep Sending Money Home Despite Job Losses." In ibid., p A7.
29 Ibid.
30 Samuel A. Stouffer, et al., *Studies in Social Psychology in World War II*. Princeton University, 1949.
31 Alexandre Abreu, "The New Economics of Labor Migration." *Forum for Social Economics*, 41, 2012.
32 See, for example: David Kretschmer, "Explaining Differences in Gender Role Attitudes among Migrant and Native Adolescents in Germany." *Journal of Ethnic and Migration Studies*, 44, 2018; and Sebnem Eroglu, "Are movers more egalitarian than stayers?" *International Migration Review*, 54, 2020.
33 Clemons, op.cit.

34 John Gibson and David McKenzie, "The Development Impact of New Zealand's Seasonal Worker Policy." In Robert E. Lucas (Ed), *International Handbook on Migration and Economic Development*. Edward Elgar, 2015.
35 For further discussion of the calculation of PPP, and its shortcomings, see The World Bank Group, *Purchasing Power Parities and the Real Size of the World Economy*. The World Bank, 2014.
36 Orley Ashenfelter, "Comparing Real Wages." *NBER Working Paper #18006*, April, 2012.
37 Ibid., p 22.
38 George J. Borjas, "Immigration and welfare magnets." *Journal of Labor Economics, 17, 1999*.
39 Aaron Ponce, "Is welfare a magnet for migration?" *Social Forces*, 96, 2019.
40 Petra W. De Jong, Alicia Adsera and Helga A. De Valk, "The Role of Welfare in Locational Choices." *Tijdschrift voor Economische en Sociale Geographie*, 111, 2020.
41 Zimmerman published several papers, and a book, focusing upon this research question. See, for example, Carle C. Zimmerman, "The migration to towns and cities." *American Journal of Sociology*, 32, 1927.
42 Thomas D. Cook and Donald T. Campbell, *Quasi-Experimentation*. Houghton-Mifflin, 1979.
43 Lieberson entitled chapter two of his book, "Selectivity." See Stanley Lieberson, *Making It Count*. University of California, 1987.
44 See Cynthia Feliciano, "Educational selectivity in U.S. immigration." *Demography*, 42, 2005.
45 Cynthia Feliciano, "Immigrant selectivity effects on health, labor market and educational outcomes."*Annual Review of Sociology*, 46, 2020.
46 For further discussion, see the essays in, Geoffrey Perkins (Ed), *Socioeconomic Status*. Nova Science, 2016.
47 See, for example, Michael S. Rendall and S.W. Parker, "Two decades of negative educational selectivity of Mexican migrants to the United States." *Population and Development Review*, 40, 2014.
48 For further discussion, see Van C. Tran, et al., "Hyper-selectivity, racial mobility, and the remaking of race." *The Russell Sage Foundation Journal of the Social Sciences*, 4, 2018.
49 Lucas Guichard, "Self-selection of asylum seekers." *Demography*, 57, 2020.
50 For further discussion of the Brazilian emigration, see Jan Brzozowski, "International migration and socioeconomic development." *Estudos Avancad0s*, 76, 2012. For a more general discussion of emigration and entrepreneurship, see Jan Brzozowski, "Entrepreneurship and economic integration of migrants." *International Journal of Entrepreneurship and Innovation Management*, 23, 2019.
51 For further discussion of the stages, see David P. Lindstrom and Adriana L. Ramirez, "Pioneers and Followers." *Annals of the American Academy of Political and Social Science*, 630, 2010.
52 For an extensive review of the theory, see Douglas S. Massey, et al., *Worlds in Motion*. Oxford University, 2005.
53 For additional information about Tonga, see Ian Campbell, *Island Kingdom*. Canterbury University, 2016.
54 John Gibson, et al., "The long-term impacts of international migration." *The World Bank Economic Review*, 32, 2018.
55 Per Engzell and Mathieu Ichou, "Status loss." *International Migration Review*, 54, 2020.
56 Similar findings concerning the continued relevance of economic conditions in migrants' home countries is reported by, Alpasian O. Akay, et al., "Home sweet home?" *Journal of Human Resources*, 52, 2017.
57 The following case studies are taken from, Allison Bowen and Alexia Elejalde-Ruiz, "Skilled immigrants often struggle to put degrees, credentials to use in U.S." *Chicago Tribune*, March 27, 2017.
58 See the discussion in Lindstrom and Ramirez, op.cit.
59 Ela Polek, Jos M. ten Berge and Jan P. Van Oudenhoven, "Evidence for a migrant personality." *Journal of Immigration and Refugee Studies*, 9, 2011.
60 Moiz Bhai and Pavel Dramski, "The Character Skills of Immigrants." *SSRN*, May 14, 2018.
61 Javier G. Polavieja, Marina Fernandez-Reino and Maria Ramos, "Are migrants seleced on motivational orientations?" *European Sociological Review*, 34, 2018.
62 Yasemin N. Soysal and Hector Cebolla-Boado, "Observing the unobservable." *Frontiers in Sociology*, 5, 2020.

3 Environmental Drivers: Climate Change and Natural Disasters

Over the past 100 years, atmospheric concentrations of greenhouse gases have led to an increase in the earth's average temperature; and without drastic changes in patterns of land use, reductions in emissions from industries and automobiles, and fundamental changes in other human activities the earth's temperature will almost certainly continue to rise. Climate change involves this long-term rise in temperatures along with greater temperature fluctuations in the short-term. The consequences are highly diverse: rising sea levels, ocean acidification, greater fluctuations in rainfall, etc. Of particular note is the tendency for climate change to result in more frequent and more severe natural disasters: storms, earthquakes, floods, and so on.

Natural disasters are classified as "fast-onset events" because they strike suddenly and tend to be of short duration. They are most likely to result in immediate displacement as the effected population flees to safer places. Climate change, by contrast, tends to involve "slow-onset events," affecting communities gradually, over long periods of time, and if emigration eventually results, it usually follows an additional, intervening driver. The proximate driver that has been most widely noted in the literature involves economic hardship; for example, climate change can slowly result in progressively worse droughts, leading to reduced agricultural production. Farmers find it increasingly difficult to make a living. Eventually, many give up, and move, but their migration may be attributed to more recently experienced economic privation rather than the environmental changes that preceded it. Political instability in conjunction with economic adversity has also been identified as a proximate driver of international migration in a causal chain beginning with slow-onset environmental effects.[1]

The coastal areas of many nations and island nations have been particularly vulnerable to the effects of climate changes. The Philippine Islands present a stark example of the catastrophic consequences of the interplay between climate change and natural disasters. This series of islands in a seismically active part of the Western Pacific Ocean has for many years been periodically battered by earthquakes and volcanoes. With global warming, however, sea temperatures have risen and warmer ocean waters have meant larger and more frequent tropical storms. Further exacerbating the environmental situation, mass deforestation along the coast has eliminated a natural barrier to wind and water. Muddy conditions are therefore typical and have frequently led to massive landslides that bury hundreds of people alive. Between 1997 and 2016 an estimated 23,000 Filipinos died from the various effects of the more powerful storms.[2]

In the mid-1980s, Lohachara, an Indian island in the Bay of Bengal, became the first island to disappear because of a combination of climate change and more severe cyclones which caused coastal erosion and mangrove destruction. Before disappearing, it had a

DOI: 10.4324/9781003158400-3

population of about 10,000 most of whom moved to the nearby island of Sagar which, again due largely to climate change, has also experienced erosion and may ultimately face the same fate as Lohachara.[3]

As bad as some of these events have been, they have not been widespread. Many scientists contend that without dramatic changes in human activities, the worst is yet to come. The most vulnerable populations – those that have already been most affected – are likely to be victimized even more in the future. The environmental shocks are, according to these many scientific predictions, expected to cause millions of people, primarily in the global South, to be displaced permanently. Two climate researchers recently concluded: "Given the overwhelming evidence about the expected adverse effects of climate change in the future, we can expect that it can become an even more important driver of migration flows in the future."[4]

Many forecasters believe that people impacted by climate change will have to choose "between flight or death" leading to the "greatest wave of global migration the world has ever seen."[5] If nations of the global North do not let the migrants cross their borders, hundreds of millions of people will be trapped. It will be "wildly destabilizing," according to many climate experts, and governments "could topple as whole regions devolve into war."[6]

While there is scientific consensus concerning the likely future consequences of climate change with respect to extreme environmental effects, the prediction of mass migration as a response is not as firmly grounded in data. As early as 2011, the UK's Office of Science published a report summarizing research on climate-linked migration. Referenced typically as the Foresight Report (the name of the government unit), it reported that migration was a much less frequent response to climate stressors because many people became poorer as a result of long-term, slow-onset changes. They were trapped. And many of those who were less adversely impacted by climate change found new ways to adapt to their altered environments as an alternative to migration.[7]

In the decade since the publication of the Foresight Report, there has been a great deal of research on climate-linked migration, conducted in nations throughout the world. We will review a representative sample of those studies in the following section, and focus upon the likelihood of people leaving their homes, temporarily or permanently, and moving across national boundaries. We will also examine the effects of varying environmental events and circumstances across different parts of the world in the hope of being able to offer generalizations about climate-linked migration.

The Status of Environmental Migrants

People forced to flee because of environmental threats have, until recently, been considered climate or environmental migrants, but were not officially designated as refugees by the UN refugee agency (UNCHR). As a result, the rights that were expected to be accorded to refugees – people forced to flee because of fear of persecution – were not extended to those who were forced to flee because of environmental events. They were also excluded from UNCHR's refugee statistical compilations despite the fact that they were a very large group of forced migrants. However, in 2016 the General Assembly of the United Nations added a "New York Declaration" which became implemented in 2018. It extended refugee status, and corresponding rights, to include people who were forced to flee or were displaced across national borders as a result of environmental disasters. Such persons are expected, in all UN member nations, to receive the same protections as all other vulnerable refugees who have been forced to leave their homes.[8]

The basic necessities to which any group of refugees are entitled, according to U.N. resolutions, are not defined in detail. In addition, there are often ambiguities in terms of which local or national entities are responsible for providing subsistence and shelter, and in any case, there are limited sanctions that can be invoked to force a reluctant host to comply with U.N. expectations. All of these limitations are illustrated by the difficult situation of a diverse group of refugees who were stranded in Bosnia, described in Box 3.1.

Box 3.1   Trying to Obtain Refugee Rights in Bosnia

In Northeast Bosnia there is a refugee camp, "Lipa" that was abandoned in December of 2020 after aid workers deemed it uninhabitable because it lacked electricity, water, etc. Migrants had been sleeping in tents and abandoned shipping containers. As they left, a fire destroyed most of the tents. Nevertheless, later that month about 700 refugees were moved into this abandoned camp. Some had fled natural disasters, others escaped from civic strife, but most qualified for refugee status. They had come from a diverse set of nations including: Afghanistan, Bangladesh, Iraq and Pakistan; and most were hoping to reach nations in the European Union when they became bogged down in Bosnia.

The Chief of Mission (CoM) in Bosnia for the U.N.'s International Organization for Migration said the refugees were in freezing temperatures, lacking basic necessities, and had to be moved to the next town where there were better facilities available. The Bosnian government said okay but did not give a moving date. In the meanwhile, the government asked local authorities to help the refugees, and to arrange a transfer. However, residents of the local towns insisted that they did not want the refugees, and moved to set up barricades to block the roads.

The CoM was not optimistic that the refugees would be moved any time soon because of the local opposition. The refugees spent New Year's Day, 2021, in freezing temperatures, trying to warm themselves around makeshift fires. The Bosnian civic protection agency agreed eventually to provide tents, but the CoM complained that leaving people in tents in icy conditions was not sustainable and went unheeded. Two weeks later the refugees were still washing themselves in snow, because there was no better alternative, and lining up barefoot to receive food.[9]

With fast-onset events, it is usually clear that the people who are fleeing floods or erupting volcanos or the like should be considered environmental refugees. Cause and effect are made evident by the close temporal connection between the environmental occurrence and the increased migration. Slow-onset events, on the other hand, tend not to produce an immediate response. The environmental changes can slowly affect the way a large portion of an effected population supports itself, but as a rule, people do not initially recognize all the potential consequences at the onset of the environmental change and so if it is going to generate an exodus, it does not usually occur until later, and as we have noted, it tends to involve an additional driver.

For host nations, and UN agencies, labeling the migrants for official purposes has posed ambiguities because of the mix of environmental, economic and other drivers attendant particularly to slow-onset events. For example, suppose that slow-onset land degradation led to declining crop yields and after a time farmers decided to migrate. One could argue that they left willingly or that they were forced; that they left for economic opportunities or because of environmental deterioration.[10]

The rights of refugees that host nations have felt obliged to honor in accordance with UN stipulations have varied according to which driver is emphasized. Prior to 2018, environmental migrations did not qualify for refugee status so a claim based on an environmental event would not then have ordinarily been recognized. Therefore official refugee migration statistics, compiled prior to 2018, almost certainly under-counted the amount of environmentally driven migration. When the slow-onset event resulted in civic conflict and that was emphasized, nations have been more inclined to accord refugee status recognizing that the migrants faced actual threats. Correspondingly, it is likely that official refugee records overstated political conflict as a migration driver. When the economic driver was emphasized, the migrants have not typically been considered refugees.[11] That has undoubtedly greatly reduced the official number of refugees in the world because, as we have noted, economic motivations can be highly salient when transnational migration is the eventual result of environmental issues.

Methodological Issues

There are a number of alternate procedures that investigators can follow in examining the relationship between migration and fast- or slow-onset events. The first decision concerns how to measure the potential environmental catalyst, and there are two basic alternatives: measures generated by objective instruments or the subjective perceptions of affected populations. Second is the question of how to assess migration, and again there are two possibilities: by inferring population changes from a comparison of data sets created before and after the environmental event, or by asking people in the affected area about friends, family and neighbors who left, and in some cases, attempting to track down and interview those who moved.

Measuring the Environmental Event

A variety of objective instruments with which to gauge the intensity of an environmental event or change are sometimes available. For example, to study the effects of severe tornados in the U.S., Ethan Raker utilized the government's Severe Weather Database. It details the latitude and longitudinal coordinates for the touchdown and dissipation points of tornados, and a tornado's magnitude is estimated at several points along its path.[12] Similarly, investigators have ascertained the magnitude of earthquakes with a seismograph, and utilized rainfall data from weather stations to examine droughts.

The validity of the data obtained from these measuring instruments depends, of course, upon their ability accurately to measure the event in question; in addition, there is the necessity of obtaining information precisely for the area assumed to have been impacted by the environmental event and that is sometimes difficult. For example, if the possibility of rainfall leading to flooding in a village is being studied and the village is located in a plain with high river density, then upstream precipitation may have a greater impact upon people living in the village than precipitation measured right at the village.[13]

Most recent studies have relied upon objective instruments of the type described here. The alternative is to rely upon people's perceptions. With slow-onset changes, analysts have been concerned that their gradualness and lengthy duration, and the frequent presence of additional, proximate drivers may lead people to underestimate the magnitude of their effect. However, a few studies have attempted to utilize questionnaires and/or interviews to assess how people view these environmental effects. For example, a group of researchers in Ghana asked goat farmers about the effects of long-term variations in rainfall. They relied mostly on questionnaires, but also conducted interviews and formed focus groups. Knowledge of rainfall varied among goat farmers in different parts of Ghana, but based upon the farmers' different adaptation strategies and the results of the focus group discussions, the researchers concluded that the questionnaires provided a reasonably valid measure.[14]

However, there are some data that suggest people's perceptions may not typically provide a very accurate measure of environmental conditions. Relevant data come from Switzer and Vedlitz's comparison of survey data pertaining to a U.S. sample's perception of drought in their area with statistics on drought from the U.S. Drought Monitor (USDM). The USDM may be the best measure of drought in the U.S. because it is a composite of numerous indicators: rainfall deficit, water shortages, and so on. The investigators placed geographical areas in the U.S. into two categories: those that experienced moderate or severe drought in the previous year, and those that did not. With their questionnaire, they asked a representative national sample whether they were aware of drought in their county. Among individuals who lived in a higher drought county, according to the USDM figures, only 31% correctly identified their country as having experienced drought in the past year.[15]

Those who were aware of the drought also were most likely to perceive it as presenting a risk. If migration were to be a response to drought, people in this category would most likely provide the migrants. Those who were less aware of the drought and its risks would be much less likely to move in response. Therefore, relying upon people's perceptions of the environment to measure the driver may not provide accurate estimates of its impact upon migration because there may be a large group of people who do not recognize its impact.

With fast-onset events, time delays in getting a research project into the field often present an additional impediment to relying upon people's perceptions to measure the magnitude of the environmental event. It may be impossible to question samples of people soon enough after a fast-onset event for them to be able to recall its impact accurately. If the event was cataclysmic, then it may be a long time before researchers can enter the setting, and they may find that many of the affected residents who survived have left. Reliance upon instruments may then be the only alternative.

Measuring Migration as a Response

The most widely used technique for inferring migration as a response to environmental events entails comparing census or other population datasets that were compiled before and after the event. A decrease in population after the event can imply that out-migration occurred. Estimating migration in this way is illustrated by a study of flooding and crop failures in rural Bangladesh. Gray and Mueller obtained three surveys, conducted in the same region over a period of ten years. They were able to trace almost all of the households in the original sample across the subsequent surveys, and thereby infer who had left. In addition, information about departed household members was obtained from administrative districts that collected data on the timing and duration of moves.[16]

When changes in data sets are used to measure migration, the causal link between migration and environmental impacts is usually not directly assessed. The timing of people's moves may suggest environmental instigation, but the linkage is circumstantial. Absent self-reports, it would be helpful at least to have migration data from similar communities not affected by environmental stress. The latter could provide a baseline with which to assess whether movement from the environmentally stressed community was greater than might be expected, and therefore more likely attributable to environmental events.

Illustrating the use of surveys and interviews is a study of the Marshall Islands (discussed in Chapter 2). The investigators gave questionnaires to several hundred respondents living in the Islands asking about where their siblings and children currently live. Those siblings and children who had residences anywhere beside the Marshall Islands were assumed to have migrated, and the respondents who remained and provided the information were asked why these people left, and specifically, whether it was due to environmental impacts.[17] Relying upon the explanations of the family members who remained can also lead to over- or under-stating the effects of environment upon migration because those who remained and provided the explanations may know only the reason they were given by the departing members of their family, or they may make incorrect assumptions about the migrants' motives.

Conclusion

In an ideal situation, an investigator would have multiple measures of the variables being studied, for example, both objective readings from properly placed instruments and subjective responses from local people. Obtaining congruent findings when using different measures is the best way to be certain that findings are not an artifact of measurement, though most studies do not have the luxury of multiple measures. It is important, therefore, to know the possible limitations of any study's design.

The Empirical Research

We begin by examining migration patterns in the last half of the 20th century from an extensive analysis reported by Beine and Parsons. They obtained a data set comprising census documents between 1960 and 2000. For this time period, they analyzed bilateral migrations between 226 origin and destination countries located in both the global South (Afghanistan, Jamaica, Namibia, etc.) and global North (Denmark, France, New Zealand, etc.). Most of the out-migration occurred from nations of the global South and it appeared to involve more internal than cross-national movement. When migration was international, the destinations were to both global South and North nations.[18]

The investigators studied both fast-onset natural disasters – the cumulative number of earthquakes, floods, etc. during a decade – and slow onset environmental stressors – measures of deviations from long-term temperature and precipitation, derived from a climate research database. International migration was inferred from changes in a nation's contiguous decennial censuses. In their analysis, they attempted statistically to control for return migration because to the degree that migrants returned to their country of origin prior to the next census, out-migration flows would be understated.

The results showed that neither fast- nor slow-onset stressors had much of an effect upon international migration. What small effects they did have in some limited conditions were dwarfed by economic and other drivers. The investigators lacked any direct measure of internal migration, but following some previous studies, they relied upon urbanization as an indicator. and it increased as expected. The logic supporting this assumption is that people in primary industries (fishing, farming, etc.) who are the ones most impacted by environmental stressors and migrate in response, are most likely to move internally, to a nearby city, increasing the urbanization of the nation. Among nations in the global South prior research has shown natural disasters to increase urbanization. In other words, where there were large vulnerable populations, when environmental stressors pushed people out of rural villages they were most likely to move to nearby cities which grew as a result, and the urban growth combined with the rural decline led to a higher degree of urbanization.[19]

Focusing upon the same time period, Cattaneo and Peri analyzed bilateral migration between 116 countries for which they were able to access data on fluctuations in temperature and precipitation, obtained from a variety of global weather stations. They found that temperature increases along with reduced precipitation led to the impoverishment of rural populations. The overall effects upon migration were not clear, however, until they statistically re-analyzed the data, dividing countries into two income categories. In the nations placed into the poor grouping, emigration was depressed. People could not afford to move and the climate stressors just kept pushing them further into poverty. In the middle-income nations, by contrast, out-migration increased in response to the climate adversities. Their moves were mostly internal, rural to urban, though there was also some international migration out of the middle-income nations.[20]

In sum, environmental stressors during the last half of the 20th century did not produce a substantial amount of international migration. When people did move in response it was more often from a rural to urban area within the same nation. The overall amount of out-migration was apparently limited by people's resources; many could simply not afford the costs of moving. They were trapped in place.

While the effects of climate change were clearly being felt in the latter decades of the 20th century, by all accounts the problems worsened in this century. In order to try to document the effects of the growing number and severity of environmental stressors, there have been a much larger number of studies conducted throughout the world in this century. The results have tended largely to mirror those of the late 20th century, though there have been some significant differences as well. We will examine the recent trends beginning with the global South.

In the Global South

Agencies of the United Nations and many associations of climate specialists have all pointed to the global South as the part of the world most likely to be strongly impacted by climate change. Correspondingly, much of the research has focused upon the degree to which migration occurs as a consequence in this part of the world. Most of the research has involved case studies, that is, analyses of whether disasters led to migration in one nation, or in specific regions of one nation.

Representative of these studies, a group of sociologists and demographers led by Barbara Entwisle focused upon how extreme floods and droughts affected out-migration from the Nang Rang district of Northeast Thailand. They found no effect. The climate stressors were associated with out-migration, but out-migration from this area had been well-established for many years. People continued to move from the district to the same places in roughly the same numbers. The investigators concluded that out-migration from droughts and floods is so tied to previously established migration patterns that absent the continuing influence of these social networks, out-migration would actually decline following environmental stressors.[21] (Social network effects on migration are discussed at length in the following chapter.)

Bangladesh is an ideal nation in which to examine the most draconian predictions concerning the impact of environmental events upon migration, and it has been very well studied. Part of the global South, it is one of the most densely populated countries in the world. It is dominated by the largest river delta in the world, helping to make its fields fertile. Farming of various types predominates, and nearly one-half of the nation's labor force works in agriculture. However, because most of the nation is less than 40 feet above sea level, it has historically been prone to flooding which, along with tornados and cyclones, have often killed thousands of people.[22]

Climate change and warming temperatures, in particular, have created the "perfect storm" in Bangladesh. It has led to more frequent and more intense cyclones that have forced hundreds of thousands of people to be relocated. In addition, melting of the glaciers and snowpack in the Himalayas has led to the swelling of the rivers that flow into Bangladesh. The rise in sea level has made Bangladesh especially prone to flooding when the already swollen rivers overflow during the annual monsoon rains. In 1998 the country experienced the worst flooding in modern history. The overflowing rivers covered an estimated 300,000 homes and killed an estimated 1,000 people. Making matters worse, the conversion of mangrove forests along coastal Bangladesh which has been cleared to support several types of farming has greatly reduced one of the nation's best natural defenses against super-cyclones which are another consequence of climate change.[23]

Some interdisciplinary groups of economists and geographers have over the past several years been studying the effects of flooding and other natural disasters in rural, coastal Bangladesh. Their research has produced a rich set of data, from a particularly vulnerable region of the world, with which to assess the prediction that worsening environmental events will lead to massive migration from the global South to the global North.

The measures utilized in the various studies have been diverse. Flooding has only been measured objectively, but it has entailed reliance upon remote sensing and satellite data for direct measures, and has been inferred from data on rainfall extremes. Mobility has been measured by changes in longitudinal data sets created specifically for the research and by changes in communities' vital statistics as compiled by the government of Bangladesh. The studies involved different, but overlapping time periods between the late 1990s and about 2010, and some of the measures that were employed were known to have flaws; however, what stands out is the very strong degree to which the findings were congruent with each other despite the studies' different methods.[24]

The most consistent finding across the studies is a surprising lack of movement in response to flooding. What migration did occur, tended to be temporary and across short distances involving moves to a nearby city. People who left their homes remained in the country, and returned to their former villages after relatively brief periods of time. When more lasting displacement occurred it was still much more likely to be internal than international. This is a typical finding: across all regions of the world, most studies have reported that internal displacement exceeds international displacement, by far, following environmental disasters.[25]

With respect to international migration, research in coastal Bangladesh has generally reported either no relationship between flooding and international migration – most people stay in place – or an inverse relationship in which fewer people are found to migrate than generally occurred in the absence of flooding. In fact, one study reported that while even modest flooding deterred cross-nation migration, very broad exposure to flooding had an especially strong negative effect upon migration.

Each team of investigators explored why flooding did not induce more people to migrate; why the apocalyptic prediction did not seem to be borne out, especially in a highly vulnerable nation of the global South. The most consistently offered explanation was that people felt trapped. Households lacked the resources necessary to migrate, especially for expensive long-distance journeys across national boundaries. And when there were repeated environmental shocks, entire villages became impoverished, and collectively lacked the means to help finance the migration of those who wished to leave.

Slower-onset environmental impacts in Bangladesh, such as increased soil salinity, also a consequence of the rise in sea level, resulted in a higher rate of movement than the faster-onset events, such as flooding. However, most people remained in place and tried to find new means of employment. Those who did leave were again much more likely to remain within the nation rather than move outside the nation. After completing several studies in Bangladesh, Chen and Mueller noted that, somehow, people have managed to adapt enough to remain in Bangladesh; but the investigators asked: What will happen as climate change makes the country less and less inhabitable over time?[26]

In a different region of the global South, rural Ecuador, Gray and Bilsborrow studied environmental influences upon migration during the first decade of this century. Because the country is located near the equator and to melting glaciers, and has a prolonged wet season, it is particularly vulnerable to climate change. Ecuador has for years experienced heavy rainfalls leading to landslides and flooding. The investigators measured slow-onset events with a composite index that included access to irrigation, agricultural land quality, etc. and one indicator of fast-onset events, annual rainfall shocks. They examined these annual environmental measures in relation to migration during the following year, defining migration as a departure from one's former household lasting for at least six months.[27]

From a household survey, they obtained data on 1,670 persons who were between the ages of 14 and 40: the ages that correspond with most international migrants. Slightly over one-half of their sample (898 people) did not move in the year following environmental stressors. Of those who did leave their households, the vast majority remained in Ecuador, often moving to an adjacent town or city. The sample of 1,670 persons included 165 who were international migrants, or about 10%.

While the amount of international migration was less than some would have expected, what was most surprising about their results was that *favorable* environmental changes in any year were more likely to be followed by an increase in internal and international migration. Perhaps such changes made moving more affordable, especially for better-off people. For land-poor households, when migration occurred in response to environmental stressors it was almost exclusively internal, and frequently entailed very short distances. The large percentage of poorer households who did not move were likely, according to the investigators, trapped in place.

As we have previously noted, internal migration – specifically, rural to urban – has been frequently observed as a consequence of environmental stressors. In 32 nations in Sub-Saharan Africa, to illustrate further, a group of researchers found that a decline in moisture availability (mostly due to decreased rainfall) led to a significant increase in subsequent years' movement out of rural and into urban areas, so long as the urban area offered industrial employment. Sub-Saharan Africa is a region that is particularly vulnerable to climate change, and the investigators predicted that increasing environmental stressors would, over the next decades, result in the region becoming substantially more urbanized.[28]

In sum, there are a substantial number of studies of nations in the global South that report that neither fast- nor slow- onset events are major drivers of international migration. Fast-onset events tend to result immediately in larger amounts of displacement, but regardless of type of onset, temporary and internal displacements predominate: people move short distances, often leaving rural areas for temporary relocations in more urban areas. And in many circumstances, slow-onset events have tended actually to reduce international migration by adversely impacting people's financial ability to afford long-distance moves.[29] These patterns are illustrated by the aftermath of two powerful hurricanes in Guatemala, described in Box 3.2.

Box 3.2   The Effects of Hurricanes in Guatemala

In November, 2020, Guatemala was hit by two ferocious hurricanes in quick succession. Thousands of homes, bridges, roads and croplands were destroyed. Government officials surveyed the impacted area and admitted they could not begin to address the devastation. They asked for other nations to help and asked the U.N. to declare their Central American region the most affected by climate change, with warming ocean waters making storms both more frequent and stronger.

When villagers slowly returned to where their homes had been, they found a sea of rocks and mud where the town formerly stood. They picked their way through the rubble to salvage whatever they could find. More than 100,000 people had no choice but to crowd into shelters that offered little. Aid workers found them to be suffering from a number of diseases due to the crowding and the lack of potable water. Despite the harsh conditions, most of the displaced Guatemalans told reporters that they could not imagine what their long-term alternatives were going to entail.

Located near the Mexican border, some people crowded into handmade rafts to cross the lakes produced by the storms; some swam. They went up and back on trips to Mexico to find whatever food they could, and bring it back. Some decided to leave the area permanently and walked hours to reach the nearest dry village in Guatemala. They were safe for the moment but saw no future there which led a few to think about migrating to the U.S. However, they had no idea how or whether they could make the trip or whether they would be permitted to enter if they did get to the U.S. border.[30]

An unambiguous conclusion regarding the effects of slow-onset stressors is not possible because there are also a few studies focusing upon nations in the global South that have found environmental stresses to be a major driver of international migration. Of particular note are several studies conducted by economist Dennis Wesselbaum analyzing migration to a sample of nations affiliated with the Organization for Economic Co-operation and Development (OECD). Introduced in Chapter 1, OECD includes many of the world's largest economies: Australia, France, U.S., etc. All the OECD studies covered the same time period, namely 1980 to 2015. Note, this 36-year time period is substantially longer than that included in many other studies of environmental effects, providing more opportunity to observe much-delayed migration. He examined different samples of origin nations in a number of studies, but all of them were in the global South.

In one study, Wesselbaum focused upon flows of migration between each of the 54 African countries and each of the 16 major OCED nations. Migration figures came from the U.N., and therefore included only legal immigration which almost certainly undercounted the true amount of migration. (Surveys and census figures, the most commonly utilized sources of migration data, simply display differences in population size, regardless of the legal conditions under which people moved.) Weather stressors were measured with a variety of geophysical data sets. He found that flooding in these African nations significantly increased population outflows, but storms and droughts did not. He surmised that the difference might arise because flooding has a more highly concentrated adverse effect on a local economy compared to storms and droughts whose effects might be dissipated over a larger area.[31] The implication is that economic adversities increased out-migration between nations in Africa and OCED nations.

In a second study, Wesselbaum and Aburn examined annual migration flows to the same 16 OCED nations, during the same time period and again relied upon a number of geophysical climate measures; but this study included a larger and geographically much more diverse group of origin nations, 198 in all. In this sample, they found that the number of weather-related disasters substantially increased international outflows from the origin nations and that temperature changes did the same. They also found that the more an origin nation relied upon agriculture, the more environmental shocks led to emigration. Presumably, it was farmers' economic losses that again were the force behind migration. The researchers also examined measures of several other possible drivers of migration but concluded that, in their sample, environmental stressors were the major drivers of cross-national migration.[32]

In conclusion, it is difficult to offer sweeping generalizations about the impact of environmental stressors upon international migration from nations in the global South. Whether such movements are heightened or depressed may depend upon: the type of environmental stressor, the relative economic distress of impacted communities, and a variety of methodological differences among studies in how they measure both environmental impacts and international migration, and how long of a delay in migration following environmental stressors can be inferred from the data set.[33]

In the Global North

In nations of the global North, neither fast- nor slow-onset events have typically led to international migration. Displacement in areas prone to natural disasters has, of course, occurred, but as in the global South, such displacements have typically involved temporary movement over short distances. Very extreme weather events have been the exception because they have sometimes caused a large segment of the affected population to flee, usually resulting in more permanent moves to nearby communities in the same nation; examples include the migratory response to a devastating hurricane (Katrina) in 2005 in New Orleans[34] and a powerful earthquake and tsunami off the east coast of Japan in 2011.

An interdisciplinary team studied the response to what has been termed the Great East Japan earthquake and tsunami, by comparing migration out of the affected area in 2010 (the year before the quake) to migration in the years following, specifically, 2012 and 2013. One group of affected residents identified as evacuees moved to nearby destinations that had not been impacted, intending to return as soon as it was possible. A second group of people who the investigators labeled as migrants remained in Japan, but moved further and more permanently away from their former homes. However, the people who migrated out of the affected area in the years following the quake left in the same relative numbers as those who migrated out in the year prior to the quake. And the pre- and post-quake destinations followed the same patterns. In both 2010 and 2012-13, people moved to areas in which they had pre-existing ties; for example, to locations where other family members had previously re-located. This finding of no major changes in emigration patterns mirrors the results reported in the previously discussed study in Northeast Thailand. The proportions of people who moved and their destinations remained relatively unaltered by the quake and tsunami because it was resources that largely determined when and where people could migrate, both previously to the quake and in its aftermath.[35]

Similar pre- and post-disaster trends have also been reported in studies of the U.S. In an ambitious analysis, Elizabeth Fussell and colleagues examined all U.S. counties that experienced a hurricane or tropical storm between 1980 and 2012. They relied upon changes in annual population estimates from the U.S. Census Bureau to infer whether people had left affected areas, and they obtained storm damage compilations from a variety of recorded measures. They found overall that damaging weather events produced few changes to the post-storm population of counties that experienced them. Specifically, when counties were growing in the years before the weather-related stressors they often experienced short-term declines in size immediately following severe storms, but over the longer term they continued to grow as a result of recovery-directed investments. The post-disaster size of counties that had not been growing prior to the severe storms showed no effect.[36]

Most studies on the effect of environmental stressors upon migration focus upon changes in the size of a community. However, if investigators only examine possible reductions in the size of affected communities, they can miss other significant changes that may occur in the composition of affected communities. A relevant study has been reported by sociologist John Logan and colleagues from an analysis of changes in the U.S. Gulf Coast. It is an area prone to severe storms, especially hurricanes. The investigators obtained hurricane damage estimates for each county and examined these estimates in relation to annual changes in each county's population size and composition, including age and race. They found that sections of the coast that have been impacted by hurricanes have lost population over the ensuing three years, presumably due to out-migration. Supporting this interpretation, they found that the reduction in population was greatest in those areas where the storm damage was most severe.

As in nations in the global South, the consequence of economic resources was again indicated by the fact that the negative impacts of storms on changes in population size

60 *Environmental Drivers*

were larger in areas with lower poverty rates. In other words, areas with a higher concentration of less advantaged people had less migration in the years after storms. Within all areas, people with fewer economic resources – such as the elderly and racial minorities – were less likely to move. Therefore, over time, the population of environmentally vulnerable areas can become poorer, and as the downward spiral continues, fewer and fewer residents of impacted areas may have the resources to leave.[37] In that sense they resemble the poor Bangladesh farmers: both are trapped in place.

What Logan and associates have termed, "segmented withdrawal" may be most likely in highly vulnerable areas, like the U.S. Gulf Coast, where climate change is heightening the risk of both additional and more severe storms. Moving may make more sense in such areas so residents who can most afford to leave do so.[38] Outside of highly vulnerable areas the choice between rebuilding in a more secure manner and relocating may be different. For example, Raker found when viewing the entire U.S. that tornados led those who lacked the resources to properly rebuild to leave affected communities. The more economically advantaged residents were more likely to remain because they could better afford to rebuild in a way that provided more protection against future storms.[39]

In sum, studies in nations of the global North show an array of responses to natural disasters. As in the global South, following even severe storms it is common for people to remain in place, and people in the affected communities who lack resources are especially likely to be trapped in place. However, in highly vulnerable areas, rebuilding can be an alternative for more affluent residents. Thus, apart from changes in the size of populations, the overall composition of affected communities often changes, sometimes becoming poorer and sometimes becoming wealthier.

Conclusion

The macro and micro studies are consistent in concluding that environmental impacts do not consistently lead to heightened levels of inter-nation migration, and that perceived economic benefits are the migrants' most salient motive. The fact that the most draconian visions of disaster-driven global migration, especially in the global South, have not occurred does not mean that they will not yet happen; nor does it signify that climate change predictions are off the mark. It simply means that in response to environmental crises, many people have been trapped, unable to move, and many others have managed to adapt, and remain in place. Migration, especially across national borders, has been of much less magnitude than expected – so far.

In addition to all of the reasons for low migration that we have already considered, we need to add to the list the sometimes serendipitous effects of natural disasters. Floods in Bangladesh, for example, have been shown in the previously discussed studies to improve the quality of soil and lead to higher crop yields in some areas. When displaced people return after experiencing floods, their farms are sometimes more successful so they are induced to stay until the next flood, then repeat the cycle. Other types of post-disaster benefits have been reported in a number of other locales. For example, in rural Indonesia Gignoux and Menendez studied the effects of earthquakes upon household incomes. They obtained household data from a longitudinal survey that covered a period of twelve years following a number of earthquakes. They also obtained precise measures of local ground tremors from a US Geological Survey database. During the first year or two after earthquakes, individuals – mostly farmers – were found to have experienced economic losses. However, by the end of the second year following the earthquakes, an influx in external recovery aid and infrastructure investments led to economic recovery for most of the affected people. In the longer run, after 5–6 years, a substantial number of the rural Indonesian farmers were economically better off than before the earthquakes.[40]

Proximate Drivers

One reason that migration, and international migration in particular, has not been shown to result from environmental stressors to the expected degree is because slow-moving events – the type most expected to result in international migration – usually involve an additional, intervening driver. When studies have found an association between environmental factors and international migration, they have concluded that "environment is rarely the sole driver."[41] When migration across borders does occur, both government officials and data analysts have often attributed it to that intervening driver, rather than the slow-onset events that began the changes that led to migration.

Economic

The proximate driver that has been most widely noted in the literature is depressed occupational opportunities or adverse impact on livelihood; stated generally, it is economic hardship. For example, a slow-moving event can: lead to reduced agricultural production and farmers cannot remain in place and make a living; or it results in the loss of marine life and fishing in the same waters becomes problematic; or the slow onset event leads to deforestation resulting in job losses in wood, timber and related industries. This pattern is illustrated by the emigration of fishermen and their families from villages around the Gulf of Guinea, described in the case study in Box 3.3.

Box 3.3 Leaving the Gulf of Guinea

Senya Beraku is a West African coastal village on the north shore of the Gulf of Guinea. Many adults in the village historically supported themselves in the fishing industry. Men in small boats went out in the Gulf of Guinea each morning and returned in the afternoon with the day's catch. Women carrying baskets waded out to meet the boats and carried the fish back to the shore. Natives and tourists waited on the beach to purchase the fish. What did not sell on the beach was brought to local restaurants and food stores. It was never a wealthy village, but people managed to support their families in this way.[42]

Over the past several decades, however, rising sea levels, due to global warming, increasingly threatened Senya Beraku (and other Gulf villages) with flooding tides and coastal erosion.[43] Their struggle was made worse when in the 1990s West African coastal countries signed agreements with Spain, France, China, and other nations giving them fishing rights in the Gulf. The European and Asian nations then brought in large capacity fleets of industrial trawlers that scooped up more fish than their allocated quotas, and the depletion of fish stocks continued to get worse.[44]

On many days, the men from the village came back in the afternoon in their small boats with nearly no fish. They grew increasingly desperate and many began to think about leaving the village. Others had left and gone to Italy, particularly the Naples area, and the villagers heard a number of emigrant success stories. Many undertook a dangerous two-part journey, first across the Sahara desert and then over the Mediterranean Sea they were smuggled into Italy. Those who survived the trip found a hostile reception. Many were physically attacked and as illegal migrants they were afraid to request government help. They also found limited employment opportunities, forcing many into drug dealing and prostitution. A few found employment in a local plastics factory and were able to make more money than they could have if they had continued to fish in Senya Beraku.[45]

How to allocate the relative responsibility for migration between the slow-onset event and economic deterioration has posed problems for analysts. Following a macro perspective, an investigator may observe a correlation among: (1) environmental stressors, e.g. long-term drought (2) local assets or resources, e.g. average income in a village or county and (3) an increase in the rate of out-migration. From a theoretical perspective, it may be reasonable to interpret the findings as indicating that economic adversity was a driver that intervened between environmental stress and out-migration. However, the presumed causal inferences may be questionable; to be specific, this type of macro study provides data involving rates and averages which may not be able to show that it was the local people who experienced the most environmental degradation or economic adversity who were the ones to migrate. Also left unanswered is the question of how the migrants experienced either environmental stresses or economic adversity and the degree to which they attributed their move to either. Finally, it would also be helpful to know how the stated experiences of migrants and non-migrants differed.

There are a few micro studies that have utilized questionnaires and/or interviews to gain insight into how international migrants, who left places that had experienced slow-onset environmental stressors with attendant economic deterioration, viewed their reasons for leaving. These studies have, for the most part, reinforced the contention that economic motivations are typically the proximate and more salient driver. To illustrate, we begin again with a study in coastal Bangladesh, one of the world's most extensively analyzed regions in climate research.

In the most relevant exploration, an interdisciplinary group of investigators interviewed individuals from a representative sample of households in coastal Bangladesh. Their sample consisted of 4456 adults who were asked about their household's members, their age and gender, experience of natural disasters, etc. They also asked whether anyone from that household had ever moved, either temporarily or permanently. This approach identified 279 migrants, nearly 90% of whose moves were both temporary (defined as less than 6 months in duration) and within the nation. Field interviewers asked the main reason(s) they moved, and found that better employment opportunities were the most frequent answer. Environmental hazards were never mentioned despite the fact the investigators knew that many had experienced significant flooding prior to moving. Those who moved anywhere, either temporarily or permanently, differed from the non-movers in several respects. Specifically, they tended to have come from more affluent households, and they were more often employed in non-agricultural jobs.[46]

There were only three permanent international migrants in the sample, too few for any meaningful analyses. There were another 31 people who left Bangladesh temporarily to move to another nation and they largely resembled the internal migrants, though they were even more likely to have been from more affluent households. Salinization in the locations they left suggested they likely experienced environmental stressors, but they also identified better economic opportunities as their major reason for moving. In sum, the investigation showed that resources were – again – an important enabler, that economic motivations were the most important driver, and that environmental stressors played a very secondary role.

A study of migration from the Marshall Islands provides a much larger group of international migrants for analysis. They are a dispersed group of islands in the Pacific Ocean with a total 2018 population estimated at 58,000 people. Between 2000 and 2018 approximately 25,000 Marshall Islanders moved to the U.S. Rising sea levels have given rise to flooding and salinity (high levels of salt), affecting drinking water and agricultural production, and these long-term environmental stressors have been assumed to be drivers of the extensive out-migration. Almost everyone who leaves the islands moves to the U.S. because of a treaty that permits Marshallese people to live in the U.S. without a visa.

Van der Geest and a group of colleagues conducted a survey on the islands and asked several hundred people whether anyone in their family had migrated and if so, why. Almost everyone had a relative who had left the Islands and gone to the U.S. The major reasons given for their moves were to obtain better earnings, education or health care, or because of ties to family members who had previously migrated (i.e. family reunification, as described in Chapter 1). Few identified flooding and related problems as an important reason. Many of the respondents who had not yet left the islands claimed they planned to emigrate in the future, and they offered the same cluster of explanations as those who had already left. Limited samples of Marshallese people living in the U.S. were also interviewed and they too stressed work and education along with health care and family considerations as having been their main reasons for leaving. Very few people who had left, or who planned to leave in the future, mentioned environmental factors as a major driver, though over 60% of those living in the U.S. did cite climate concerns as a possible reason not to return.[47]

Types of Entrapment

The economic disparities associated with people's different responses to environmental stressors suggest the usefulness of distinguishing between two types of entrapment. In the preceding pages we have frequently referred to people exposed to environmental events, but unable to afford to move, as "trapped." However, a survey conducted in vulnerable regions of global South nations turned up some interesting results on this matter. Non-migrants were asked why they had not left, and many replied that they "had to stay." This response was interpreted as indicating the person or household was trapped by limited resources. As expected, in most of the countries it was people in the lowest income categories in their nations who were most likely to say that they had to stay.

However, in some of the nations it was people in the highest income categories that offered the trapped response to the question of why they had not moved. They had the resources, though. The analysts concluded that the homes and lands they owned may have led them to decide that they would have to give up too much if they left. So, some people in vulnerable communities are trapped in place by a lack of income, savings and tangible possessions while others are trapped by their ownership of immobile assets.[48]

64   *Environmental Drivers*

Civil Conflict

There have been some widely described instances in which long-term climate stressors have been followed by civil unrest and large numbers of people leaving the country. It has been common for economic hardships also to have been involved, making it difficult to disentangle hardship and conflict as proximate drivers. After reviewing a large number of relevant studies, Katherine Mach and associates have concluded that climate effects upon civil conflict operate primarily through economic shocks related to climate.[49]

Prolonged drought due to climate warming has in some nations in Sub-Sahara Africa, for example, sharply reduced agricultural production. The resulting food shortages have led to rioting, political instability and civic conflict and have also been associated with large-scale migrations. Many of the out-migrants have left their distressed countries and moved, permanently or temporarily, to Greece, Italy and other European nations.[50] However, the question that remains unresolved is the degree to which this pattern is confined to a limited sample of nations in Sub-Saharan Africa and just a few other places in the world. In other words, to what extent is:

environmental stress --> civic conflict --> out-migration

a causal sequence that can be generalized across nations.

The first issue concerns how frequently environmental hazards lead to civic conflict. In one attempt to address this issue, utilizing data for nations in Sub-Saharan Africa, Hendrix and Glaser examined both long-term (land degradation) and short-term (rainfall variations) climatic variance as precursors to civil conflict (measured by the number of battle-related deaths in civil wars). They found that both types of climate stressors, but especially the short-term measures, were associated with the likelihood of armed conflict. For example, decreases in rainfall during one year were associated with a greater likelihood of deaths from civil conflicts in the country during the following year.[51] It must be noted, however, that their sample was confined to Sub-Saharan nations and that geographical area includes some of the poorest and most conflict-prone countries in the world. Before further pursuing the generalizability of the possible environment-conflict association we turn to studies of the second half of the sequence, that is, the possible connection between civil conflict and out-migration.

Most of the studies examining whether civic conflict is a proximate driver of emigration are case studies, focusing upon one specific nation, or region of a nation. Some research supports the connection. For example, Aree Jampaklay and associates examined unrest in the southern provinces of Thailand, where between 2004 and 2016 over 15,000 people were killed or injured due to violent unrest. Both unrest in the provinces and migration, especially across the nearby border into Malaysia, increased during the first decades of this century. Are the two connected? The investigators used a database that provided information on the exposure to violence of each village in the provinces and obtained data on migration by comparing surveys of household residents conducted in 2014 and 2016. The results indicated that individuals who lived in a village that experienced a violent event during a year were more likely to leave than those persons living in villages without such experiences.[52]

On the other hand, Agadjanian and Gorina obtained different results in a study of Kyrgyzstan, a Central European nation, formerly part of the Soviet Union, in which there were violent border disputes during the first decades of this century. The investigators noted that there were yearly fluctuations in both internal and international migration, the latter tending to be temporary. However, neither form of migration was found to be associated with political unrest. Rather, international migration was found to be related primarily to economic downturns and to involve residents of urban rather than rural areas.[53]

Finally, we turn to a study that examines the entire climate-unrest-migration sequence, with a sample that is more generalizable than case studies. This is a research project whose results were reported by Guy Abel and a group of demographers and economists. Because their study provides data that are highly relevant to the issues under consideration in this section we will discuss it in some detail. We begin by describing its sampling and measurement.[54]

Sample: Asylum seekers requesting international protection as refugees, according to data provided by the UN's High Commissioner for Human Rights. The applicants came mostly from throughout Africa and Asia, and many applied for asylum in Western European countries. The applications occurred during the time period 2006 to 2015. Note, this sample does not include all international migrants; only those seeking asylum. Such a sample is more likely to include persons fleeing conflict. Therefore, there is a bias toward confirming the causal linkages with this sample.

Conflict data: Yearly battle-related deaths for the entire period taken from a variety of global data sets. (Many studies rely upon annual deaths as the measure of conflict intensity. Such deaths are an aggregated variable and when such data are correlated with the behavior of individuals – that is, migration decisions – it tends to ignore individual decision-making. Individuals' agency is not taken into account; but as we have noted previously, individuals' perceptions of macro events are not always accurate either. So, the measurement decision is always difficult and consequential.[55])

Climate data: A drought index compiled from a number of climate databases that provided specific data on precipitation, rivers, etc.

With these data, the investigators statistically analyzed the climate-conflict-migration association at a global level. Over the full-time period (i.e. 2006–2015) they found little evidence of causal linkages, despite the sample bias noted above. A few significant relationships were observed between 2010 and 2012 that mostly involved refugee flows from Syria and Sub-Saharan Africa during this time period. The investigators concluded that the climate-conflict-migration association is highly confined to specific times and places.

In sum, there are findings supporting a connection between environmental stressors and civil conflicts in a small sample of nations, and there are findings supporting a connection between civil conflict and migration, also in a small sample of nations. However, as a generalization, the entire causal sequence – that is, the contention that environmental stress leads to civic unrest leading to international migration – does not have a great deal of empirical support.

Adaptation

Some places that due to global warming face the threat of ever more severe floods, tornados, or other disasters have tried to adapt, as an alternative to mass migration. Some of these adaptations have involved minimal changes to their social organization. For example, some places have simply added protective bulwarks, such as sea walls and stormwater storage basins. These projects have the potential to reduce ecological vulnerability, but many of the areas that are most in need of protective undertakings cannot afford them. Further, where resources have been available, studies have reported a tendency for these projects to disproportionately impact poor residents – the ones most likely to live in impacted areas – often leading to their displacement. In addition, the long-term efficacy of these projects may be suspect because the effects of future climate changes may overwhelm even these defenses.[56]

A more extensive change entails modifying traditional practices without an extensive transformation of the social organization. For example, farmers in some regions have responded to the threat of continuing natural disasters by changing crop management practices: when they plant and what they plant, how they manage water and other natural resources, etc. These new, hopefully more adaptive practices and technologies are often described as constituting "climate smart agriculture (CSA)." There have been a few notable successes, but a review of attempts to innovate CSA practices and technologies in the agricultural regions of countries around the world has typically reported low rates of adaptation. People's traditional practices are typically resistant to change and innovation often requires investments that environmentally impacted people cannot afford.[57]

The most complete form of adaptation involves transforming the way large numbers of residents earn their living. In these places, the impacts of climate change have been so drastic that former modes of production cannot continue. The choice that then confronts people is to migrate to a place where their former practices can still be followed if there is such a place to which they could go; or to substantially alter how they will survive. Box 3.4 describes a town that attempted a very ambitious adaptive transformation.

Box 3.4   A Missouri Town Adapts to the Loss of Geese[58]

Sumner, Missouri is a small rural town that for many years billed itself as the "Wild Goose Capital of the World." A 40-foot-high fiberglass goose overlooked the town and the annual social highlight was the Wild Goose Festival. Because geese from Canada settled near Sumner every winter, the town attracted hunters whose spending on food, lodging and so on were the heart of the local economy. Most of the hunters were white, working-class men who were viewed as sportsmen which gave them leeway to act in a rowdy manner, especially in the Sportsman Club bar. Their boisterous behavior was accepted because of the importance to the town of their spending.

But then – as a result of climate warming, the geese moved further north and Sumner could no longer attract the goose hunters so vital to the local economy. In response, the town tried to remake itself, flooding a nearby refuge in order to attract ducks and duck hunters. The women then took over activities around hunting, and gave the Festival a family-friendly feel: a pie auction, quilt show, Festival Queen competition, etc.

Local farmers, for whom corn was a major crop, were adversely impacted by the addition of moisture to the soil in an attempt to attract ducks. Meanwhile, the attempt to replace goose hunters with duck hunters has had limited success. Never a large town, when the Goose Festival and related activities began in the 1950s, Sumner's population was just over 300 people. Once the geese stopped coming, and the farmers' corn crops were affected, the town slowly, but continuously, lost population. As people kept leaving, by 2020 it population was estimated at fewer than 100 people, one-third of whom were living in poverty.

Sumner's disappointing experience with total adaptation appears also to characterize other towns' experiences. For example, after devastating tornados struck the Japanese town of Onajawa in 2011, the town moved to re-establish its traditional fishing industry by building a seafood processing plant. With private and public funds over the next decade they built commercial activities around the plant, hoping to turn the area into a tourist attraction. In the interim, residents continued to leave, and by 2020 it still remained unclear whether Onagawa would make a comeback from the devastation or slowly become a ghost town.[59]

Notes

1 For an overview of a great deal of relevant research, see The White House, *Report on the Impact of Climate Change on Migration*. October, 2021.
2 Hannah Beech and Jason Gutierrez, "Typhoon Spares Philippine Capital." *The New York Times*, November 2, 2020, p A9.
3 Ilan Kelman, et al., "Viewpoint paper, Islander mobilities." *International Journal of Global Warming*, 8, 2015.
4 Dennis Wesselbaum and Amelia Aburn, "Gone with the wind." *Global and Planetary Change*, 178, 2019.
5 From the introduction to, Abrahm Lustgarten, "Where Will Everyone Go?" ProPublica, July 23, 2020.
6 Ibid. See also, Betsy Hartmann, "Rethinking climate refugees and climate conflict." *Journal of International Development*, 22, 2010.
7 Government Office of Science, "Migration and global environmental change." Final Report, London, 2011.
8 United Nations High Commissioner for Refugees, "Climate change and disaster displacement." *U.N.* March, 2019.
9 Elian Peltier, "Migrants Chilled to Bone, Lacking Shelter in Bosnia." *The New York Times*, January 15, 2021, p 11.
10 Alison Heslin, et al., "Displacement and Resettlement." Chapter 10 in Reinhard Mechler, et al. (Eds), *Loss and Damage from Climate Change*. Springer, 2019.
11 For further discussion, see Lawrence A. Palinkas, *Global Climate Change, Population Displacement and Public Health*. Springer, 2020.
12 Ethan J. Raker, "Natural hazards, disasters, and demographic change." *Demography*, 57, 2020.
13 For further discussion, see Joyce J. Chen, et al., "Validating migration responses to flooding." *American Economic Review*: Papers & Proceedings, 107, 2017.
14 Bright K. Tetteh, et al., "Perceptions of weather variability and climate change on goat producers' choice of coping and adaptation strategies." *Climate and Development*, 12, 2020.
15 David Switzer and Arnold Vedlitz, "Investigating the determinants and effects of local drought awareness." *Weather, Climate, and Society*, 9, 2017.
16 Clark L. Gray and Valerie Mueller, "Natural disasters and population mobility in Bangladesh." *PNAS*, 109, 2012.
17 Kees van der Geest, et al., "Climate change, ecosystem services and migration in the Marshall Islands." *Climate Change*, 161, 2020.
18 Michel Beine and Christopher Parsons, "Climactic factors as determinants of international migration." *Scandinavian Journal of Economics*, 117, 2015.

19 For a review of studies, see Michael Berlemann and Max F. Steinhardt, "Climate change, national disasters, and migration." *CESifo Economic Studies*, 63, 2017.
20 Christine Cattaneo and Givani Peri, "The Migration Response to Increasing Temperature." *Working Paper 21622*, National Bureau of Economic Research, October, 2015.
21 Barbara Entwisle, Nathalie Williams and Ashton Verdery, "Climate change and migration." *American Journal of Sociology*, 125, 2020.
22 For further discussion, see Part One in, William van Schendel, *A History of Bangladesh*. Cambridge University, 2020.
23 See Robert Glennon, "The Unfolding Tragedy of Climate Change in Bangladesh." *Scientific American*, April 21, 2017.
24 This discussion is based upon: Clark L. Gray and Valier Mueller, *op.cit*; Joyce J. Chen, et al., *op.cit*; and Joyce Chen and Valerie Mueller, "Sea level rise will likely prompt migration in Bangladesh." *Nature Climate Change*, 8, 2018.
25 For further discussion, see International Organization for Migration, "Environmental migration." *Migration Data Portal*, 27 October 2020.
26 Joyce Chen and Valerie Mueller, "Behind the Paper." *Behavioural and Social Sciences at Nature Research*, October 22, 2018.
27 Clark Gray and Richard Bilsborrow, "Environmental influences on human migration in rural Ecuador." *Demography*, 50, 2013.
28 J. Vernon Henderson, Adam Storeygard and Uwe Deichmann, "Has climate change driven urbanization in Africa?" *Journal of Development Economics*, 124, 2017.
29 For a review of the studies, see Cristina Cattaneo, et al., "Human migration in the era of climate change." *Review of Environmental Economics and Policy*, 13, 2019.
30 Natalie Kitroeff, "After Two Merciless Hurricanes, Rising Fear of a New Refugee Crisis." *The New York Times*, December 4, 2020, p A1.
31 Dennis Wesselbaum, "Revisiting the climate driver and inhibitor mechanisms of international migration." *Climate and Development*, 10, 2020.
32 Wesselbaum and Aburn, op.cit., p 109.
33 For further overview, see Reiko Obokata, Luisa Veronis and Robert McLeman, "Empirical research on international environmental migration." *Population and Environment*, 36, 2014; and Lore Van Praag and Christiane Timmerman, "Environmental migration and displacement." *Environmental Sociology*, 5, 2019.
34 See, for example, Katherine J. Curtis, Elizabeth Fussell and Jack DeWaard, "Recovery migration after hurricanes Katrina and Rita." *Demography*, 52, 2015.
35 Mathew E. Hauer, Steven R. Holloway and Takashi Oda, "Evacuees and migrants exhibit different migration systems." *Demography*, 57, 2020.
36 Elizabeth Fussell, et al. "Weather-related hazards and population change." *Annals of the American Academy of Political and Social Science*, 669, 2017.
37 John R. Logan, Sukriti Issar and Zengwang Xu, "Trapped in place?" *Demography*, 53, 2016.
38 For further discussion, see Mariana Arcaya, Ethan J. Raker and Mary C Waters, "The social consequences of disasters." *Annual Review of Sociology*, 46, 2020.
39 Ethan J. Raker, op.cit.
40 Jeremie Gignoux and Marta Menendez, "Benefit in the wake of disaster." *Journal of Development Economics*, 118, 2016.
41 Reiko Obokata, Luis Veronis and Robert McLeman, "Empirical research on international environmental migration." *Population and Environment*, 36, 2014, p 119.
42 Hans Lucht, *Darkness Before Daybreak*. University of California, 2012.
43 Caleb Mensa, Amos T. Kabo-bah and Eric Mortey, "Assessing the effects of climate change on sea level rise along the Gulf of Guinea." *JENRM*, 4, 2018.
44 Neil Munshi, "The fight for West Africa's fish." *Financial Times*, March 13, 2020.
45 Lucht, op.cit.
46 Amelie Bernzen, Craig Jenkins and Boris Braun, "Climate change-induced migration in Coastal Bangladesh?" *Geosciences*, 9, 2019.
47 Kees van der Geest, et al., "Climate change, ecosystem services and migration in the Marshall Islands." *Climate Change*, 16, 2020.
48 International Organization for Migration, *Making Mobility Work for Adaptation to Environmental Changes*, 2017.

49 Katherine J. Mach, et al., "Directions for research on climate and conflict." *Earth's Future*, 8, 2020.
50 B.S. Levy, et al., "Climate change and collective violence." *Annual Review of Public Health*, 38, 2017.
51 Cullen S. Hendrix and Sarah M. Glaser, "Trends and triggers." *Political Geography*, 26, 2007.
52 Aree Jampaklay, Kathleen Ford and Aphichat Chamratrithirong, "Migration and unrest in the Deep South Thailand." *Demography*, 57, 2020.
53 Victor Agadjanian and Evgenia Gorina, "Economic swings, political instability and Migration in Kyrgyzstan." *European Journal of Population*, 35, 2019.
54 Guy J. Abel, "Climate, conflict and forced migration." *Global Environmental Change*, 54, 2019.
55 Correlating aggregate data with individual behavior has been previously discussed as risking the "ecological fallacy." For further discussion of this problem in studying conflict and migration, see Unit Seven, "Armed conflict, violence, and the decision to migrate." *Migration and Development*, 2020.
56 Eric Klineberg, Malcolm Ataos and Ux Koslov, "Sociology and the climate crisis." *Annual Review of Sociology*, 46, 2020.
57 Pramod K. Aggarwal, et al., "The climate-smart village approach." *Ecology and Society*, 23, 2018.
58 The following description is based upon, Branden T. Leap, *Gone Goose*. Temple University, 2019.
59 Camille Cosson, "From a tsunami-devastated zone to an attractive fishing town." *Urban Geography*, 2020.

4 Connections Between Origins and Destinations

This chapter explores the extensive interconnections between emigrants' origins and destinations. We begin with variations in the similarities between the nations' languages and cultures, noting that the closer they are to each other the more attractive a potential destination. We will also note how origins and destinations are connected by migration chains that involve concerted migrations by families, friends and people who share lifestyles. These linkages provide the pathways for both out-migration and return migration. Return migration is also prompted when migrants reach the financial goals they had set before moving, or become disillusioned or lonesome in the destination nation and decide to retrace their steps and go back home. In addition to these connections that are based upon the movements of people, there are flows of money routed from destinations to origins in the form of remittances that are of crucial importance to people left behind in many origin nations.

By way of review, recognize that the topics to be considered in this chapter correspond to theoretical perspectives that were introduced in earlier chapters. To be specific, language and culture are usually conceptualized as macro level variables, and as such they are associated with the earlier push-pull and neoclassical macro perspectives. Migration chains into and out of nations are examples of meso, or network, considerations that are emphasized in the new economics of labor migration (NELM). Finally, the focus upon individuals' assessments of costs and benefits in deciding whether or when to go or stay is associated with the micro perspective, and neoclassical micro theory in particular.

Cultural and Linguistic Distance

The most historic connection between many origins and destination nations is a cultural affinity involving similarities in their customs, values and language. The source of the similarity may lie in a former colonial relationship between the nations, a historically large-scale migration between them or a change in the legal boundaries that divided what was once a single nation. This topic was very briefly introduced in Chapter 2 where we noted that potential destination nations with cultures and languages similar to origin nations could attract migrants despite offering less economic advantages than other potential destinations where the culture was very different from their own.

Culture and Its Measurement

Culture has been broadly defined as a people's way of life, encompassing both patterns of behavior and the norms and values which guide that behavior, and the preferred means people follow and the implements they use, such as forks or chopsticks. At the macro level, every culture has been defined by the nature of its social institutions, customs and beliefs concerning art and architecture, clothing, etc. At the meso and micro level, culture involves roles and relationships, and offers widely shared values and norms about what should constitute appropriate behavior in diverse institutional settings, such as schools, workplaces, churches, and so on.[1]

Most definitions of culture are abstract and amorphous, so if it is going to be possible to compare origin and destination cultures (or any two cultures), formal methods have to be followed, and a number of procedures have been used to assess the degree to which any two cultures are alike. Some studies have selected specific cultural traits to compare, implicitly assuming that if two cultures are alike on the selected traits they are probably similar in other respects as well. For example, Docquier and associates focused upon two such cultural traits: the importance of religion and belief in gender equality. From a global survey of people's values, they selected several questions that appeared to measure each trait. If, for example, respondents from a nation tended to say that religion was an important part of their daily life, then it was assumed that religion was highly valued in that culture. Similarly, if people agreed that men and women should have equal rights, then the investigators assumed that the culture had gender-equalitarian values. Finally, based upon differences between nations in the importance of religion and belief in gender equality, the cultural distance between any two nations could be inferred.[2]

There are also several established inventories of cultural traits that investigators can utilize to compare nations. One of the most widely used in migration studies is the Hofstede scale. It originally contained four cultural dimensions and was later extended to six. It is utilized to assign values to nations based upon their scores on as many as six cultural dimensions:

  Individualistic versus collective orientations;
  People's tendency to accept power associated with hierarchies;
  Feminine or masculine approach (e.g. inclined to compromise or to fight);
  Desire to avoid uncertainty;
  Emphasis upon restraint versus indulgence;
  Orientation to the long-term or short-term.

Societies are given scores of zero (low) to 100 (high) on each dimension, with 50 considered the mid-point. To illustrate, a society in which people felt a strong responsibility to their families would have an individualistic score below 50. The quantitative scores that are assigned to each nation make it relatively easy to compare the cultural similarities between any two nations.[3]

Language as Culture

In research, a nation's language is sometimes used as a proxy for its culture. The underlying rationale is that languages are major components of culture and therefore likely to be related to other major components. Further, languages are the principal medium through which distinctive cultures are transmitted and maintained. Associated with the linguistic practices are cognitive styles and patterns of thought. Thus, a language is intimately tied to the characteristic ways of viewing the world which are signature features of every culture.

72 Origins and Destinations

While there is theoretical support for viewing language as a proxy for culture, and many studies do, a word of caution is also in order. Two societies could have historically shared essentially the same language, but if each subsequently had different experiences and had developed different institutional arrangements, then their languages might remain more similar to each other than their cultures.[4] (While cultures often change slowly, they are not static.)

Language and Its Measurement

From a measurement standpoint, how language is viewed in relation to culture is of little consequence. Further, given the importance of a migrant's ability to converse in a destination nation's language, some analysts have focused upon measuring the similarity between nations' languages without emphasizing the fact that language can also be viewed as an integral component of any culture.

Most language comparisons between nations make use of an established linguistic tree which consists of: *families* (meaning they are languages that share an ancestral history), *branches* (which are clusters within families) and *groups* (languages within clusters that are very similar in grammar and vocabulary). For example, the largest family is Indo-European and among its largest branches are Romance (which includes French, Spanish, etc.) and Baltic-Slavic (which includes Russian, Polish, etc.) Groups usually consist of very similar to each other languages that relatively recently split from each other (e.g. Danish and Norwegian). Nations whose primary languages are in the same families, branches or groups are assumed to be more alike linguistically – and perhaps culturally as well – than nations whose languages are in none of the same categories.[5]

Linguistic proximity indices usually assign values based upon how many levels of the family tree two languages share. For example, the highest score would be given to two nations that shared the same language (e.g. France and Belgium). The next highest score would go to two nations in the same group, next most for two nations only in the same branch, still less for two nations whose language was only in the same family. A score of zero would go to two nations whose languages were in separate families. See the illustration in Figure 4.1.[6]

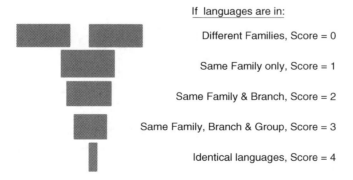

Figure 4.1 Linguistic Similarity Scoring.

Cultural Distance and Migration

There have been both case studies and comparative analyses focusing upon the effect of cultural distance on emigration flows, and the results have usually been consistent in showing that cultural disparities are a barrier to emigration. How large a barrier appears to vary with the economic development of the origin nation.

Docquier and associates examined emigration aspirations in a sample of nations in the global South, specifically in the Middle East and North Africa. Respondents were asked if they hoped to emigrate to one of the OECD nations, all of which are in the global North, and if so, to which one. They measured cultural distance between the respondent's origin and hoped-for destination with two previously described dimensions: religiosity and belief in gender equality. Those people who had OECD migration aspirations exhibited lower levels of religiosity, especially when compared to others in the same nation who did not intend to migrate. Because lower levels of religiosity are typical characteristics of OEC nations, these people were self-selecting on the dimension of cultural affinity. However, the differences between would-be migrants and those planning to stay were relatively small indicating that people who hoped to migrate selected destinations where they would fit better culturally with respect to religiosity; but only to a small degree. Some of the aspiring migrants also expressed more gender egalitarian views than non-migrants, but this difference was confined to people under 30 and single women, and again the differences between them and non-aspirants were not large.[7]

The investigators did not attempt to compare cultural and economic drivers, but in light of the research on economic drivers, described in Chapter 2, we can surmise that for many of the people hoping to emigrate out of nations in the global South income and employment opportunities would be paramount considerations. Cultural differences would remain relevant in choosing a specific destination, though they would likely be less salient than economic opportunities. Studies of people emigrating from nations in the global North to other global North nations – where economic differences among potential destinations are relatively small – support this contention because under these conditions cultural distance takes on much greater importance.

Relevant data come from a case study of Romanian migration to other European Union countries. Mikai and Novo-Corti obtained inter-EU migration data from The World Bank and measured the cultural distance between Romania and each other EU nations with the previously introduced six dimensions Hofstede scale. They found a strong negative relationship between Romanian emigration flows and the cultural distance between Romania and each destination nation. The less the cultural disparity, the greater the amount of migration. They concluded that for people emigrating within the EU, where economic differences among nations were not very large, cultural similarities were a crucial determinant.[8]

Focusing upon a broader sample of global North nations, Belot and Ederveen viewed migration flows among 22 OECD nations. They measured cultural distance with an early version of the Hofstede scale as well as two other indicators dealing with traditional values and similarities in religion. (Two nations would have a low religious distance score if the distribution of religious adherents was similar in each.) The three indicators might have been expected to be positively related to each other given that all were presumably measuring the same concept (i.e. culture). However, the correlations among them were very low and sometimes negative in direction: a puzzling finding that raises questions about the validity of some of the measures.

Despite not finding strong and positive relationships among the cultural indicators, each of them was nevertheless negatively correlated with migration flows, as expected. In other words, regardless of how cultural distance was measured, greater similarities among nations were associated with more migration between them. In addition, the investigators included measures of the differences between OECD nations in income and employment, and their analysis showed that cultural barriers did a better job of explaining inter-nation migration patterns than economic differentials in this economically relatively homogeneous sample.[9]

In sum, people who leave their nations seem to prefer moving to a nation whose culture is similar to their own. This cultural driver becomes particularly salient when economic differences among the nations are not pronounced, for example, when people are emigrating within the global North. South to North emigres, however, may be relatively less influenced by cultural similarities and more attuned to the possibility of better economic possibilities in choosing destinations.

Linguistic Distance and Migration

Language disparities have been expected to act as a barrier to migration because language skills are often a pre-requisite for finding employment. Correspondingly, a number of studies report that migrants able to speak the destination nation's language tend to receive at least a modest "fluency return" in the form of higher wages.[10] In addition, language facility is one of the most important ways through which migrants culturally assimilate in a new nation. Research suggests that prior to emigrating, people are aware of the effects of language dissimilarity and act accordingly in choosing destinations.

The previously discussed analysis reported by Belot and Ederveen examining the effects on migration of cultural distance also examined the effects of linguistic distance. To review, their sample consisted of 22 OECD nations, and they were trying to explain migration flows between these nations. They relied upon two measures of linguistic distance: whether origin and destination nations shared the same language; and the proximity between a sample of words selected from each nation's language. The latter measure produced scores close to those that would be obtained by a family tree analysis as illustrated in Figure 4.1. Both indicators were found to have significant effects on migration flows. Specifically, lacking a common language decreased migration between nations and, in addition, the greater the distance between the nations' languages the less the migration between them.[11]

Adsera and Pytlikova reported similar results, but their study is particularly noteworthy because of its expanded sample which enabled them to examine migration flows from over 200 origin nations to 30 OECD nations. They also increased the number of linguistic indicators to three: a language tree index; the phonetic similarity of words in the two languages; and the similarities among samples of words from the two languages. In addition, they examined the diversity of languages in destination nations, hypothesizing that nations where people spoke many different languages would present migrants with a more difficult adjustment, hence acting as a migration barrier.[12]

The investigators found that all three of the linguistic proximity indices were strong predictors of migration flows to non-English speaking nations. The indices also explained migration flows to English-speaking nations, but the effects were smaller. They assumed the difference arose because many migrants from non-English speaking nations learned some English in school, from movies, or other sources prior to emigrating so leaving a non-English speaking nation to move to an English-speaking nation would be less of a handicap than moving between nations that spoke different non-English languages. Linguistic diversity in the destination nation, as expected, also acted as a barrier, discouraging emigration.

In sum, despite relying upon highly diverse indicators the studies we have reviewed are congruent in reporting strong suppressing effects of cultural and linguistic dissimilarity on migration. The suppressing effect appears to be so strong that it continues to be visible regardless of what dimension of either culture or language is reflected by the indices relied upon by investigators.

Chain Migration

Chain migration describes a widely observed pattern of movement in which prospective migrants decide to move, and choose where to move, according to the paths that were forged by people they knew, or knew about, who moved previously. Once migration between an origin and destination nation begins it can eventually create a social network, with multiple interpersonal ties that link former and future migrants. New migrants tap into these ties and receive help in moving, finding employment and housing, etc. Then each new migrant expands the network's connections, leading to still more migration in the same footsteps.[13] These processes are illustrated by a migrant stream from a few Bangladesh districts to some cities in Northeast Italy, as described in Box 4.1.

Box 4.1   Chain Migration from Bangladesh to Italy

During the mid-1990s most European nations tightened their immigration restrictions more than Italy did. A few cities in Northeast Italy then became main destinations for a growing number of Bangladeshi migrants, large numbers of whom left a few specific districts in Bangladesh – a pattern which suggests that chain migration was involved. As the migrants explained to Morad and Sacchetto, the role of social ties was very significant in their choice of destinations.[14]

The social connections – based upon family, friendship and neighborhood – between previous emigres and later emigres were often in place for long periods of time. One young recent migrant explained:

"Some Bangladeshi from my home region were living in Italy.

I have always kept in touch with them by telephone."

Other Bangladeshi who lacked direct contact with others who had emigrated to Italy were able to benefit from information provided by others in their home district who did have direct contacts with Bangladeshi who had emigrated to Italy. Information that was passed on in the network involved work and housing opportunities and it was the basis for numerous migrants' decisions to move to Italy.

"My friends who have relatives in Italy told me that 'Italy is the

only country in Europe where you can .. work without documents."

> As new migrants arrived they, in turn, facilitated the movement of still others from their home districts. One young man who came to Italy with the help of his cousin explained how he later helped others to follow.
>
> "The number who came here .. with my help is around 100. They were my brothers, my cousins, husbands of my nieces, my neighbours and some others."

Chain migration has usually been invoked to describe the migration links connecting people based upon kinship ties, or people who lived in close proximity in the sending society. However, essentially the same process occurs among people who share a distinctive lifestyle that set them apart. For example, in the Northern Italian town of Cremona there is a concentration of highly dedicated artisans who completely devote themselves to making extremely well-crafted stringed musical instruments: violins, violas and cellos. Since the 15th century, this center has been widely known for its innovative artistry and the craftsmen's total immersion in their creative work. This reputation led to a cross-national social network that for hundreds of years has brought young people to Ceroma who wanted to be part of a community of artisans whose lifestyle revolved around their shared passion for their craft.[15]

Contemporary social media amplify the spread of information concerning whether people who share a distinctive lifestyle will find a place to be attractive. Twitter or Facebook, for example, can efficiently set a migratory chain in motion which can sometimes trigger the vigilance of people who take responsibility for monitoring who enters a place. To illustrate, a young American woman who with her female partner had been living in Bali and found it to be "queer friendly" posted that information on a thread on Twitter. She and her partner also offered to help other gay and lesbian couples settle in Bali, providing direct links to helpful visa agents. Fearing an influx of other gay Americans would be attracted to the conservative nation, Balinese immigration officials removed their Twitter accounts and gave them a few hours to pack their bags and leave the country.[16]

The way that a lifestyle chain of the type that had Balinese officials worried has operated in other nations is described in Box 4.2.

Box 4.2 Chain Migration of Mexican Gay Men

Sociologist Hector Carrillo and a team of assistants interviewed and observed 150 men in gay bars and clubs, and at gay-themed events, in San Diego. The men they observed and interviewed consisted largely of Mexican-born gay immigrants and their U.S.-born male partners, all of whom were then living in San Diego. (From the Mexican border, it is about 25 miles to the city.) The objective of the research was to illuminate international migrations that were largely motived by the men's distinctive sexual interests: a "gay culture of migration."[17]

> A majority of the Mexican-born immigrants, according to Carrillo's findings, believed they would be more able to live "openly gay lives" in the U.S. and perhaps even legally marry. These were not options in more conservative Mexico. In addition, being further away from the Mexican families in which they were raised – where their sexual orientation was generally disapproved – also protected both them and the families they left behind from the "stigma" that all of them would have experienced if they had openly remained in their hometowns.
>
> The Mexican migrants followed an established gay network of friends and acquaintances that over time came to provide a link between San Diego and a number of Mexican cities and towns. After migrating, they relied upon what the investigators termed, a network of informal cultural ambassadors. These men, who had previously migrated, and were more integrated in the gay community, introduced them to the people, places and activities that were at the center of Mexican American gay life in San Diego.

In studies of economic, environmental and other migration drivers, chain migration has probably often been a complicit, but unrecognized, variable. Assume, for example, that one person, a pioneer, decides to emigrate to another nation. The specific destination may have been selected for its economic opportunities, its linguistic similarity, or to escape floods or droughts. Some people connected to this original mover – because they had lived in the same village or were kin – will be inclined to follow, and a subsequent macro analysis will find that most of the migrants moved to a new locale that offered better economic opportunities, linguistic similarity, or a safer environment. And while such conclusions are not incorrect, they may fail to recognize the chain effect that was also influencing migrants' choice of pathways. In one notable study, a team of sociologists and demographers found that the effects of climate change on patterns of out-migration in Thailand were heavily dependent upon previously established social networks. While climate change was a proximate driver, where people chose to move was strongly related to their links to previous migrants.[18] However, most studies of migration in response to climate change, or to economic or cultural drivers, do not also take these possible network influences into account.

Migration Chains as Stimuli

Sometimes implicit and sometimes explicit in formulations of the chain migration thesis is the assumption that previous migrants not only influence the destination of subsequent migrants but actually encourage emigration. In other words, the information they provide and the potential assistance they can offer may act as a stimulus to move to those left behind. Data with which to test this assumption has generally been lacking, though. Empirical study of this hypothesis has been hampered because a relatively very small proportion of any population actually emigrates, and an even smaller number would have a connection to a prior émigré. Hence, it would require a very large sample to include sufficient numbers of such people; and for a complete assessment, it would also be necessary to obtain a "control group" consisting of similar people from the same place who did not emigrate.

A Swedish demographer, Anna-Maria Eurenius, created a unique database from the Swedish National Archive with which to test the chain-stimulus hypothesis. From this database, she selected a random sample of 250 people who lived in a specific county in Sweden in 1890 and left the country to move to the U.S. in 1891. From the same county, she took a random sample of 500 people similar in age to the migrants who did not move. For both the movers and the stayers she was able to obtain the emigration history of their close family members.[19]

Eurenius' main finding was that the chances of a person emigrating increased substantially with each increase in the number of previous family emigrants. The same direct relationship held for both males and females, and it was when they were in their middle 20s in age that both were particularly likely to follow the lead of previous family emigres. There were no data on the effects of previous emigres who may have been friends or neighbors but did not share a kinship relationship so their possible influence could not be assessed. And the study's time interval (i.e. one year) was highly condensed so that if it took people more than one year to follow family emigres that data would not be available either. Despite these limitations, the results provided strong support for the chain-stimulus hypothesis.

The Chain Multiplier

In most nations, regardless of how restrictive their immigration policies, certain categories of family members (spouses, children, parents, etc.) are typically admitted under family reunification programs (as described in Chapter 1). This is a type of chain migration and it has been labeled a migration multiplier because of the way following family members entering a nation to join an "initiating" migrant increases the total size of the destination nation's immigrant pool. In the U.S., for example, since about 1990, chain migration has exceeded new migration almost every year. On average, each new immigrant sponsored about three and one-half additional migrants. According to a 2017 report from the Center for Immigration Studies, over 60% of all people admitted into the U.S. were added as a result of a migrant chain, mostly under family reunification policies.[20]

The nation with the highest rate of chain migration into the U.S. was Mexico, averaging over six additional people for each initiating migrant, with family chains the major component. For example, among Mexico's large émigré population – virtually all of whom moved to the U.S. – sibling networks have been especially active. Pairs of brothers were the typical initiators followed by sister migration, and these connected moves were often generated over very short periods of time.[21] As we have previously described, however, streams of Mexican migration to the U.S. follow a number of different informal networks.

Cumulative Causation

Cumulative causation refers to a frequently observed tendency for international migration flows between the same origin and destination to be self-sustaining over a lengthy period of time. Chain migration is the principal force behind this tendency as a result of the informal recruitment networks that link migrant groups across time and space. One question that has been of particular interest to migration analysts concerns whether there is an upper limit to cumulative causation; a point after which the inflow slows or stops, if the destination's initial attractiveness fades.[22]

At some point, network resources can become strained or exhausted. Among people from the African nation of Cape Verde, for example, there was a migration chain linking to the Netherlands. People who for years had helped other family members and friends to follow in their footsteps – obtaining legal documents, finding places to live and work – often eventually came to feel burdened and frustrated because they felt that people back home did not appreciate the fact that they could not help everyone.[23]

In addition, there are often built-in forces that can lead to deteriorating conditions in the destination nation. The range of jobs that emigres from a specific place can perform is likely to be limited. At some point the continuing influx of migrants can saturate the local job market, leaving later arrivals with fewer opportunities. At the same time, because of the tendency for people in a migrant stream to settle in close proximity to each other, their sustained inflow raises the demand for a relatively fixed supply of housing, leading to rent increases. Despite facing less income and higher costs migrant flows have often been observed to continue. At what point will the chain network eventually be shut down? Mexican emigrants to the U.S. are the group that has been most studied in relation to this question.

Focusing upon Mexico is suggested because the nation has experienced very large rates of out-migration, and it has almost all entailed moving to the U.S. The data set that has most often been utilized is the Mexican Migration Project (MMP). It began by accumulating data on four Mexican communities as origin sites in 1982, and has periodically added sites since. By 2020 it included 93 rural and 61 urban communities. About one-half of the latter were in metropolitan areas with over 100,000 inhabitants. For each community included, the database contains data for households, including their composition, assets, migration history, etc.[24]

Fussell and Massey proposed that changes occurring in Mexico would reduce the migratory chain. Specifically, they noted that Mexico was becoming more urban and that more of the migrants were coming from urban areas while they were previously much more likely to be leaving rural areas. Relying upon classical theories about rural-urban differences, they assumed that urbanites were more selective and limited in their friendship and neighborhood circles and so less likely to be connected to migratory social networks. Even if someone from the same residential block were to migrate, they probably would not even notice. The typical urbanite is also thought to be less likely than the typical rural resident to be involved in an extended kinship network.[25]

Some years later, utilizing data from the MMP, Paredes-Orozco examined rural-urban changes in U.S.-bound migration from Mexico. He noted that, as Fussell and Massey had anticipated, the composition of the flow out of Mexico had changed in recent years to involve more urban origination. However, the likelihood of people migrating was not lower in small urban or even metropolitan areas than it was in rural areas, and in some conditions it was actually higher. Further, the same social processes appeared to be operating across all the different potential origin areas. Migrants from both small and large communities were found to rely upon community and family ties to reduce the risks and costs of moving to the U.S. In short, cumulative causation had apparently not been limited by increasing urbanization in Mexico.[26]

There is, however, some evidence to suggest that while the social network-driven migratory chain to the U.S. has not been compromised, deteriorating local conditions for migrants may have resulted in more dispersal of Mexican migrants in the U.S. During the last decades of the 20th century, there was an especially large migration from Mexico to Los Angeles. Ivan Light has argued that Los Angeles reached a saturation point, making it more difficult for later arrivals to find jobs and housing, and also exposing them to the resentment of locals, objecting to the growing number of poor migrants. The self-perpetuating movement of Mexican migrants to Los Angeles markedly slowed, and was redirected to other U.S. cities and towns that had not previously attracted large numbers of Mexican migrants.[27] Social networks continued to generate migration out of Mexico, but the chain linking Mexico and some particular destinations (e.g. Los Angeles) apparently reached an upper limit.

Family as Compensation

Migrations analysts, as we have noted, have been puzzled by the way chain migration can continue even after economic conditions deteriorated at the destination. Perhaps that seemed puzzling because some analysts focused too narrowly upon economic motivations. Ties to family can be important motivators for non-economic reasons. For example, studying a British sample, Ermisch and Mulder found that people who lived far from their parents were likely to move long distances to be close to them, even after they had lived for five years or more at the same residence, and were socially integrated into their neighborhoods.[28]

The strong pull of family, parents and siblings in particular, obviously has an emotional component, and being close enough to be able to actualize family relationships may compensate for some loss of income if people are unable to duplicate their economic situation after the move. Gillespie, Mulder and Thomas analyzed a large Swedish sample of working-age individuals for whom they had survey data concerning their reasons for moving. When living closer to family was the primary motive, their labor market outcomes were generally worse after the move, and the relative losses were especially pronounced for the migrants who had children of their own.

There were compensations, though. Having family close by could be a source of childcare, providing parents with workplace flexibility, and eliminating some childcare costs. However, even if it did not have these benefits, the investigators noted that the migrating parents might be quite willing to sacrifice economic returns for family contact. Moving to connect with family could also, under some conditions, eventually have economic benefits. Among those who were unemployed immediately prior to the move, the investigators inferred that families must have been a source of information and contacts because those who moved primarily for family were more likely to find employment in their new locale than previously unemployed migrants who moved for other than family reasons.[29]

Stepwise Migration

Stepwise migration, sometimes also referred to as multiple or serial migration, describes a frequently observed tendency for people not to remain in one destination nation, but rather to move to several destinations. Sometimes a return to the origin nation is interspersed between the various destinations. Additional moves often occur when migrants confront adverse economic conditions in the initial destination, but a sequential pattern of moving to new destinations can also be an established part of a migratory chain. While many variations are possible, underlying all of them is a tendency for many international migrants to settle temporarily in more than one destination nation.

Studies of migrants' life courses showing multiple destinations began to appear regularly during the first decade of this century and bourgeoned during the second decade. Many of the studies concluded that migrants shared a hierarchical ranking of destination nations and tried to accumulate sufficient resources along the way eventually to reach the nation(s) they considered to be most desirable. The ranking, according to anthropologist Nina Glick Schiller is multi-dimensional. A city's economic opportunities, as one would expect, were one of the ranking criteria. In addition, from her interviews with migrants, Schiller concluded that the migrants, along with their friends and families, shared a ranking of cities based upon their cultural diversity, openness and lack of political surveillance. At the top of their rankings were the leading cities of the global North which they viewed as offering both economic opportunities and cultural openness: London, New York, Paris and Toronto.[30]

While many migrants from the global South would prefer to move to the highest-ranked cities, it can be prohibitively expensive and difficult to do in a single move. It very often takes a series of moves as described in Box 4.3.

Box 4.3 Stepwise Migration of Multinational Maids

Anjou Paul interviewed 160 Filipina and Indonesian domestic workers who had left their homes and migrated to Singapore and Hong Kong. For some, it was a first move, for others a step along a way that they hoped was going to continue, while for others it was a last stop after multiple moves. She found that they shared a hierarchy of destinations, ranked according to desirability, and that they aspired to keep moving up the hierarchy. Paul later enlarged her study with a survey of 1200 domestic workers and interviews with their agencies and employers.[31]

The Filipinas were especially hoping eventually to reach Canada, or the U.S., however, they faced difficulties. Placement agencies demanded large fees, often creating "debt bondage" because the fees were so large relative to their modest salaries, and indebtedness slowed their movement. There were also immigration barriers and costs that combined to make it nearly impossible for them to move to their most desired locations in a single move. At each step, they acquired more information and help from enclaves of fellow nationals who had remained in that place, at least temporarily. And they tried to save enough money to finance their next step.

The patterns of movement were variable. For example, some moved to Singapore, then on to Italy or Bahrain and then to Canada. Others moved to Hong Kong and then to the U.S. And some remained at stops along the way, unable to move up the hierarchy; or they found they could make enough in a place like Hong Kong to send remittances back to family in the Philippines, and so they chose to stay.

Stepwise migration can also occur as a result of unanticipated circumstances that migrants confront. For example, a large group of Latin Americans migrated to Spain, largely in hopes of finding better employment opportunities. In Spain they also received European Union (EU) citizenship, enabling them to move freely across much of Europe. When their employment conditions in Spain deteriorated, they took advantage of their EU citizenship to move to England (when England was still part of the EU).[32] Similarly, when EU citizens born in Somalia, Iran and Nigeria confronted discrimination and racism in Sweden or Germany, they moved on to England in anticipation of better treatment there.[33]

For some migrants, however, the serial moves may not have been part of a long-term plan envisioned at the onset. Crawley and Jones interviewed over 100 migrants from Syria, Nigeria and Afghanistan who were living at the time in Greece, Italy and Turkey. Many of them have lived in other places along the way: Libya, Iran, etc. They explained that they believed they might have remained at any of their previous locations had conditions been different; for example, if their economic situation had not deteriorated or if civic conflict had not increased. They became serial movers without really intending to continue to move. In other words, everywhere in-between their home country and their final destination was not, as they remembered it, meant simply to be a stepping stone.[34]

Transnational Families

In Chapter 2 we described a common tendency in the global South for one household member to migrate, usually to the global North, in hopes of finding better wages. For the family, this is a strategy of "hedging their bets" because it is less risky than if the entire family were to move. The one who migrates, if successful, sends remittances to the family that stayed behind. This arrangement can last for many years, or the one who migrated can return home; or if the migrant obtains better wages than could be expected back home, then the rest of the family may follow. In any case, an integral member of a family is away for an extended period. In this section, we will examine some of the likely consequences.

Anthropologist Caroline Brettell, in an overview, writes that the most common pattern of migration by one spouse is for the male partner to migrate and the wife (and children, if there are any) to remain in the sending community. Sometimes, the overall situation of the family members left behind improves; but often, the absence of the husband/father creates additional burdens for those who remain.[35] What data are available also show a new tendency has been increasing in the global South in which it is the wife/mother who is the family member that migrates. This recent trend modifies an historical pattern in which it had almost always been the husband/father who left, if only one family member migrated.[36]

As women migrate from nations in the global South to live and work in nations in the global North, they are exposed to different cultures, with new ideas and values. Of special significance is the "modern" view of women that is widely held throughout the North. It emphasizes much more gender equality than women from patrilineal societies in the South previously experienced. When these women return home their husbands typically expect them to resume the subordinated role traditionally prescribed in their culture, and conflicts over different expectations can ensue. However, the recent increase in the amount of female migration has, in many nations of the global South, gradually weakened patrilineal structures and slowly altered gender relations.[37]

Men Left Behind

When a female family member migrates, like the previously described transnational domestic workers, she is the one who ordinarily sends remittances. The wife's new role in helping to support her family can create stress for the husband left behind, but apart from finances, the absence of the wife-mother also tends to create special strains for everyone in both the nuclear and extended families left behind. The men who stayed typically reported that they missed their wives, and they also expressed dissatisfaction with the extra responsibilities of child care and domestic household chores, both of which they found to be difficult. How one group of men left behind coped with an absent wife/mother is described in Box 4.4.

Box 4.4   Husbands Left Behind in Ghana

An international team of sociologists was able to find 12 men who were living in Ghana's principal city, Accra, and were willing to sit for extensive interviews. All of these men were married to women who had been overseas for at least two years. Most of their wives were either in the U.S. or the U.K., and their average stay at the time of the study had been about four years in duration. Most of the husbands left behind were in professional positions (lawyers, lecturers, businessmen, etc.).

To handle domestic chores, the men with adolescent daughters at home relied upon the girls to do most of the cleaning, cooking and taking care of younger siblings. Those without adolescent daughters relied mostly upon other female relatives, female friends or they paid female domestic workers. (Most of the men could afford to pay for services, if necessary.) Note, they maintained a rigidly gendered division of labor, common in nations in the global South, in which child care and household chores were considered women's work, even when wives/mothers were absent.

The separated husbands and wives maintained regular phone and text contact, and some were also able to travel up and back for regular visits. Some of the men – the investigators did not note the number – felt so emotionally or sexually deprived that they found "girlfriends" to temporarily replace their wives. Overall, however, the investigators concluded that the men in their sample effectively handled their wives' absence by employing a number of coping strategies.[38]

Absent mothers tend to remain involved in "mothering from afar," calling their children regularly and wanting detailed information about their lives, but in many instances studies report that the children resented their mothers' absence and felt emotionally less attached to her.[39] The young children who remain home usually receive much of their daily care from "other mothers," female relatives including older sisters and aunts, and grandmothers, in particular.[40] It is apparently commonplace for these substitute caregivers to try to encourage these children to be independent and take care of themselves as much as possible. The grandmother of a young Filipina girl whose mother had migrated explained that she (i.e. the grandmother) had been getting the little girl ready for school each day, but that she planned to help less in the near future.

> "I told her to learn how to do the things I've been doing for her … so that when her mom comes back she will be happy to know that her daughter can take care of herself."[41]

Females who migrate, according to several studies, tend to remit a larger share of their earnings than males, though the absolute amounts they send are often less due to a discriminatory tendency for women to be paid less than males. The relatively large remittances the women send probably indicate that the norm of family obligation is stronger among females than males in the global South. However, as the remitting female demonstrates an ability to help support a family, at least in some nations it raises their status in the family.[42]

The children in many cases do benefit from the migrant mother's remittances, especially with respect to enhanced educational opportunities. However, there is a good deal of evidence that indicates children are adversely impacted by the absence of a migrating mother. A meta-analysis that involved thousands of children and adolescents who were originally included in studies conducted across nations of the global South found that children typically suffered more depressive and anxiety disorders, and physically were more likely to be under- or over-weight when their mothers migrated. This analysis included every published study the investigators could find through 2018.[43] In addition, at least one other study compared the effects of migrating fathers and mothers on their children's school performance and found that children lagged further behind their peers when it was the mother who was away.[44]

The consequences for parents, when a grown daughter migrates, appear to vary according to the daughter's marital status. From several small studies it appears that when unmarried daughters migrate, left behind parents are typically the beneficiary of remittances, though in some instances daughters are more concerned with trying to save for a prospective marriage, and parents feel they are not getting as much as they should. With married daughters, most of the remittances go to their husbands and children, unless the grandparents need assistance in paying for the children's education. The daughter's separation from her own nuclear family, however, is a frequent matter of concern to her parents. They often feel that her children miss her and they worry that her marriage will not survive the separation.[45]

Women Left Behind

When husbands leave, the consequences for their wives left behind have until recently been the subject of a lot of speculation, and a few limited studies from which it is difficult to generalize. Theorizing about how wives fare when their husbands emigrate has been driven by two polar hypotheses: (1) the first holds that women who under the best of circumstances tend to be overburdened in many nations of the global South are further weighed down by having to pick up husbands' work while continuing to handle their own responsibilities, or (2) which argues that wives' household status improves when their husbands are gone, especially in patrilineal societies, and that they have more autonomy with which to pursue leisure activities.

In this writing, the most complete empirical assessment has been reported by a team of sociologists and demographers utilizing a unique dataset in Nepal. A panel study – which follows the same selected participants across time – has been ongoing in a rural area of south-central Nepal since 1996. It provides a wealth of data on migrations, remittances, household and community characteristics. In recent years, hundreds of thousands of people have left Nepal every year due largely to the nation's high level of unemployment, and most of them are young, married men. The data that have been collected by the panel study provide an ideal data set with which to examine whether wives' situations improved or deteriorated when their husbands migrated. The analysis showed that the husband's absence typically had both positive and negative consequences for the left-behind wives. On the one hand, the time used calendar each wife completed showed that the women usually spent more hours toiling on their farms because of the loss of the male's labor; difficult work, usually on top of their other chores. On the other hand, the remittances sent by the absent husbands gave many wives a new degree of financial freedom and enabled them to participate more in leisure activities outside of the home.[46]

The children of a migrant father may benefit from his remittances which can increase household assets. This can translate into better nutrition and more educational opportunities for them. At the same time, studies in Pakistan, Thailand and elsewhere also report that the children of fathers who emigrate miss the guidance and support they otherwise could have received, and may be more likely to be unhappy and anxious. Other studies that compare the offspring of families with both migrant and non-migrant fathers are consistent in showing that children in households with a father who emigrated are more likely to have behavioral problems and display hyperactivity and inattention.[47]

Remittances

Remittances from international migrants who left nations in the global South steadily increased from the mid-1990s to 2019, reaching a high point of (U.S.) $554 billion. These remittances became an important source of income, reducing overall poverty in the nations that received them. COVID-19 reductions in work and travel subsequently led to several years of decline, and total remittances for 2021 were estimated to decline to approximately (U.S.) $470 billion.[48] Even when the scale was reduced, remittances continued to be a large and important part of nations' economies in the global South, and the economic growth of many nations continued to be positively related to the size of remittance inflows.[49]

Philippine migrants present a good illustration of the importance of remittances. In 2020, an estimated ten million Filipinos, almost ten percent of the nation's population, lived and worked outside of the country. The government of the Philippines has for many years encouraged and facilitated work-related emigration by establishing a number of boards and bureaus to promote and manage the export of labor. The government made these investments both to ease domestic unemployment and because migrants' remittances made an important contribution to the nation's economy.[50] In total, according to World Bank figures, the emigres sent back about (US) $35 billion in 2020 which was approximately ten percent of the nation's GDP. Only in Guatemala (13%) and Ukraine (11%) did remittances constitute a larger share of the nation's GDP. The migrants worked at casinos in Marrakesh, car washes in Macau, as nurses in the U.S., as maids in Taiwan, and on global cruise ships; and in many families, more than one member of the family migrated and sent remittances.[51]

With so many members of families away from each other for extended periods of time, maintaining family ties can become problematic. However, Anthropologist Ina Zharkevich contends that remittances are an important means by which a separated family member reinforces kinship bonds with those who remained behind. Because many migrants from nations in the global South earn money from physical labor – as maids, farm and construction workers, etc. – the remittances they send are viewed as meeting their obligations by "blood and sweat." The toil that the money represents makes these

86 *Origins and Destinations*

remittances more intimate to the recipients than monetary conferrals acquired in other ways. At the same time that remittances can reinforce family ties, they can also be a source of conflict among extended family members who remain behind. In other words, they can both bind and divide. One day, in a local court in Nepal, Zharkevich witnessed a dispute over remittances brought by an older woman, Sapana, against her daughter-in-law. It is described in Box 4.5.[52]

Box 4.5   Conflict Over Remittances in Nepal

Sapana accused her daughter-in-law of taking all of the remittances sent by her son, the husband of the daughter-in-law. Even though the two women lived in a joint household, worked together in the same family fields and ate from the same hearth, they had different "money pots." Sapana felt that she was entitled to a portion of her son's remittances because she had taken out a loan to pay for his travel, and she was still making payments. She was a widow and finding it difficult to make ends meet.

In the emotion-charged court hearing, each woman accused the other of failing to show proper respect. The quarrel made apparent the strains between the nuclear and extended family. The women were part of a joint family as a result of Nepal traditions, and not by choice. Keeping all of her husband's remittances, and excluding her mother-in-law, provided the daughter-in-law with a tangible way of asserting the salience of her nuclear, rather than extended, family.

In Nepal, Zharkevich noted that there were also frequent conflicts over remittances within transnational nuclear families. Wives often complained that migrant husbands were not sending enough money; that they were failing to meet their traditional male obligation to provide for their wives. Arguments about money over the phone could grow so frequent and so heated that emigrant men sometimes avoid phoning, and some of them stated that they would like to get rid of their phones altogether to avoid the conflict that they thought was likely to recur in future conversations.

Studies conducted in a number of nations in the global South have focused upon the recipient households, and tried to chart precisely how remittances affect household budgets. The results have varied. Some household expenditures will almost invariably increase, given the infusion of external funds, but differences are reported in which budget categories receive increased expenditures. Some recent studies illustrate the absence of an overall pattern:

1   In Bangladesh, Raihan and associates found that remittances increased household expenditures on health, food and housing, but not on education, and it did not increase durable investments (e.g. farm equipment).[53]
2   In Senegal, Randazzo and Piracha found that cross-national remittances increased household expenditures across every category; and that the increases were roughly proportionate to previous allocations. In other words, marginal

spending patterns did not change as a result of the infusion of additional funds from remittances.[54]

3   In Mexico, Aysa-Lastra found that remittance–induced changes in household spending varied completely according to the gender of both the sender and the recipient. Men and women remitted for different types of expenditures, and men and women who received remittances put them to different uses.[55]

Return Migration

Return migration, also referred to as remigration, is a difficult concept to operationalize because of the complexity of many migration patterns. To illustrate, suppose that I move from nation A to B then later to C. If I go back to B, does that constitute return migration, or must I go all the way back to A? The answer depends upon a lot of considerations: Has my family remained in A, or did they also move to B? Is my citizenship in A? How long did I stay in B before moving to C? Most data sets do not include a level of detail adequate to answer all of the above questions, so studies of voluntary return migration typically involve a degree of measurement error. When a nation forces migrants to leave, some data on the deportees are usually collected by statistical offices, border protection and immigration law enforcement agencies, but many nations' records are incomplete. Voluntary returns at a global scale are tracked by the International Organization for Migration (IOM) and by some nations' agencies, but the total number of returnees is almost certainly under-counted.[56] Because of the deficiencies with "official" return migration records, most studies rely upon specially designed surveys or datasets that were initially collected for other purposes but include relevant migration data.

Aspirations and Plans

People who move to a nation different from the one they grew up in frequently hold on to the idea that they will eventually return home. For those who migrated in search of better employment opportunities, retirement is often viewed as the time when they will be able to return. As they grow older, however, many realize that returning home was a dream they cannot actualize. Some settle for the hope that they can be buried in their home country, though even this is out of reach for most. Despite their hopes and long-term aspirations, a number of considerations keep most migrants from returning. If they had children in the destination nation, remaining close to them for support may be compelling.[57] In addition, many of their extended families and friends – the people they would return for – may have in the interim died or moved elsewhere.

Over time, many migrants come to feel that the destination nation is almost home, while changes in the origin nation make it feel less like the home they have been missing. Erdal has summarized these alternatives by writing that "home" for the migrant can have four possible locations: here or there, both or neither. And where home really is can fluctuate among the four choices.[58] So, for people who have migrated, an opportunity to return to a previous home can present a complex set of issues to consider, as illustrated in Box 4.6.

> **Box 4.6   Deciding Whether to Return to Liberia**
>
> The violence of a prolonged civil war in Liberia during the 1990s resulted in thousands of people fleeing their homes and traveling about 750 miles west to Ghana. When the conflict ended the UN High Commissioner for Refugees (UNHCR) began an active assistance program (in 2008) to provide the refugees with some alternatives. UNHCR offered to help them to better integrate in Ghana, repatriate in Liberia, or resettle in a third nation. The migrants needed to weigh their options and make a decision.
>
> A married couple, Jack and Shetha initially argued about whether to stay in Ghana or go back to Liberia. She was sure she wanted to return and said:
>
>> "I am tired of my life here! We are just wasting time … It is better to restart our new life in Liberia."[59]
>
> Jack was afraid he could not duplicate his current teaching position in Liberia so Shetha made a month-long "go-and-see" visit where she turned for help from her family that had remained. They agreed to help the couple find work and housing so Jack relented and they returned home.
>
> Other migrants with no family or friends remaining in Liberia to assist them were more reluctant to move back. That was the situation of a 41-year-old single man who said:
>
>> "If I go back I will have to rebuild my network … If I return to Liberia there will be a big gap in my life."
>
> Some families hedged their bets, with one member returning to Liberia while the other remained, and based upon the experience of each the couple would later make a decision. Still other migrants were enticed by a dream of going to the U.S. or Canada or Australia, but this was a realistic possibility only for those with family already in those countries so they could apply for family reunification.

A substantial percentage of all returning migrants appear to be following a plan to return that they laid out in advance. Some initially left home planning to remain in the destination nation for only a limited period of time, for example, until they could save enough money to send their children to school, or buy a farm or a store, or until the violence that led them to flee is over. In other instances, readmission agreements with countries of origin were negotiated with the destination nation in advance, stipulating migrants' lengths of stay. Of course, many migrants also return home unexpectedly because they face problems in the destination nation – such as loss of a job or racial-ethnic hostility – or because their family at home needs them (e.g. due to illness or natural disaster). For some migrants, the return home is involuntary. In most destination nations they can be expelled if they have been convicted of a crime or if they over-stayed their visa – or simply because a new political regime does not want them to remain. For these involuntary returnees reintegration is especially difficult, as described in the following section.

There are limited data concerning whether migrants' voluntarily return home in greater or lesser numbers than they initially expected. Most research on the issue has been confined to case studies of small groups of migrants from a single nation. A large, unique dataset on return migration exists for the U.S., though the time period it covers is 1917 to 1924, making its contemporary applicability questionable given how many dynamics have changed over the past 100 years. Nevertheless, the completeness of the data makes them difficult to disregard. Zachary Ward, an Australian economist, found that between 1917 and 1924 the Bureau of Immigration asked migrants entering the U.S. if they planned to stay permanently or, if not, how long they planned to stay before returning home. The government also collected information on departures, but again, only during this time period.

Ward took a 1% random sample of the many ships coming from Europe to the U.S. between 1917 and 1924, and obtained information on plans and departures for that ship's passengers. Comparing what the migrants said they planned on arrival with the actual departure information, he found that only 15%, or less (depending upon the specific year) of the entrants initially intended ever to return home. They considered it a permanent move. However, 40% or more actually did return. It was single men from Southern and Eastern Europe whose rate of return most exceeded their initial plans. They arrived with fewer skills than migrants from Western or Northern Europe and appeared to return home because they found good-paying jobs more difficult to obtain than they anticipated.[60]

Ward's finding that, on socioeconomic considerations, the return migrants were negatively selected is consistent with other findings of studies that focused upon more contemporary groups. For example, an analysis of recent return migration to nations in the global South from the Netherlands found that the lowest income group had the highest rate of return. Next highest were migrants in the highest income group. The middle-income group was lowest, producing what Ward and others have described as a U-shaped return pattern.[61]

Generational Differences

Return plans and aspirations have also been shown to vary by immigrant generation. One of the most relevant studies came from a large survey in France which included a representative sample over 12,000 immigrants and their offspring, all between 18 and 50 years of age. The survey, among other items, asked about the immigrants' onward mobility intentions: Did they think they would move back to their (or their parents') home country, or did they intend to go to a third country (i.e. not their ethnic homeland).

Demographer Louise Caron classified the people in her sample according to their immigrant generation, and then analyzed their onward mobility intentions in relation to their generation. The analysis showed that foreign-born migrants who were not French citizens at birth, first generation (G1), were the ones most likely to consider returning to their ethnic homeland, if they were to move. The offspring of immigrants, G2, who were raised in France were much less likely to report intentions to return to their parents' origin country but much more likely to plan to live one day in a third country. Regardless of generation, those with more educational attainments or/and fluency in multiple languages were also more inclined to move to a new and different country. There was also a generational difference in how these people responded to perceived discrimination. First-generation immigrants responded to feeling discriminated against in

France by intending to move to a third country. They were disappointed in France, so inclined to move, but not back home under these conditions. However, the second generation, G2, responded to perceived discrimination by intending to move back to their parent's country of birth. Caron proposed that this expressed their disappointment with France and was also a way for them to signify their identification with their (parents') homeland.[62]

Similar findings come from a study of Chinese families in Toronto in which the investigators concluded that whether and where young people migrate depends upon their kin networks. When the first generation maintained transnational ties to their countries of origin the children built upon those networks and these connections became the pathways back to the nation of their ethnic origins.[63] Thus, return migration and out-migration paths are highly duplicative of each other. They are, according to Entwisle and associates, "interconnected steps in a migration system."[64]

The assertion of ethnic identification in the second generation has been widely described in other studies and referred to as, "reactive ethnicity." The G2 returnees are often disappointed with what they find in their parents' homeland, though. For example, Christou and King interviewed 64 second-generation people of Greek descent. They all moved back to Greece, from either Germany or the U.S. as a result of having grown up with a strong Greek identity. They found many conditions in Greece different from what they expected, and also felt that they were not accepted by natives as being sufficiently Greek. They were considered "hyphenated Greeks." Disappointed, a number of the returnees were contemplating going back to their birth nations, i.e. either the U.S. or Germany.[65] Similarly, a group of men of Korean descent who were born and raised in China then moved to South Korea felt that their Korean ancestry was not fully accepted in South Korea. They discovered that birth citizenship counted for more than coethnicity, and that where, outside of Korea, people were born strongly influenced the kind of reception they experienced in Korea. For example, Korean Americans were accorded higher status and more accepted than Korean Chinese.[66]

Drivers of Return

A large percentage of voluntary migrants are in pursuit of economic gain. Their immediate gain, as described in Chapter 2, can be in the form of increased wages in the destination country. However, what can be termed economic migration is often also part of a long-term mobility strategy. The objective is for migrants to accumulate savings to enable them to open their own businesses when they return home. In many nations of the global South, there are elevated rates of self-employment among returning migrants. Others who migrate acquire technical, social and language skills on their jobs in the global North which qualify them for higher wage positions when they return.[67]

On the other hand, of course, some migrants are not successful in obtaining the kind of wages that they expected before they moved. Whether that leads them to pack their things and move back home has been examined with inconsistent results. Some studies report that economic disappointment leads to remigration, but other studies report no relationship between them. Caron and Ichou have tried to reconcile the different findings by focusing upon the conditional effects of migrants educational attainments before they moved, assuming that these attainments would be positively related to their economic expectations. Their data involved long-term migration out of England and Wales, and they found that it was migrants who were relatively well educated who were the most likely to return if they faced employment difficulties in the destination nation. This educational effect was especially pronounced for males and for relatively new arrivals. Migrants with lesser educational accomplishments, with lower economic expectations, who could not obtain employment did not experience the same mismatch between expectations and outcomes, and so were less likely to remigrate.[68]

In addition to economic considerations, a number of other types of variables have been shown to effect the likelihood of remigration. In several studies, experiencing discrimination has been cited by returnees as their reason for leaving. For example, in the previously discussed study of migrants intentions to leave France, they mentioned discrimination as a reason they would want to leave. In a study of 40 people who actually returned from Germany to Turkey, Sener found that the migrants stated that discrimination was a major reason for their remigration. The group studied by Sener all had relatively high socioeconomic status; they were physicians, engineers, professors, etc. However, they did not feel that their professional status protected them from widespread discrimination in Germany because of their ethnic identity. Because of their credentials they believed they could still make a good living in Turkey, but even if returning meant economic sacrifices they felt it was worth it to "feel at home."[69]

Reintegration

Many people who migrate, as we have noted, leave with the intention of someday returning "home." For those who do return, there is the question of how well and how quickly they will be able to reintegrate. The process of reintegrating has usually been defined in terms of carving out new roles and relationships – at work, in families, etc. – that fit the returnees based upon how they have changed as a result of their experiences as migrants. Flahaux defines it as migrants finding their place in society, back in their country of origin.[70]

For forced returnees, reintegration can be especially problematic. In a number of global South nations, including Cambodia, Egypt, Honduras, and others, migrants who are expelled from the E.U. or the U.S. are regularly detained, imprisoned, put on parole. In a number of less repressive nations, returnees who were either expelled or forced for economic reasons to return, are not formally punished, but they are stigmatized, labeled as lazy failures.[71] Even in nations where non-voluntary returnees are neither punished nor stigmatized, there tends to be few government programs designed to facilitate their reintegration. They might receive some assistance from family members or from poorly funded NGOs, but they are largely on their own. In all of these situations, it is extremely difficult for the returnees to reintegrate and many aspire again to migrate.[72]

Voluntary returnees include a range of people who were not expelled, but the "voluntariness" of their return can be highly variable. At the low end of the continuum are people who felt they had no choice but to return because they felt isolated and became desperately lonesome or wound up unable to support themselves. At the high end of this continuum are people who emigrated with a specific objective in mind. After reaching that objective it was always their plan to return home. While they were away, it was typical for these people to keep one eye on the people at home, and try to assure that a comfortable place would be waiting when they returned.

Migrant Filipina domestic workers illustrate the importance of maintaining contacts. After years of working overseas many return home impoverished, even after years of earning more than they could have if they remained in the Philippines. The explanation is that they remit a large percentage of their earnings, leaving little for savings. In addition to relatively large remittances, they return home for visits with their families as often as they can. After interviewing a small sample of Filipina migrant household workers, Saguin concluded that they are renegotiating a space for their return from the very moment that they decided to migrate.[73]

Notes

1. For an overview of major theories of culture, see Jerry D. Moore, *Visions of Culture*. Rowman & Littlefield, 2018.
2. Frederic Docquier, Aysit Tansel and Ricardo Turati, "Do emigrants self-select along cultural traits?" *International Migration Review*, 54, 2020.
3. G. Hofstede, "Dimensionalizing cultures." In *Online Readings in Psychology and Culture*, 2, 2011.
4. For further discussion, see Yoshihisa Kashima, Emiko Kashimo and Evan Kidd, "Language and Culture." In Thomas M. Holtgraves (Ed), *The Oxford Handbook of Language and Social Psychology*, Oxford University, 2014.
5. For further discussion of language families, see James Stenlaw, Nobuko Adachi and Zdenek Salzmann, *Language, Culture, and Society*. Taylor & Francis, 2017.
6. A similar measurement procedure was employed by, Alicia Adsera and Mariola Pytlikova, "The role of language in shaping international migration." *The Economic Journal*, 125, 2015.
7. Docquier, et al., *op.cit.*
8. Iuliana Mikai and Isael Novo-Corti, "Cultural distance and migration patterns in the EU." *European Research Studies Journal*, 23, 2020.
9. Michele Belot and Sjef Ederveen, "Cultural barriers in migration between OECD countries." *Journal of Population Economics*, 25, 2012.
10. For data on the fluency return, see Ying Zhen, "English Proficiency and Earnings of Foreign-Born Immigrants in the USA." *Forum for Social Economics*, 45, 2016; and Abdihafit Shaeye, "Dynamics of English fluency return for refugees." *Journal of Immigration & Refugee Studies*, 17, 2019.
11. Belot and Ederveen, *op.cit.*
12. Adsera and Pytlikova, *op.cit.*
13. The term was initially described by, John S. McDonald and Leatrice D. McDonald, "Chain migration, ethnic neighborhood formation, and social networks." *The Milbank Memorial Fund Quarterly, 42, 1964*. It has been extensively refined by Massey in a series of papers on Mexican migration to the U.S. See, for example, Douglas S. Massey, "Understanding Mexican migration to the United States." *American Journal of Sociology*, 92, 1987.
14. All of the following quotes are taken from, Mohammad Morad and Devi Sacchetto, "Multiple migration and use of ties." *International Migration*, 58, 2019.
15. Simone Guercini and Diego Ceccarelli, "Passion driving entrepreneurship and lifestyle migration." *Journal of International Entrepreneurship*. Published online: 14 January, 2020.
16. Richard C. Paddock, "She Called Bali 'Queer Friendly'." *New York Times*, 1/21/2021, P A8.
17. Hector Carrillo, *Pathways of Desire*. University of Chicago, 2017.
18. Barbara Entwisle, Nathalie Williams and Ashton Verdrey, "Climate change and migration." *American Journal of Sociology*, 125, 2020.
19. Anna-Maria Eurenius, "A family affair." *Population Studies*, 74, 2020.
20. Jessica Vaughan, "Immigration Multipliers." *Center for Immigration Studies*, September, 2017.
21. See Fernando Riosmena and Mao-Mei Liu, "Who goes next?" *The ANNALS of the American Academy of Political and Social Science*, 684, 2019.
22. Elizabeth Fussell and Douglas S. Massey, "The limits to cumulative causation." *Demography*, 41, 2004.
23. Jorgen Carling, "Making and Breaking a Chain." In Oliver Bakewell, et al. (Eds), *Beyond Networks*. Palgrave Macmillan, 2016.
24. For further description, see Jorge Durand and Douglas S. Massey, "Evolution of the Mexico-U.S. immigration system." *The ANNALS of the American Academy of Political and Social Science*, 684, 2019.
25. Fussell and Massey, *op.cit.*

26 Guillermo Paredes-Orozco, "The limits to cumulative causation revisited." *Demographic Research*, 41, 2019.
27 Ivan Light, *Deflecting Immigration*. Russell Sage Foundation, 2006.
28 John Ermisch and Clara H. Mulder, "Migration versus immobility, and ties to parents." *European Journal of Population*, 35, 2018.
29 Brian J. Gillespie, Clara H. Mulder and Michael J. Thomas, "Migration for family and labour market outcomes in Sweden." *Population Studies*, 74, 2020.
30 Nina Glick Schiller, "A comparative relative perspective on the relationships between migrants and cities." *Urban Geography*, 33, 2012.
31 Anju Mary Paul, *Multinational Maids*. Cambridge University, 2017.
32 Rosa M Giralt, "Onward migration as a coping strategy?" *Population, Space and Place*, 23, 2017.
33 Jill Ahrens, Melissa Kelly, and Ilse Van Liempt, "Free movement?" *Population, Space and Place*, 22, 2014.
34 Heavan Crawley and Katherine Jones, "Beyond here and there." *Journal of Ethnic and Migration Studies*, 47, 2021. See also the overview in, Kellynn Wee and Brenda SA Yeoh, "Serial migration, multiple belongings and orientations toward the future." *Journal of Sociology*, 57, 2021.
35 Caroline Bretell, "Marriage and migration." *Annual Review of Anthropology*, 2017.
36 International Labour Organization, "Who are the women on the move? ILOSTAT," December 18, 2020.
37 This pattern has been widely observed and described. See, for example, Maria Aysa-Lastra, "Gendered patterns of remitting and saving among Mexican families." *ANNALS of the American Academy of Political and Social Science*, 684, 2019.
38 Gervin A Apatinga and Faustina A Obeng, "The coping strategies of 'men left behind' in the migration process in Ghana." *Migration and Development*, 10, 2021.
39 Eric Fong and Kumiko Shibuya, "Migration patterns in East and Southeast Asia." *Annual Review of Sociology*, 46, 2020.
40 See Elspeth Graham, "Parental migration and the mental health of those who stay behind." *Social Science and Medicine*, 132, 2015.
41 Theodorea Lam and Brenda A. Yeoh, "Parental migration and disruptions in everyday life." *Journal of Ethnic and Migration Studies*, 45, 2019.
42 Fong and Shibuya, *op.cit*.
43 Gracia Fullmeth, et al., "Health impacts of parental migration on left behind children and adolescents." *Lancet*, 392, 2018.
44 Patricia Cortes, "The feminization of international migration." *World Development*, 65, 2015.
45 For a study of 37 left behind parents of migrating daughters in Indonesia, and a review of the literature from other nations in the global South, see M. Faishal Aminuddin, et al., "The social and economic impact of international female migration on left-behind parents in East Java, Indonesia." *Asian and Pacific Migration Journal*, 25, 2019.
46 Dirgha Ghimire, Yang Zhang and Nathalie Williams, "Husbands' Migration." *Journal of Ethnic and Migration Studies*, 10, 2019.
47 Benjamin Penboon, et al., "Migration and absent fathers." *Asian and Pacific Migration Journal*, 28, 2019.
48 The World Bank, *Covid-19*. October 21, 2020.
49 Shijun Cao and Sung Jin Kang, "Personal remittances and financial development for economic growth in economic transition countries." *International Economic Journal*, 34, 2020.
50 For further discussion, see Jason DeParle, *A Good Provider Is One Who Leaves*. Penguin, 2020.
51 Jon Emont, "Countries Lose Billions Sent Home From Workers Abroad." *Wall Street Journal*, July 6, 2020, P 1.
52 Ina Zharkevich, "Money and blood." *American Anthropologist*, 121, 2019.
53 Selim Raihan, Mahtab Uddin and Saki Ahmed, "Impact of foreign remittances on the household spending behaviour in Bangladesh." *Migration and Development*, 10, 2021.
54 Teresa Randazzo and Matloob Piracha, "Remittances and household expenditure behaviour." *Economic Modelling*, 79, 2019.
55 Aysa-Lastra, *op.cit*.
56 IOM, "Return Migration." *Migration Data Portal*, February 19, 2021.
57 For further discussion of one such exile group – Turkish women in Denmark – see, Anika Liversage and Gretty M. Mirdal, "Growing old in exile." *Journal of Ethnic and Migration Studies*, 43, 2017.

58 Marta B. Erdal, "This is my home." *Comparative Migration Studies*, 2, 2014.
59 All quotes are from, Maohiko Omata, "The complexity of return decisions." *Journal of Ethnic and Migration Studies*, 39, 2013.
60 Zachary Ward, "Birds of passage." *Explorations in Economic History*, 2016.
61 Govert Bijwaard and Jackline Wahba, "Do high-income or low-income immigrants leave faster?" *Journal of Development Economics,* 108, 2014.
62 Louise Caron, "An intergenerational perspective on (re)migration." *International Migration Review*, 54, 2020.
63 Janet W. Salaff and Arent Greve, "Social Networks and Family Relations in Return Migration." In Chan Kwok-bun (Ed*), International Handbook of Chinese Families.* Springer, 2013.
64 Entwisle, et al., op.cit, p 1476.
65 Anastasia Christou and Russell King, *Counter-Diaspora*. Harvard University, 2015.
66 Helene K. Lee, *Between Foreign and Family*. Rutgers Univerity, 2018.
67 For further discussion, see Jacqueline M. Hagan and Joshua T. Wassink, "Return migration around the world." *Annual Review of Sociology*, 46, 2020.
68 Louise Caron and Mathieu Ichou, "High selecttion, low success." *International Migration Review*, 54, 2020.
69 Meltem Y. Sener, "Perceived discrimination as a major factor behind return migration." *Journal of Ethnic and Migration Studies*, 45, 2019.
70 Marie-Laurence Flahaux, "Reintegrating after return." *International Migration*, 59, 2020.
71 Jacqueline M. Hagan and Joshua T. Wassink, "Return migration around the world." *Annual Review of Sociology*, 46, 2020.
72 Camille Le Coz and Kathleen Newland, *Rewiring Migrant Returns and Reintegration*. Migration Policy Institute, February, 2021.
73 Kidjie Saguin, "Returning broke and broken." *Migration and Development*, 9, 2020.

5 Undocumented Migrants

In prior chapters, we have touched upon how various events and processes impact migrants who lack legal status in their destination nation. This chapter is exclusively devoted to them: the routes they travel, how they are received, and the ways that they adjust. We will refer to them as undocumented or unauthorized migrants, and use the terms interchangeably. Some analysts and some agencies also refer to them as irregular migrants, but regardless of the term used, it is the same group of migrants that are being denoted. They will not be referred to here as "illegals" because illegal is a descriptor that should not be applied to people, even if they lack legal standing in a nation.

To complete this picture of migrants' legal status we should add that some migrants also violate laws in their origin nations when they leave without proper authorization. There are a few nations, all of which tend to have authoritarian regimes – examples include Cuba, Iran and North Korea – that limit the rights of their citizens to emigrate without the government's prior approval. If people depart these nations without authorization and later return, they can be fined or imprisoned.[1]

Whether or not nations should restrict prospective migrants from exiting or entering raises philosophical questions that could be important to consider, but are not usually addressed by social scientists. An exception is Political Scientist Sarah Song who notes that there are potentially strong arguments in favor of open borders. How can nations morally justify preventing people from moving as they wish, particularly when most of them are simply trying to make better lives for themselves?[2]

Those cosmopolitan advocates who support open borders also tend to emphasize universal norms and supranational authority. In disagreement, people who are opposed to open borders and want to maintain legal restrictions justify their position by arguing that immigration threatens a nation's cultural identity or its racial, ethnic and religious mix, and the values associated with that mix. And of course there is the familiar argument that immigration must be controlled to protect a nation's labor force from unfair competition. (These claims are systematically examined in Chapter 8.)

While a number of groups claim to fear labor force competition from migrants, the reality is that in many of the wealthier nations employers need a low-paid group of workers will to perform the arduous work the native labor force rejects. Admitting temporary workers has been widely viewed as the best compromise: it makes the migrant workers available to employers, but the nation preserves the right to reject as permanent residents those that "do not fit." In many nations this compromise has resulted in an increase in the proportion of residents with temporary rather than permanent status; and as a consequence, agencies have to be empowered to routinely monitor those with temporary status.[3]

DOI: 10.4324/9781003158400-5

In Chapter 8 we will examine in detail the costs and benefits of migrants to destination nations. For now we can simple note that, to date, in virtually every country in the world, governments have decided that it is both necessary and legitimate to exert control over their borders. Given widespread public support, without too much debate about moral or philosophical issues, designated officials go about routinely determining who is admitted, where and how they are admitted, and placing labels implying varying degrees of legality upon different categories of migrants.

Estimating Undocumented Populations

Most broadly defined, unauthorized immigrants are people who are living in a nation in which they are not citizens *and* are lacking valid entry and/or residency permits. How they come to occupy this status varies, but there are a few categories that are the most heavily populated:

1. Migrants who cross a border surreptitiously, without permission. In most instances they go voluntarily, sometimes without assistance, and sometimes with the assistance of smugglers. In other cases migrants are trafficked, meaning their exodus is not voluntary. Regardless of these variations, these migrants are universally considered to be undocumented, and subject to deportation or imprisonment.
2. People who overstay their visas after legally entering a nation for a delimited period as students, guest workers, etc. Migrants in this category are also universally considered to be undocumented, though there are variations in how governments deal with them.
3. Migrants who are seeking asylum, and in the nation while awaiting an entry decision. Some nations do not apply an undocumented label to people while they are in this waiting position, but others do. As a result, comparing figures from different nations can be misleading.
4. Children born to unauthorized parents are, in many nations (e.g. most of Europe), also considered to be unauthorized, but in other nations (e.g. the U.S.), anyone born in the country, regardless of their parents' status, is automatically given citizenship. Again, these differences can make it difficult to compare figures across nations.

Migrants who are lacking documentation are typically apprehensive and try not to come to the attention of government officials of any type because of fear of arrest or deportation. The police are the ones they are most likely routinely to encounter, but given that all kinds of mundane daily activities, such as working and driving, are in many nations illegal for undocumented migrants, they tend to be generally apprehensive about the possibility of being under surveillance by anyone in an official capacity.[4] Immigration control responsibilities have also been delegated to physicians, landlords, employers and others who have varying degrees of responsibility to report residents they believe to be undocumented. In the UK, for example, Back and Sinha have described how this widespread policing restricts the spaces in which undocumented migrants can feel comfortable.[5]

Furthermore, apprehensiveness is not confined to the unauthorized migrants. It is also exhibited by their grown children. In a study of thousands of immigrants and their adult offspring in Los Angeles, a group of sociologists found that the adult children of undocumented parents were more inclined to avoid "surveilling institutions" than their peers whose parents were authorized. Specifically, they were more inclined to avoid situations in which formal records were kept, so they disproportionately sought informal, "off the books" employment and were less likely to open bank accounts. Fear of deportation because of their family member's legal vulnerability was their central motivation. The differences between the children of unauthorized and authorized parents, the investigators found, were not due to more general differences in the offspring's institutional attachments. Thus, both sets of offspring were equally likely to belong to social or religious organizations as long as those records were unlikely to be examined by government agencies.[6]

There are also a large number of families whose members' immigration statuses are mixed. For example, one spouse-parent may have legal status while the other does not. Siblings may also have different legal statuses. Under these conditions all of the family members, regardless of their own status, are usually very careful to protect the family member(s) who are undocumented.[7]

The deportation anxieties of unauthorized immigrants and their spouses, siblings and grown children can even extend to a desire to avoid researchers wishing to interview them for surveys or censuses. Their avoidance leads to undercounting which obviously complicates efforts to estimate the number of unauthorized migrants residing in a nation. A variety of different approaches have been developed to estimate this difficult-to-count population, and we will briefly review some of the more widely used.

One of the most extensively utilized procedures for estimating the size of the unauthorized population in a nation is the "residual method." It has been employed in studies of the U.S. for many years, and more recently it has been utilized in a number of European nations as well. This method requires two sets of figures: (1) the total foreign-born population living in a nation on a specific date and (2) the legally resident foreign-born population living in the nation on the same date. Then (2) is subtracted from (1) and the resultant figure provides the estimate of the nation's unauthorized immigrant population. The data necessary for the two figures are usually compiled from a variety of sources including national sample surveys, censuses and administrative records from government agencies.[8]

While the final calculation is quite straightforward, preparing the data to get there can involve a number of complex steps. To illustrate, in the U.S., the Center for Migration Studies (CMS) relies upon the American Community Survey (ACS) conducted by the Census Bureau. It is an annual survey of several million people used to describe local communities and provide a yearly snapshot of the nation. From year to year, the total for the foreign-born population and the undocumented population is calculated by subtracting the number of arrivals from the number who left the population (due to emigration, death, etc.). In addition, CMS estimates how many undocumented residents may not have been counted in the ACS surveys, and adjusts the number upward according to weights that have been developed over the years. To evaluate their accuracy, CMS periodically compares their estimates to those independently developed by government agencies.[9]

Alternatively, some nations and some analysts try to rely upon the number of people apprehended at a nation's borders to estimate the number of unauthorized migrants living in a nation. The Internal Organization for Migration has written that apprehensions can be a reliable indicator, even while noting that they are prone to double-counting because agencies may include multiple captures of the same individuals.[10] Furthermore, it is often impossible to derive an overall unauthorized migrant estimate from apprehensions because in many nations there are a large number of migrants who entered legally, but overstayed their visas. They no longer have legal status, but they are not subject to border apprehension unless they go home, and then try to return. In many nations, these overstayers are the single largest group of undocumented migrants. These limitations make apprehension data of reduced use in global estimates of the number of undocumented migrants.

When neither the requisite data for the residual method nor apprehension figures are available, demographers have improvised a variety of other methods to take advantage of what data are available. This can entail taking unauthorized migrant figures from the latest available census, population register, national survey, or the like, and adjusting them with more up-to-date statistics on new migration, return migration, migrant deaths, etc. Of course, the updated estimations are no more accurate than the pre-adjusted figures with which one begins.

When all else fails, there is a "proportional ratio method." To use it in nation A, an investigator identifies a more-or-less "matched" nation, B, based upon its historical similarity to A's migration patterns and for which there is an estimate of its unauthorized immigrant population. The ratio of unauthorized to authorized immigrants in B is then calculated, and that ratio is applied to the non-citizen population of A to provide an estimate of the unauthorized population in A.

In addition to specially formulated methods, such as those described above, there are a number of sample surveys that have been employed in a number of nations to try to surmount the estimation problems. Despite methodological innovations, however, accurate sampling of this population remains difficult. After reviewing a wide range of methodological alternatives, Massey and Capoferro have concluded that all of them tend to fall short in providing a completely accurate overall picture of nation's immigrant population, and are especially likely to undercount the undocumented population.[11] They recommended "ethnosurveys" of representative origin communities which entail taking a random sample of the community's residents and interviewing them in depth concerning the migration activities and experiences of people in their household, other family members, neighbors, etc. The objective is to discern how migration out of a community fluctuates across time, how documented and undocumented migrants compare in terms of their backgrounds and progress after they arrive. This approach has been followed in the previously introduced Mexican Migration Project.[12] However, in studying migration in most other parts of the world it has presented an expensive model that takes years to implement and it has not frequently been followed.

Undocumented Migrants in Leading Destination Nations

In many of the leading destinations of international migrants, the data with which to describe their current (or even recent) undocumented migrant population is lacking. With respect to Canada, for example, there does not appear to be any data other than border intercepts by the police that have been published within the last 15 years (as this is written in 2021). Where data are available in many other nations, they are often incomplete or subject to sizeable estimation errors. There are a few nations with large immigrant populations for which there is relatively reliable and recent data with which to estimate the size of their undocumented population. Most of this research has been conducted by the PEW Research Center.

The U.S.

The U.S., with the world's largest immigrant population, appears also to have had the largest undocumented population. Investigators at the PEW Research Center began with data from the ACS. PEW adjusted the ACS data to account for likely undercounts in the number of undocumented migrants and then followed the previously described residual method. The PEW investigators estimated that the total immigrant population of the U.S. in 2017 was about 46 million, and that just under one-fourth of them were unauthorized. Looking back, they noted that there was a steady increase in the size of the undocumented population between 1990 and 2007, reaching a peak of over 12 million persons. The number then continually declined, falling to just over 10 and one-half million by 2017. The Center's estimate in 2017 included about 1.5 million immigrants who had temporary permission to remain in the U.S. but were liable to deportation by changes under consideration by the government. The bulk of the drop was due to a decrease in overall emigration from Mexico, the nation that provided the largest single group of immigrants and unauthorized immigrants to the U.S. During the decade of decline, more Mexicans returned home than migrated to the U.S.[13]

A later study conducted by Robert Warren of the Center for Migration Studies extended the time period under analysis to 2019. Also relying upon ACS data, he found the decline in undocumented migrants from Mexico continued, and it was only partially offset by an increased flow from several other Central American nations.[14] A summary of undocumented migration to the U.S. at selected points in the 2010 decade is presented in Table 5.1.

The data indicated that undocumented immigrants were employed across every broad occupational grouping in the U.S., though they were concentrated in a few areas. In particular, they comprised more than one-third of all U.S. workers in unskilled manual industries, including agriculture, mining, construction, etc. Further, analyses indicate that they experienced very little upward mobility out of their less-skill required positions. Compared to migrant workers with authorization and to their native-born counterparts, the unauthorized workers showed a relative absence of upward mobility even when they changed jobs or employers. The investigators describe their transitions as "occupational churning" in which they cycle between similarly low-status positions.[15] Several examples are described in Box 5.1.

Table 5.1 Estimates of the Undocumented Migrant Population in the U.S. 2010–2019

	Population in the U.S., 2010–2019 (in millions)		
	2010	2015	2019
Total	11.7	11.1	10.3
From Mexico	6.6	5.3	4.8
From Other Central America*	1.5	1.6	1.9
From Asia**	1.6	1.6	1.7
From All Other	2.0	2.6	1.9

Notes

* Throughout the decade, the largest in-flows from Central America, other than Mexico, were from El Salvador and Guatemala.

** Throughout the decade the largest in-flows from Asia were from India and China.

> **Box 5.1   Churning Among Jobs in New York**
>
> At the end of 2020, there were an estimated one-half million undocumented immigrants living in New York City. Lacking legal papers their work opportunities were severely limited. Many had to move among different, but similarly low-paying jobs in the informal (off-the-books) economy. Some typical examples follow.[16]
>
> Christina, an undocumented Latina, worked folding clothes at a dry cleaning store. She earned just enough to sublet a room for $60 per week and send a small remittance back home for her children's education. When the cleaner's business declined, she was laid her off, and had difficulty finding any other job. She went through her savings, and then was evicted. A friend let her sleep in his living room couch, and another friend helped to obtain products from a wholesale distributor, and she became a street vendor.
>
> Manuel worked at several short-term jobs through most of every year. At income tax season, for example, he dressed in a costume associated with an icon of a tax preparation firm and stood on a street corner handing out advertising fliers to passing pedestrians. After the tax season, during a Covid outbreak, he found someone who would sell him boxes of personal use face masks. He tried with little success selling them at a few outdoor locations and finally settled under a subway station where he said he could earn enough to send some money to his children. When Covid declined and the demand for masks declined with it, he would again be searching for another way to earn money.

Germany

At the same time that PEW researchers were estimating the undocumented immigrant population in the U.S., PEW colleagues were tabulating the same figures for Germany, and a number of other European nations. The time period, again, extended to 2017, and these were the latest figures available for Germany as this was written. The raw data used in the analysis came from national labor force surveys from Eurostat, the statistical office of the European Union (EU), as well as several other affiliated European nations. To compensate for some likely omissions in the Eurostat data, the PEW researchers added cases from the German government's administrative records on asylum seekers who were in the country waiting for entry decisions on their applications. The number of non-citizens who were authorized to be in Germany was then subtracted from the total number of non-citizens – the residual method – to arrive at a final estimate.[17]

The investigators found that the number of unauthorized immigrants living in Germany more than doubled between 2014 and 2016, after increasing slowly prior to 2014. The number then declined between 2016 and 2017 to a total of between 1.0 and 1.2 million persons. As such, they comprised about 20% of all German non-citizens in 2017, a percentage that was a little lower than that then found in the U.S. (24%). The number of unauthorized immigrants living in Germany appeared to be the largest of any nation in the E.U. The U.K., then in the E.U., was a close second, and the two combined were home to about one-half of all unauthorized immigrants that were living anywhere in the E.U.[18]

A Hamburg economist, Dita Vogel, estimated Germany's undocumented population every few years, and in 2014 placed the figure at between 180,000 and 520,000 people. In that same year, PEW – using the procedures we have discussed – put the number at between 500,000 and 600,000. The upper limit of Vogel's estimate was, therefore, quite close to PEW's figure. Vogel's data came from the statistics published by Germany's Federal Criminal Agency which show the number of persons without German citizenship or legal residence who were arrested during the preceding year. Based upon how under- or over-represented undocumented migrants are expected to be in a particular police data set, Vogel infers a multiplier to convert the number of undocumented persons arrested to the total undocumented population.[19] If the upper limit of Vogel's estimate was found to consistently generate estimates close to PEW's more cumbersome figures then it would provide a less complicated alternative. However, further evidence of such consistency is lacking.

The records of the German Federal Police also provide some information concerning how undocumented migrants enter the country. During 2018, the police caught 38,000 people trying to enter Germany without authorization which the police stated was likely only a fraction of those without authorization who managed to enter successfully. However, if we assume that arrest figures are representative and the police figures can be generalized, then Germany and the U.S. also appear similar in the type of routes undocumented migrants followed. Almost three-quarters of the undocumented migrants who were caught trying to enter Germany came by land, the largest group coming from neighboring Austria. Most of the remainder were apprehended at an airport. The preponderance of undocumented migrants entering the U.S. also traveled over land routes. On the other hand, the undocumented German migrants' countries of origin were more diverse than those linked to the U.S. No one nation predominated as Mexico did with the U.S. About one-third of Germany's unauthorized immigrants came from a number of Southern and Eastern European nations and nearly another one-third were from Middle East-North Africa region.[20]

Australia

In Australia the Department of Immigration and Border Protection (DIBP) regularly selects a sample of the visas of migrants, noting whether they have expired, and then looks for evidence that the holders of the expired visa are still living in the country. From these figures, they offer a projection of the total number of overstayers which the government claims is the single largest group of undocumented migrants in the country. In 2019 DIBP put the number of overstayers at about 64,000, and speculated that as many as 12,000 of them could be legally over-extended by 20 years or more. Migrants from Malaysia followed by Chinese nationals were the groups with the largest number of overstayers.[21]

Working from the DIBP numbers, the total undocumented population living in Australia could be estimated at something over 64,000 people; but how much more? One possible answer came from a government analysis of the labor force which produced an estimate that there were about 100,000 undocumented people working in Australia in 2019, and that about three-quarters of them worked in agriculture.[22] So perhaps there were as many as 100,000 people living in the country who lacked proper documentation, and that was in a nation that had a total of 7.5 million immigrants.

For the overstayers who were able to find jobs in Australia despite their undocumented status, working conditions were typically very difficult, and wages were often meager. The migrants who lacked legal standing felt that they had no recourse, though, if they wanted to remain in Australia; and they did want to stay because conditions were even worse in the nations they left. Some typical situations are described in Box 5.2.

Box 5.2 Undocumented Workers in Australia

Marie Segrave, an Australian criminologist, sat around a table with eight men who were unauthorized migrants living and working in Australia. She encouraged them to talk about their experiences which she later summarized in an article.[23] The undocumented migrants told her that they were always aware that they had no legal rights of any kind. They worried that if they were detected they would be deported, and their employers knew this, and were able to take advantage of their vulnerability.

Most of the men told Segrave that they originally came to Australia on (temporary) tourist visas that provided no work rights, but because of their very limited opportunities at home they remained in Australia after their visas expired. The primary motivation for most was to earn enough to be able to send money back home to help support their children or their parents or their siblings, etc. Work in Australia presented the possibility of earning enough to send remittances. They had no commitment to the country. Their orientation was purely instrumental. As one man said,

> "We don't want to spend the rest of our lives here. We just came here for money to assist our people back home."

Segrave reported that she found widespread evidence of exploitation by employers in the men's stories. They came for jobs that often turned out not to be as promised. However, the men recognized that if they complained they could be reported to DIBP and deported. One man shrugged and explained,

> "We just accept whatever wages paid ... We have no choice."

What is missing from the equation that could produce an estimate of the overall size of the unauthorized population in Australia is an estimate of the number of migrants who entered Australia without authorization. People who entered under the radar. These data are missing because Australia refuses to publish them out of concern that the information will be of value to smugglers. The government of Australia puts substantial restrictions on the release of capture and detention figures to make it more difficult for smugglers to monitor the success of various routes and methods. While the numbers are not published, Australia has apparently managed to keep the number of illegal entries much lower than in other major immigrant destination nations.

Australia has managed to keep down unauthorized migration by having its navy vigorously patrol the waters off Indonesia, the most likely water crossing to reach the island nation. Ships carrying migrants are stopped and forced to return. As a further deterrent, the government has widely publicized its position of permanently barring "queue jumpers" – anyone attempting illegal maritime travel – from ever settling in Australia.[24]

Most of the migrants who slip past the navy patrols and reach the mainland, or who are taken off of intercepted ships, are moved into offshore detention centers that former occupants describe as prison-like. They are sometimes kept there for many years in conditions that are so bad that children have attempted suicide and women have developed psychosomatic symptoms, becoming paralyzed or blind.[25] When migrants in these detention centers become seriously ill they are often brought to the mainland and put in hotels where they are under locked guard. A former medical officer said that many of the migrants did not receive adequate medical care and that their mental health deteriorated because they were locked in their rooms for 23 hours a day. He said, "the government is sending a message."[26]

Surreptitious Border Crossing

Migrating to a wealthier nation is often perceived by people in a poor nation as the best, or only, way to escape from extreme poverty. Given that legal entry into wealthier nations is frequently blocked or is very limited, many desperate people attempt to circumvent the legal route, and sneak across a border into a wealthier nation. They hope to find jobs that pay better than any that are available to them in their current nation. Often it is one member of a family who makes this attempt, hoping to be successful enough to help support the family that remained behind. They climb mountains, swim rivers and go to great lengths to avoid detection at the border, relying upon information from established social networks, as described in Chapter 4.

A good deal of Mexican migration to the U.S. has historically fit the above pattern: individuals or small groups, following the advice of previous migrants, attempt to elude border patrols and enter the U.S. Poor Cambodian farming families, especially those living close to the Thai border, similarly expect that some members of their families will risk arrest or physical danger in order to sneak into Thailand with its more prosperous economy. That nation offers jobs in construction, manufacturing and agriculture that pay unskilled workers nearly double what they could expect in Cambodia. Those jobs have been described as exerting a nearly magnetic force on desperately impoverished Cambodians, even though they know that without documentation they will have no legal protections and there will be severe restrictions on their movements.[27]

An unknown percentage of attempts to enter a nation without documentation fail, mostly due to the migrant being apprehended at the border. A number of nations do not regularly provide statistics on arrests and detentions, so no global figures are available. During the second decade of this century, the greatest number of border apprehensions among reporting nations was in the U.S. where there were about 400,000 in a typical year. The vast majority were young adult males from Mexico, and their numbers, along with authorized migration from Mexico, were decreasing.

There has also been a growing number of unaccompanied minors, usually boys between the ages of 14 and 18, that have been apprehended trying without documentation to enter the U.S. and a number of European nations. The youth that are designated as unaccompanied are not traveling with parents, but they are frequently part of a group, and are often traveling with other relatives, family friends or neighbors. In most instances, unaccompanied minors are traveling to re-unite with members of their families that migrated earlier. When apprehended at a border crossing they are often holding a slip of paper containing the phone number of a relative living in the country. However, desperate families have sometimes sent these youngsters ahead as "pioneers," with other family members hoping soon to follow.[28]

Unaccompanied Minors From Central America

When Joe Biden replaced Donald Trump as President of the U.S. in January, 2021, the new administration promised a more welcoming reception of migrants and the number of migrants from Central America substantially increased. There was, in particular, a surge in the number of unaccompanied minors. During the first six months of the Biden presidency, an estimated 50,000 children traveling without a parent crossed through Mexico and reached the U.S.'s southwest borders, at Texas or California, where they were detained by customs officials who had difficulty figuring out where to put them.

Many of the minors were accompanied by relatives other than their parents, however, some were being escorted by a paid smuggler. Most of the children were hoping to be re-united with a parent who had previously migrated to the U.S. but lacked legal status. As a result, the parent could not apply for family reunification or serve as a migration sponsor. Paying a smuggler to transport their child was their only recourse, even though some smugglers had been known to take money then leave children in the desert, let them drown, or the like. An unknown number of the smuggled children survived the trip, evaded the border patrol and were re-united with their parents. Many did not get past the border, though, and they were typically placed in overcrowded and understaffed shelters designed to be temporary; but they sometimes remained for months until they were either sent back across the border or permitted to go with parents. Some illustrative examples are presented in Box 5.3.

Box 5.3   Unaccompanied Minors in U.S. Detention

Maria Ann Mendez left Honduras in 2011 to come to the U.S. to earn money to better support her then six-year-old daughter, Cindy, who remained with her grandmother. Ms Mendez regularly sent remittances for 10 years until she was ready to send for her daughter. She paid a "guide" $8,000 to bring Cindy from Honduras, a trip of nearly 2,000 miles. Three weeks after they left, she first heard from Cindy: she had crossed the Rio Grande River near the U.S. border in a raft and U.S. customs officials put her in a temporary camp in Texas. She had not showered in days, she told her mother, and was sleeping on the ground, and did not feel well. Several weeks then passed with no additional contact or information for the worried mother and then Ms Mendez was notified that she could pick up Cindy who had been moved from Texas to California.[29]

Ann Parades left Guatemala for California in 2014 when her daughter, Melissa, was three. She regularly sent remittances to help her mother feed and clothe Melissa and buy some appliances for herself. Seven years later her brother, who also lived in California, was trying to bring his adult daughter, her husband and child to the U.S. Melissa, now 10 years old, could join them if Ms Parades paid her share. She contributed $3,400 to the smuggler who was bringing the group through Mexico to the U.S. For 10 days they rode in the back of an old truck, slept on the floors of filthy shacks and finally reached the U.S. border where they were apprehended. Melissa was placed in a shelter for a couple of weeks and then released to her mother's custody. When she got out she complained about the crowding – having to share a mattress – limited time outside of the tent, too little food and too few blankets when they were cold. When Melissa was released she was not accorded legal status, but placed in "removal proceedings" and it was not certain whether she would be granted a reprieve.[30]

Conditions in the detention centers for unaccompanied minors improved after Biden became president, but children still remained, for lengthy periods, with 1,000 crammed in a tent facility, 40 in a partitioned room. The youngest children slept in playpens, the older ones squeezed together on mats. Border patrol agents gave the children over 14 years forms to sign and notices to appear in court where they will be considered for deportation or asylum. The children complained that they did not understand what they were asked to sign.[31]

Access to the children in the camps was extremely limited so information about conditions in the camps comes mostly from interviews with the children after they were released. The descriptions given by the children presented in Box 5.3 are typical of those provided by children who were released to a parent. A description of conditions in the shelters for the children who were sent back to Mexico is provided by a group of academics who in 2016 and 2017 interviewed 97 minors who were apprehended at the U.S. border and returned to Mexico. Most of these children similarly complained that they were not adequately fed, endured cold temperatures, did not receive medical care when they were ill, and some reported having been physically or verbally abused. They also complained about being forced to sign forms that they poorly understood.[32]

Smugglers

For people wishing to migrate and enter another nation without prior authorization, some type of paid, off-the-books assistance is often required. The migrants may plan to request asylum or seek admittance as refugees, or they may wish to avoid surveillance and enter surreptitiously. Regardless of their eventual entry plan, they may need transportation, information about the best routes to travel, help in avoiding dangers, etc. The range of services offered by smugglers, and their corresponding fees, are highly variable.

At the low end of services provided, part-time smugglers may only offer a river crossing or a truck ride. The people offering these limited services typically operate alone rather than as parts of an organization, and their fees are usually small. At the high end of the services hierarchy are well-organized professional operations, often with international criminal connections, and their services tend to include transportation plus accommodations along the route, help in crossing borders, counterfeit documents, etc. They sometimes also provide assistance in resettling in the destination nation. Their fees, as might be expected, are very high, typically requiring that migrants or their families are willing to assume long-term debts to pay for the services. There are also a wide range of smuggling operations that are intermediate to the two extremes.[33]

Many of the professional, full-time smugglers operate out of hubs, places where a lot of migrants and transportation routes converge. They may openly advertise their services, on billboards and social media, and like any other business adjust their fees to supply and demand. In some cases, smugglers insist upon up-front payment, but an extended payment arrangement is more common. When the cost is very high, it is typical for the smuggler to make long-term payment arrangements with the migrant's family that remains behind. Another alternative is to rely upon a person trusted by both parties to guarantee payment when the migrant reaches the destination, or to make pro-rated payments as the migrant's journey proceeds. The trusted party is in many parts of the world referred to as a "hawaladar," and the arrangement is part of a hawala system.[34]

In some nations with extensive out-migration there are also special institutions that provide loans for people who wish to leave, need to pay a smuggler, but are unable to pay the fees. In Guatemala, for example, there is Banrural: a private bank with ties to the government. Its green and white storefronts are located throughout the nation. Borrowers approach the bank requesting a loan to improve their property or buy farming machinery, the types of loans Banrural is authorized to provide. However, the loaned money goes straight to a smuggler. As collateral, borrowers usually put up their land, their only possession of value, which creates a burden for the family that remains behind, often leading to a downward spiral of debt.[35]

When the destination nation can be reached by land, smuggled migrants usually follow land routes. According to U.N. data, the most heavily traveled smuggling route in the world has been land routes from Central America into North America, and the U.S. in particular. About three-quarters of a million migrants were smuggled annually along these routes, with smugglers' revenue estimated at about $4 billion annually. The only other routes that were estimated to generate over one billion dollars annually were land routes from Sub-Saharan Africa to North Africa, and they carried just under one-half million people annually, according to the U.N. estimate.[36]

From a large number of studies, published around 2017, the U.N. Office of Drugs and Crime compiled a list of reported smuggling fees. In the years since these figures were obtained, the costs have most likely increased. A sample of their compiled findings, showing origins and destinations as well as routes are presented in Table 5.2.

While land routes are the most common mode followed by smugglers, as border control measures change or as routes become more dangerous, smugglers often change their modes of travel: for example, from land to sea or from land to air. For example, the horn of Africa is a major origin for smuggling migrants into Southern Africa, and the nation of South Africa, in particular. They can be transported over land or by sea passage along the coast or by flying to a neighboring country and then traveling over land. The perceived probability of success at any particular time is the major determinant of the choice.

Some smuggling attempts fail as a result of fatalities on route. Although most migrants are smuggled on land routes, the most known fatalities occur on sea routes. In 2017, the latest figures available as this is written, there were about 3,000 deaths globally among

Table 5.2 Smugglers' Routes and Fees

Origin and Destination	Type of Route	Reported Cost
Libya to Italy	Sea	$500 to $2500
Afghanistan to Western Europe	Land	Around $10,000
Central America to U.S.	Land	$14,000 to $15,000
Nepal/India to U.S.	Air	$27,000 to $47,000

migrants being smuggled that were due to drowning and about 2,000 that occurred on land routes due to accidents, homicides, etc. If migrants are injured or fall ill along the way, smugglers often provide little care which increases the fatality rate.[37] Worse yet, in some instances people who hope to make a quick profit buy a boat and pack as many migrants as possible into it. They demand up-front payment, and offer only transportation. Once they leave the shore, however, the smugglers have thrown dozens of migrants overboard in order to reduce overcrowding, even though they deliberately crowded more people in than the boat could accommodate.[38]

On the other hand, Icduygu argues that smuggling can be highly functional. It is often a direct result of crises that cause large numbers of people to try to flee conflict, persecution, environmental disasters, etc. After studying people migrating between Turkey and Europe's Southeast periphery, Icduygu concluded that migrant smugglers have been invaluable. He also reported that many of the migrants described helpful exchanges with smugglers, and the establishment of positive relationships. One Afghan man who migrated to Turkey said, "I even became friends with one of the smugglers; we shared a lot on the way."[39]

Any attempt to smuggle people across national borders is potentially dangerous and its success is problematic. Many end in failure, for one reason or another, and yet from towns in Mexico to villages in West Africa people continue to turn to smugglers. Part of the reason, of course, is that they are desperate, know they will need assistance to migrate, and legal channels are not available. Additional insight into why failures do not diminish smugglers' business comes from an ethnographic study in West Africa. Alpes conducted in-depth interviews with people who had undertaken risky migrations or who knew about others who had. From these interviews, she concluded that some smugglers develop relationships with families and with entire communities. These relationships are crucial in establishing the smuggler as a knowledgeable, caring and trustworthy person. If an attempt to reach a destination fails, people tend to attribute it solely to bad luck, and it does not reflect poorly on the smuggler or deter future attempts.[40]

There are no reliable data showing how smuggled migrants differ from undocumented migrants who do not travel with a smuggler. Young adult males do again appear to predominate according to apprehension data, but these data are of limited value because, in addition to previously noted limitations of such figures, smugglers are often connected to migrants' social networks. Apprehended migrants are therefore reluctant in many cases to admit that they are being smuggled in order to shield the smuggler from arrest. As a result, apprehension figures of people being smuggled and of smugglers are severely under-reported.[41]

Distinguishing Between Smuggling and Trafficking

There is a historical distinction between migrant smuggling and human trafficking with only the latter involving coercion. However, the distinction sometimes blurs because people who are being smuggled are in highly dependent situations which introduces the possibility of exploitation. What begins as a straightforward smuggling arrangement sometimes winds up with the migrant being deceived and coerced along the way so that smuggling comes to resemble trafficking. In addition, migrants who start out with smugglers have on occasion been abducted along the way and then trafficked.[42]

When children appear to be the victims, trafficking can be even more difficult to distinguish from smuggling. In the global North, there is a widespread assumption that children grow up in their parents' home and attend school until they reach adulthood. However, across the global South a huge proportion of children are forced, by economic necessity, to begin to work years before they reach adulthood, and finding work often means migrating to a higher-wage nation. Because legal entry is limited, these children who migrate are often undocumented; but are they smuggled or trafficked? When apprehended, officials have often considered them to be the victims of traffickers, based upon assumptions that may not fit well with children from the global South. For example, hundreds of undocumented Vietnamese boys have been apprehended in the UK working on cannabis farms, in nail bars, in restaurants serving Vietnamese food, etc. Officials have often presumed that they must be the victims of traffickers, even though in many cases they were neither lured by false promises nor taken from their homes by force.[43]

Trafficking

Human trafficking is widely defined following the UNODC as entailing deception or coercion in attracting or capturing people who are transported to a place where they will be exploited. The abuse to which trafficked persons are exposed takes a variety of forms. They may be forced into prostitution or related sex trades, kept as slave labor, coerced into an arranged marriage, conscripted into an army, sold for the removal of their organs, etc.[44]

While trafficked people are exploited in a wide variety of ways, the two general types that comprise most of the known cases are sexual exploitation and forced labor. During the first years of this century, among identified victims, forced labor far exceeded sexual exploitation as the motive of traffickers. The difference between them further increased until 2014 or 2015 when forced labor began to decline as a proportion and sexual exploitation began to increase. By 2016 sexual exploitation became the dominant motive of traffickers and its ascendance grew in the following years.[45]

The most complete descriptions of traffickers and of trafficked persons come from apprehension figures and the accounts of victims, even though these data have very serious limitations. It is estimated that only a small fraction of trafficked persons are apprehended and the victims of trafficking, even though they are key witnesses, typically lack an overall view of the process.[46] These shortcomings should be borne in mind as one reads the figures on the following pages.

During the second decade of this century, over one-half of the detected victims of trafficking were apprehended in their own countries. Cross-border, as opposed to domestic, trafficking was especially likely coming into high-income European countries and was more inclined to involve adults (at least 18 years old). The largest group consisted of women who were designated for sexual exploitation. In many parts of Asia in particular, where trafficking is more likely to be domestic, there are a larger proportion of child and adult male victims, and they are less likely to be sexually exploited and more likely to be taken for forced labor.[47]

About 80% of the apprehended young women – who were the largest group of victims of inter-nation trafficking – were transported through official border points, such as airports and border control stations. About two-thirds of them had experienced some form of exploitation even before they were apprehended at an official border point and most of the remaining one-third were still unaware of their situation; that is, they believed they were traveling abroad for new opportunities they had been promised. Fraud or deception was commonly employed in order to obtain the initial cooperation of the trafficked women. Physical violence was rare; recruitment was typically dependent upon fake and lucrative promises.[48]

About three-quarters of the persons convicted of trafficking, as recently as 2018, were citizens of the country in which they were tried. Even the one-quarter who were foreigners tended to come from the same region in which they were apprehended. These figures correspond with the previously noted tendency for more trafficking to be domestic than inter-nation. They also correspond with the use of fraud and trickery to entice many victims because people are more inclined to trust others from the same nation. Among those persons convicted of either domestic or inter-nation trafficking in 2018 or 2019, only about one-third were female, but when the victims were female and the perpetrator's objective was sexual exploitation, female traffickers were employed in more than one-third of the cases.[49]

UNODC identifies several types of traffickers based upon their organizational form and mode of operating. There are individual traffickers who usually operate on their own but sometimes work with each other if an opportunity presents itself. They are especially likely to rely more upon guile that force in recruiting victims. Some common examples include young males enticing unsuspecting young females into what the females incorrectly believe is a romantic relationship; poor parents offering a child to a trafficker falsely believing the child is to be given an economic opportunity that will benefit the family. Physical force is more likely with criminal organizations, though even here overt violence is reported in only about one-half of the cases. Also characteristic of some of the larger trafficking organizations is a high degree of specialization with some groups focusing upon the recruitment of specific targets and other groups specializing in their exploitation. For example, one group recruited young women in Hungary and then sold them for exploitation to a second group in Switzerland.[50]

There is relatively little information regarding the financial returns to traffickers. What data there are come mostly from court records, and they report a very wide range of values. Across the world, a person being trafficked across national borders can be worth anything from a few hundred dollars (U.S.) to twenty thousand dollars or more, depending upon how the person is to be exploited and the location. Additional profits for traffickers after the initial sale can also be substantial. For example, one group paid $2,800 for each woman "recruited" out of Southeast Asia with the promise of a job in Belgium. When they arrived the traffickers insisted that the women had each accumulated a debt of $12,000 which they had to repay while working under exploitive conditions. To illustrate further, over a period of several years, thousands of trafficked children were brought to Europe where they were taught to become pickpockets and forced to work in the streets. Their criminal activities were estimated to have yielded over one million dollars for the traffickers who exploited them.[51]

Sexual Exploitation

As we have noted, the most prevalent form of inter-nation trafficking involves women and girls as the victims. They are forced into marriages by purchase, or into working as hostesses or prostitutes or as performers in the pornography industry, etc. The common element is that they are treated as commodities to be bought and sold, and kept in positions in which they are subordinate to men. The thread that runs through the experiences of trafficked women and girls is their devaluation. In many cases it is cultural;

families in Afghanistan, Pakistan, Nigeria and elsewhere have been willing to sell females who they regarded as expendable.[52] In other countries individual females who had emotional difficulties and/or had been abused were vulnerable to the promises of a trafficker. They are sometimes manipulated to such a degree by traffickers that they do not perceive themselves as abused or exploited.[53]

In many other cases, it is severe economic deprivation that makes females susceptible to the promises of traffickers or leads their relatives to be willing to offer them for sale. Particularly notable has been a steady stream of women and girls from Afghanistan that have been trafficked into Pakistan for forced marriages. Most were sold to traffickers who in turn sold them to their future husbands. Because they are viewed as commodities they are usually treated poorly by their husbands and his family. A few manage to escape and find refuge in a shelter, but because they are undocumented they have few rights, and if apprehended they are liable to be jailed. The experiences of some representative women are described in Box 5.4.

Box 5.4   Trafficking Afghan Women for Forced Marriages in Pakistan

A group of researchers were able to locate and then interview a sample of the women who had been trafficked from Afghanistan to Pakistan for forced marriages. The interviewers were especially interested in their earlier experiences when they were trafficked as girls, and upon their current health status.[54]

One 32-year-old woman described her trip from Afghanistan to Pakistan when, as a girl, she was sold for a forced marriage in Pakistan. She believes her parents sold her for a small amount of money to what turned out to be a group of traffickers and smugglers. They led her on a difficult trip across the border. It was an especially arduous trip for her because she suffers from asthma, but she was given no medical assistance. A lot of the time she thought she would not survive the trip. Upon arriving in Pakistan she was handed over to a man who was going to be her husband – an arrangement over which she had no choice.

One 27-year-old woman stated that as a young girl she had been forced into marrying an old man, and because she had been sold, her in-laws felt free regularly to abuse her, both physically and mentally. Her husband condoned their actions, and personally considered violence as the best way to keep her in line. She now suffers from headaches, nervousness and insomnia, making her life, as she describes it, miserable.

A 24-year-old woman explained that she has no national identity. Having been sold and trafficked as a young girl, she does not know exactly where in Afghanistan she is from. That excludes obtaining Afghan citizenship or of returning home as an option. In any case, lacking citizenship she cannot travel. In addition, not having identity papers meant that she cannot be treated in a hospital or receive the free health care accorded to Afghan citizens. She is – unhappily – totally dependent upon her husband.

Sex Workers

Many trafficked women are forced into prostitution or related sex work. The conventional view has been that these women are coerced into working as prostitutes, strip club dancers, pornographic performers, or the like, and that they are exploited. They remain in these positions, according to the conventional view, only because they are closely monitored or fear reprisals if they try to leave. Sometimes "escorts" oversee their activities 24 hours a day, and resort to violence, if necessary, to keep them in line. Sometimes their families back home are threatened if the women do not comply.

One of the more esoteric threats was employed with Nigerian women who were trafficked into Italy to be sex workers. The traffickers took samples of their hair and/or nails. The women believed that a voodoo woman back in Nigeria could mix these personal effects into a powder and then perform a ritual which would ensure that the trafficked woman would be seized by madness or sudden death if she were to try to leave.[55]

Agency?

There is little doubt but that many trafficked women have been constrained to remain as sex workers. On the other hand, there is a feminist perspective that views sex work as being like other occupations except for the patriarchal-based stigma placed upon it. Some women, they argue, may view prostitution or performing in pornographic films or the like as a form of self-employment that can lead to economic independence. To illustrate, after escaping from a coercive situation with a trafficker, two Mexican women in the U.S. voluntarily turned to sex work as being their best alternative. It offered more money and more autonomy than other jobs that were available to undocumented migrants like themselves.[56]

Sociologist Rhacel Parrenas has proposed a middle ground between constraint and agency in describing the thousands of Filipina women who have been sex workers in Japan. She describes their experience as "indentured mobility." Those women who were trafficked did work under difficult conditions and were able to keep little money from their work. However, they felt that they had escaped from worse poverty at home and while they lived as "invisible aliens" who were subject to exploitation in Tokyo, they did not see themselves simply as powerless victims. Parrenas, herself, worked alongside the hostesses she interviewed and wrote that they had some choice in who they had sex with, did not consider themselves to be prostitutes, and viewed their situation as preferable to the women like them who were foreign domestics or migrant farm workers because they had better mobility possibilities.[57]

Visa Overstays

There are a variety of rules concerning visa requirements for people traveling between nations. Ordinarily a visa is required that stipulates a reason for the visit (work, education, tourism, etc.) and the length of time the visa holder will be permitted to stay in the country. There are exceptions: Some nations permit visitors from specific nations to stay for a period of months, without a visa. If the holder of a visa remains in the nation beyond the stipulated date, then the person's status changes to undocumented.

Although nations routinely record visa information, most have a limited capacity to accurately estimate the number of visa overstayers. In the U.S., for example, the Department of Homeland Security (DHS) reports on potential status violators, relying primarily upon entry and exit data. The agency counts these border transactions, not individual travelers. So, if a traveler who is compliant enters and exits the U.S. three times in a year, then three is added to the denominator of the overstayers/non-overstayers ratio. Because most frequent travelers are especially compliant with their visa requirements, DHS' calculation of the overstay rate is artificially low.[58]

Despite the deceptively low official overstay count, the number of overstayers apparently comprises a large percentage of the U.S.' unauthorized population. In 2017, for example, people who overstayed their visas were estimated to account for 62% of the newly undocumented residents. Most of the remaining 38% had initially entered the U.S. without authorization.[59] Note that the 62% estimate is probably understated given the government's artificially low count of overstayers.

Some of the figures involved are not as precise as one would hope but suggest that visa overstays are probably a very large percentage of the undocumented migrants in many of the leading destination nations. In Australia, for example, we previously reviewed figures that indicated visa overstayers likely comprised about two-thirds of that nation's undocumented population – a figure very close to that estimated for the U.S.

In 2020, an estimated 92,000 migrants overstayed their visas in the U.K. However, this figure did not include the non-visa visitors from countries whose citizens were able to stay without visas for up to six months. Their number, in recent years, has been estimated to be an average of about 250,000 people,[60] but the accuracy of this number is unknown, though their inclusion could bring the yearly total number of visa overstayers to about 350,000. The latest PEW figures for the UK (2017) put the total unauthorized immigrant population at between 800,000 and 1.2 million, and that range had been stable for several years.[61]

The U.S. provides the most complete breakdown of visa overstayer rates. The report for 2019 indicated that the highest rates were for student and exchange visa visitors which involved about 1.95 million visitors. About 3% of them overstayed, and about 20% of the overstayers were at least 12 months over their allotted time. The largest number of student and exchange visa overstayers were from Asian nations.[62]

Enforcement and Detention

In many nations routine monitoring of overstays by the government agency that keeps visa records is relatively lax, and limited largely to notifying visitors if their authorization is about to, or has, expired. In fact, a number of nations rely largely upon ordinary citizens to notify the appropriate agency if they suspect someone in their country lacks authorization. For example, both the UK and Australia have run campaigns encouraging people to anonymously use special hotlines or dedicated websites to report anyone they think may be living or working illegally in their nation.

On the other hand, enforcement is not usually lax if an overstayer is brought to the attention of officials. Immigration control agencies in many nations maintain regular contact with various local enforcement bureaus to learn if anyone on their overstayers list (or any other unauthorized immigrants) are suspected of having breached any laws, no matter how minor. For example, a driving-related conviction, or other misdemeanors, has been adequate to begin removal processes in the U.S. for thousands of cases every year.[63] Any routine contact with law enforcement personnel can be a trigger leading to detention and deportation proceedings, as illustrated in Box 5.5. It is not surprising, therefore, that unauthorized immigrants – given their precarious legal status – tend to fear and avoid the police.[64]

Box 5.5   An Overstayer's Detention in Japan[65]

Wishma Rathnayaka, a migrant from Sri Lanka, entered Japan with a residency permit in 2017 and began to study Japanese at a school outside Tokyo. There she began a relationship with a young man who was also a student and also from Sri Lanka, and the two moved into an apartment together. Soon after she stopped attending classes, which school officials reported to immigration authorities who then denied her request to renew her residency permit, but she was not detained at the time.

Officials lost track of her until August 2020, when she came into a police station in central Japan and asked for protection from her boyfriend who she said was abusing her. The police noted that her residency permit had expired so she was in Japan illegally. They sent her to a detention center to await deportation, and that was initially fine with her. While there her former boyfriend, who was now back in Sri Lanka, wrote and threatened her life if she returned to Sri Lanka. She then decided to try to stay in Japan but felt that her request only antagonized the staff at the detention center who did not take her request seriously.

After several months in the center, she fell ill with a fever. The staff told her she was just anxious, and a nurse suggested she start a diary by writing about everything she had to be thankful for. She grew progressively weaker, unable to eat and then unable to walk. She begged to go to a hospital. When they finally took her, months later, it was too late. Two days later she died, the 24th such detainee to have died in a Japanese detention center. Months later her sisters in Japan had still not learned the cause of her death, despite repeated requests.

In most nations, when an unauthorized immigrant comes to the attention of officials the immigrant is placed in a detention center. Amnesty International and other human rights groups have been very critical of conditions in most centers, accusing nations of intentionally maintaining harsh conditions in order to deter unauthorized immigrants from trying to return after they are deported. For example, in recent years thousands of Ethiopians have migrated to Saudi Arabia either to find work or escape violence, or both; and some have entered with authorization and some without. In 2019, at least one-half million Ethiopians were estimated to be in the country without authorization. To deter this influx, Saudi Arabia began to place hundreds of thousands of Ethiopians (and other undocumented immigrants) into one of a dozen detention centers. In 2019 there were nearly two million migrants in these centers where ex-detainees told of being abused, chained together, and claimed to have witnessed numerous deaths.[66]

After release from detention, if they are not deported, immigrants sometimes continue to be monitored electronically. As a condition of release, they are required to wear an electronic monitor (EM) on their wrist or ankle. In principle, releasing immigrants from detention could give them an opportunity to re-integrate into their communities. However, in-depth analyses of a sample of 30 immigrants released from detention with EM ankle shackles in Los Angeles led an investigator to conclude that EM was little more than extended punishment. It marked the people wearing it with a criminal stigma that led members of their formerly supportive ethnic community to shun them. Labeled as "undocumented criminal aliens," they were hardly better off than when they were in detention.[67]

Deportation

Non-citizens, whether or not they are authorized residents, are subject to deportation if they are convicted of a serious crime. However, unauthorized immigrants are especially vulnerable to deportation because an arrest or conviction brings them (with their unauthorized status) to the attention of immigration officials. In addition, in most nations they also lack the legal rights accorded to authorized immigrants in challenging a deportation order.

Most nations have laws concerning the removal of authorized non-citizens convicted of certain types of crimes. In New Zealand, for example, if an immigrant has been in the country for less than two years, they face deportation if convicted of a crime which carries a three-month or more prison sentence. A drunk driving conviction could qualify. In the UK, an unauthorized immigrant sentenced to 12 months in jail faces mandatory deportation; a less than 12-month sentence is assessed on an individual case by the immigration agency. A conviction for shoplifting items valued at less than 200 pounds would be sufficient to trigger a recommendation for deportation.

Immigrants convicted of a crime make up a large percentage of the deportees, and many nations' statistics include a deported criminals category. Remember, though, that unauthorized immigrants have usually committed the crime of entering the nation without documentation or overstaying their visas. For example, the most serious crime committed by the largest proportion of deported immigrants in the U.S., in February of 2020, was their illegal entry or re-entry. The next most frequent involved driving and traffic offenses.[68]

In metropolitan Nashville, Tennessee, for example, beginning in 2006, unauthorized immigrants were no longer able to obtain driving permits. The following year, the city and county began to participate in a federal program that allowed local law enforcement agents to become deputized to enforce federal immigration laws. Then local police increased the number of routine traffic stops for minor violations. What followed was a marked increase in the number of unauthorized Latino immigrant drivers who were arrested following a traffic stop, and then deported.[69]

In a number of nations that report relevant statistics, deportations increased during the early decades of this century, but then began to decline around 2015. In the UK, the number fell to 7,400 enforced returns in 2019, the lowest number the government ever recorded.[70] Similarly, in the U.S., comparing monthly deportations in February of each year, the number of deportations fell from about 20,000 in 2014 to about 11,000 in 2020.[71] Deportation figures also fell in Germany, from over 25,000 annually in 2016 to 20,600 in 2019. However, in Germany, the government intended to deport a much larger number of persons, but they were unable to locate them or they lacked identity papers so their home country could not issue travel documents enabling them to return.[72] Similar bureaucratic problems have been reported in Sweden and Switzerland as well. All three countries acknowledge a deportation gap: the difference between the number of people who were ordered to leave the country, and the actual number for whom the government was able to implement deportations.[73]

When a nation decides to deport a person who lacks travel papers from their home nation, it can put the person into legal limbo. In Denmark, for example, the government decided to deport a number of Syrian refugees, but the Danish government had no diplomatic relations with Syria which prevented arranging for them to return. The Syrians were taken to "departure centers" where they were held for months. An official of the Danish Refugee Council said they would be in the centers, "for the indefinite future, with no prospect of being sent back forcibly, but no chance of living their lives in Denmark either."[74]

When an immigrant is arrested and faces deportation, the costs to the family that tries to mount a legal defense can be substantial. There are the lost wages of the person in detention, and also the out-of-pocket costs of posting an immigration bond and hiring an attorney. A large percentage of households in parts of the U.S. contain both documented and undocumented residents so there are a lot of households at risk. These households have been found to lose about one-half of their income when an immediate family member is arrested and threatened with deportation.[75]

In the U.S. where the largest number of immigrants, both documented and undocumented, come from Mexico, deportation back to Mexico is associated with continued financial losses for the deportee as well as his or her family, and a long-term struggle to remain connected with kin who were not deported. The people who have been removed, in particular, have been found to experience a great deal of psychological stress over a period of many years as they continue to try to maintain meaningful relationships with their families who remain back in the states.[76]

While there are laws in most nations that stipulate the conditions under which noncitizens convicted of a crime are to be removed – the combining of criminal and immigration law often referred to as "crimmigration" – there are sometimes cases that fall between the cracks and require judicial review. To understand how judges in the U.S. reach decisions, sociologist Asad L. Asad spent hundreds of hours in Dallas (Texas) Immigration Court in 2015 interviewing judges, prosecutors, private attorneys and family members. From this research, Asad concluded that the judges justified their removal decisions in one of two ways. There was a "scripted approach" associated with by-the-book decisions and an "extemporaneous approach" that entailed digging into the noncitizen's history. The latter was most commonly invoked when a judge was looking for ways to grant temporary relief to a person considered to be deserving. However, the scripted approach predominated and during the year in which Asad's research was conducted, the Dallas Immigration Court provided relief in fewer than five percent of the cases brought before it.[77]

Notes

1 Jacqueline M. Hogan and Joshua T. Wassink, "Return migration around the world." *Annual Review of Sociology*, 46, 2020.
2 Sarah Song, "Political theories of migration." *Annual Review of Political Science*, 21, 2018. See also the essays in Pieter de Wilde, et al. (Eds), *The Struggle over Borders*. Cambridge University, 2019.
3 David Cook-Martin, "Temp Nation?" *American Behavioral Scientist*, 63, 2019.
4 See, for example, Amada Armenta and Rocio Rosales, "Beyond the fear of deportation." *American Behavioral Scientist*, 63, 2019.
5 Les Back and Shamsen Sinha, *Migrant City*. Routledge, 2018.
6 Sarah Desai, Jessica H. Su and Robert M. Adelman, "Legacies of marginalization." *International Migration Review*, 54, 2020.
7 Heidi Castanada, *Borders of Belonging*. Stanford University, 2019.
8 For further discussion of the residual method and other techniques, see Phillip Connor and Jeffrey S. Passel, *Europe's Unauthorized Immigrant Population Peaks in 2016*. Pew Research Center, November, 2019.

9. See the Appendix in, Robert Warren, "In 2019, the US undocumented population continued a decade-long decline." *Journal on Migration and Human Security*, 9, 2021.
10. IOM's Global Migration Data Analysis Centre, *2015 Global Migration Trends Factsheet*.
11. Douglas S. Massey and Chiara Capoferro, "Measuring undocumented migration." International Migration Review, 38, 2004.
12. Jorge Durand and Douglas S. Massey, "Evolution of the Mexico-U.S. migration system." ANNALS of the American Academy of Political and Social Science, 684, 2019.
13. Jeffrey S. Passel and D'Vera Cohn, "Mexicans decline to less than half the U.S. unauthorized immigrant population." *PEW Research Center*, June 12, 2019.
14. Warren, op.cit.
15. Matthew Hall, Emily Greenman and Youngmin Yi, "Job mobility among unauthorized immigrant workers." *Social Forces*, 97, 2019.
16. The following is taken from, Juan Arrendondo and David Gonzalez, "No Papers And No Jobs." *The New York Times*, November 19, 2020, p A16.
17. See Jens M. Krogstad, "How we estimated the number of unauthorized immigrants in Europe." *Pew Research Center*, 2019, and Phillip Connor, Jeffrey S. Passel and Jens M. Krogstad, "How European and U.S. unauthorized immigrant populations compare." *Pew Research Center*, 2019.
18. Phillip Connor and Jeffrey S. Passel, "Unauthorized Immigrants in Germany." *Pew Research Center*, 2019.
19. Dita Vogel, *Update Report Germany*. July, 2015.
20. DW News, January 29, 2019.
21. M.L. McAuliffe and F. Laczko (Eds), *Migration Smuggling Data and Research*. International Organization for Migration, 2016.
22. Department of Agriculture, Water and the Environment, *National Agricultural Workforce Strategy*. 2020.
23. Marie Segrave, "What it's like to live and work illegally in Australia." *The Conversation*, July 24, 2017.
24. Jane McAdam, "Australia and asylum seekers." *International Journal of Refugee Law*, 25, 2013.
25. Julie Machen, "The melancholic torturer." *Journal of Sociology*, 56, 2020.
26. Livia Albeck-Ripka and Tariro Mzezewa, "Australia Detained Refugees in Locked Hotel Rooms." *The New York Times*, January 22, 2021, p A11.
27. Robert Nurick and Sochanny Hak, "Transnational migration and involuntary return of undocumented migrants." *Journal of Ethnic and Migration Studies*, 45, 2019.
28. Ibid.
29. Miriam Jordan, "A Border Overwhelmed and Parents Desperate for News." *The New York Times*, April 10, 2021, p A10.
30. Miriam Jordan, "'Will I Recognize You?' A Girl's Long Road to See Her Moher." The New York Times, May 9, 2021, p A19.
31. Miriam Jordan, "'No Place for a Child': Inside a Packed Tent Camp." The New York Times, March 31, 2021, p A16.
32. Kiera Coulter, et al., " A Study and Analysis of the Treatment of Mexican Unaccompanied Minors." *Journal on Migration and Human Security*, 8, 2020. There is anecdotal evidence that conditions improved after Biden became president but still remained inadequate.
33. U.N. Office on Drugs and Crime, *Global Study on Smuggling of Migrants 2018*. U.N., 2018.
34. For further discussion and some examples, see Giovanni Legorano and Joe Parkinson, "Following the Migrant Money Trail." *The Wall Street Journal*, December 30, 2015. The hawala system is also used in various criminal activities, to launder money, smuggle gold and other commodities, etc.
35. Emily Kaplan, "Guatemalans Achieve the American Dream with a Loan and a Smuggler." *The New York Times*, November 8, 2019, p 9.
36. U.N. Office, op.cit.
37. Ibid.
38. Richard Perez Pena and Abdi Latif Dahir, "Migrants Put Overboard By Smugglers." *The New York Times*, March 24, 2021.
39. Ahmet Icduygu, "Decentring migrant smuggling." *Journal of Ethnic and Migration Studies*, 47, 2021.
40. Maybritt J. Alpes, *Brokering High Risk Migration and Illegality in West Africa*. Routledge, 2019.
41. McAuliffe and Laczko, op.cit.
42. McAuliffe and Laczko, op.cit.

43 Mike Dettridge, "Between theory and reality." *Anti-Trafficking Review*, 16, 2021.
44 UNODC, *Global Report on Trafficking in Persons* 2020. UN, 2020.
45 Migration Data Portal, *Human Trafficking*. Updated 6 May, 2021.
46 IOM, *Traffickers and Trafficking*, UN, 2014.
47 UNODC 2020, op.cit.
48 Ibid.
49 Ibid.
50 Ibid.
51 Ibid.
52 Bandana Purkayastha and Farhan N. Yousaf, *Human Trafficking*. Polity, 2019.
53 M. Verhoeven, et al., "Relationships between suspects and victims of trafficking." *European Journal of Criminal and Policy Research*, 12, 2013.
54 The following summaries of the women's interviews are taken from, M.M. Kakar, et al., "Irregular migration, trafficking into forced marriage, and health insecurity." *Global Regional Review*, 5, 2020.
55 Ronald Weitzer, "Human trafficking and contemporary slavery." *Annual Review of Sociology*, 41, 2015.
56 Purkayastha and Yousaf, op.cit.
57 Rhacel S. Parrenas, *Illicit Flirtations*. Stanford University, 2011. South Korean sex workers in Australia, who migrated voluntarily, have expressed the same advantages of their work. See Julie Ham, Kyungja Jung and Haeyouing Jang, "Wilence, movility and 'rational values'." *Sexualities*, 19, 2016.
58 Jessica M. Vaughan and Preston Huennekens, "Analyzing the New Visa Overstay Report." *Center for Immigration Studies*, September, 2018.
59 Robert Warren, "US Undocumented Population Continued to Fall from 2016 to 2017." *Center for Migration Studies*, 2019.
60 Daniel Waldron, "UK visas overstayers double in five years." *Workpermit.com*, February 25, 2021.
61 "Unauthorized Immigrants in the United Kingdom." *PEW Research Center*, November 13, 2019.
62 DHS, *Fiscal Year 2019 Entry/Exit Overstay Report*, March 30, 2020.
63 Margot Moinester, "A look to the interior." *American Behavioral Scientist*, 63, 2019.
64 Armenta and Rosales, op.cit.
65 The following is taken from, Ben Dooley and Hisako Ueno, "Japan Shanken After Detainee, Wasting Away, Dies Alone in a Cell." *The New York Times*, Mary 19, 2021, p A8.
66 Global Detention Project, "Saudi Arabia." 2020.
67 Miriann G. Martinez-Aranda, "Extended punishment." *Journal of Ethnic and Migration Studies*, 46, 2020.
68 Syracuse University, *Transactional Records Access Clearinghouse*, 2020.
69 Amada Armenta, *Protect, Serve, and Deport*. University of California, 2017.
70 The Migration Observatory, "Deportation and Voluntary Departure from the UK." 07 July 2020.
71 Syracuse University, *op.cit.*
72 "Germany: Number of asylum-seeker deportations fall in 2019." *DW News*, 2020.
73 Lisa M. Borrelli, "They know the procedure." *Journal of Ethnic and Migration Studies*, 47, 2021.
74 Jasminia Nielsen, "After Years in Denmark, Some Syrians are Forced Back." *The New York Times*, April 15, 2021, p A9.
75 Geoffrey A. Boyce and Sarah Launius, "The household financial losses triggered by an immigration arrest." *Journal of Migration and Human Security*, 84, 2020.
76 Beth C. Caldwell, *Deported Americans*, Duke University, 2019.
77 Asad L. Asad, "Deportation decisions." *American Behavioral Scientist*, 63, 2019.

6 The Social Integration of Migrants and Their Offspring

The social integration of immigrants and their offspring involves the degree to which they converge with natives on a number of discrete, but inter-related, dimensions. There is a social structural aspect that entails how closely their attainments match natives in education, occupation and other aspects. The degree to which an immigrant's group is spatially segregated is also included here as a social structural dimension. In addition, social integration also encompasses cultural aspects involving the values, customs and lifestyles that people adopt. This dimension is typically measured by such indicators as people's acquisition of new language preferences, increased rates of inter-marriage, new tastes in food, music, etc.[1]

There are a number of major theorists who prefer to use the term assimilation rather than integration as the master concept.[2] However, the dimensions they include under the assimilation rubric ordinarily correspond very closely with the dimensions conventionally included under social integration, and because integration is the more widely utilized term in the migration literature we will favor it here as well.

Conceptualizing Integration

One of the most complete listings of the dimensions of social integration was prepared by Ager and Strang at the behest of the UK Home Office. The investigators began by spending time at two British sites that had substantial immigrant populations, conducting interviews and observations. They also carried out an extensive review of the integration literature, noting how other investigators had measured the concept. Then they subjected the variables they had identified to a number of statistical analyses to see what kinds of groupings and linkages there were among the variables. Ager and Strang concluded that there were 10 "domains" and that they were clustered into four overarching areas.[3]

The first three clusters that they identified correspond mostly with what we have identified as structural considerations, the fourth is primarily cultural. The concepts and indicators that they associated with the four most encompassing areas are as follows:

1   Markers and Means – refers to immigrants' achievements in various realms, most importantly in employment. Other important markers of integration include attainments in education and ability to obtain adequate housing and health care.
2   Citizenship and Rights – involves activities related to attaining inclusion and equality. Ager and Strang thought that the specific indicators to be employed would

vary according to different nations' conceptions of citizenship and rights. Ensuing studies have emphasized such measures as civic participation and enrollment in citizenship courses.
3   Social Connection – entails the relationships across different racial or ethnic groups; the bonds, bridges and links among them. The indicators that have often been employed to measure this domain include the geographical separation of immigrant groups and immigrant membership in mainstream organizations.
4   Facilitators and Barriers – refers to factors that either encourage or inhibit social integration. Here the authors included two sub-dimensions: (a) sufficient language skills to be able to communicate with people outside of one's own group and the ability to understand cultural expectations and (b) feelings of safety and security in one's community.

The core concepts of integration and assimilation have a long history in anthropology and sociology. They were originally formulated in studies of pre-industrial societies and in the small towns of more contemporary nations. These earlier studies focused upon how well the components of entire societies or communities fit together. For example, were the society's religious beliefs compatible with its technology? Contemporary studies of integration, by contrast, examine individuals and groups of immigrants and their relationship to their new societies. Because of this difference in focus, Willem Schinkel argued that the concept of integration is applied inappropriately in contemporary studies. Integration made theoretical sense in relation to the parts of societies, but not in relation to individuals, he contended, and claimed that its unsuitability was indicated by considering its antonym: disintegration. How could an individual be considered to be disintegrated, he asked?[4]

Schenkel made some interesting points, but what he overlooked is that the early theorists for whom social integration was a core concept – Durkheim, Parsons and others – also focused upon the connection of individuals to society; and that connection was, in fact, central to their conceptions of social integration. Schenkel also raised other serious theoretical and policy issues with respect to integration, and they warrant consideration, but they are beyond the scope of this text. More recent studies, at least since the 1990s, have also noted a number of complex issues surrounding the concept of integration and they have led contemporary analysts to develop some new terms in order to account for variations not encountered in the earliest formulations.

The first of the more contemporary issues to be considered concerns the question of: Into what are migrants integrated? Historically, theories of social integration or acculturation assumed either implicitly or explicitly that there was a mainstream – a single core or dominant – culture into which newcomers would be more or less absorbed. Integration was like a melting pot. However, modern societies, and especially those that are the leading destinations for immigrants, are multi-cultural. They are a pastiche of many different sub-cultural groups whose customs continue to shape what might be considered the mainstream. To some degree, in other words, integration is a two-way street. Immigrant groups take on some of the ways of the core culture at the same time that they contribute to its continued unfolding. To illustrate, consider the way that pizza, bagels and egg rolls are staples in the diets of many people, in many nations, but at an earlier time were largely confined to the diet of one particular immigrant group. Recognizing this two-way street between immigrant groups and the mainstream made the earlier melting pot imagery a not very good fit.[5]

In addition, the diversity of modern societies provides newcomers and their offspring, in particular, with different paths they could follow. Some will strive to assimilate into the mainstream, and find that there are few obstacles. They adopt the practices associated with the mainstream and strive to attain upward mobility. However, some are pushed or pulled in a different direction because they find the mainstream path blocked and/or develop an attachment to the values or practices of a non-mainstream group. For example, some of the dark-skinned children of Haitian immigrants in Miami, after experiencing racial discrimination, felt an affinity to lower-class Black culture, and that is the direction in which they assimilated. Following the writings of Alejandro Portes, the different sectors of a society into which immigrants and their offspring have assimilated are usually referred to as segmented assimilation.[6] It has been a particularly useful concept in explaining the downward mobility of some in the second generation.[7]

Another issue arises because becoming integrated into a new society does not mean that the first or later generations have to leave behind all facets of their group's former ways of life. Because of modern means of travel and communication and the ubiquitous social media, people are able to remain connected to more than one place, and one implication of this is that various aspects of their lives are likely to be differentially integrated in the new society. They may, for example, be active participants in the politics of their new nation, but continue to be committed members of the church associated with their former nation. This variability in individuals' institutional attachments is usually described as selective assimilation or selective acculturation, and it too has been widely utilized in contemporary studies.[8]

Dimensions of Integration

Because the most common pattern of global migration involves people moving from nations in the global South to nations in the global North, migrants typically have less education and lower occupational standing than natives in the destination nation. Due to a combination of lower socioeconomic standing and native prejudice, new arrivals also tend to live in physically segregated communities. While segregation can thereby be a consequence of low socioeconomic standing, it can also inhibit future socioeconomic mobility and cultural assimilation. A great deal of research has focused upon how long immigrants and their offspring remain divergent from the native population, and we will review this research with special attention to the experiences of the second generation. We will specifically examine three of the most widely studied indicators of integration: socioeconomic standing, segregation and inter-marriage.

Socioeconomic Standing

We begin this section with an analysis of integration with respect to socioeconomic standing, focusing upon occupation and education, the most widely studied dimensions. We will review relevant research historically, and also examine how socioeconomic integration is affected by where people live, and by their gender and race. The occupational standing of immigrants and their offspring has been measured in a variety of ways, the most common of which include: wages or income, amount of unemployment and blue-collar (lower) versus white-collar (higher) positions. Education has typically been measured both by educational aspirations and levels of actual attainment. Because of the high correlation between education and occupation, indices of each have frequently been used interchangeably.

An important research question concerns how long the consequence of the first generation's typical socioeconomic deficit lasts. For example, does it span immigrants' entire working lives? Does it continue to depress the successes of the second generation? One answer comes from an interesting historical study that examined the effects of the pre-migration occupational standing of Italian, German and Russian men who immigrated to the U.S. between 1880 and 1900. From the manifests of the passenger ships that brought them to the U.S., Peter Catron was able to obtain occupational data for a large number of male passengers. (The ships did not record this information for female passengers.) From U.S. census records the investigator also obtained occupational data for both the same men and their sons in 1910 and 1940.[9]

The 1910 census reports disclosed the then-current occupation of the immigrants who had arrived between 10 and 30 years earlier (i.e. from as early as 1880 or as late as 1900). The pre-migration occupational differences among the men from different countries had been large. For example, many of the Germans were in white-collar occupations (professionals, managers, etc.) that paid substantially more while many of the Italians had been concentrated in low-skilled blue-collar occupations (factory workers, laborers, etc.) that paid substantially less. Analyzing the 1940 records which covered most of the immigrant' working lives showed that most of the pre-migration differences had persisted among the first-generation men.

There was also a direct correlation between the relative rankings of fathers and their sons, that is, the further fathers were below their native U.S. counterparts the further below were their sons; but the magnitude of the differences in the second generation was much smaller. So, while a gap remained, the occupational standings of the second-generation sons began to converge with the standing of natives indicating movement toward integration on this dimension, with little indication of segmented assimilation. For the descendants of immigrants, Catron concluded, background was not destiny. Note, however, this conclusion applies to a sample comprised entirely of white males.

Studies of educational integration among first and second generations, in more contemporary U.S. samples, show a similar pattern in which the second generation closes the gap between themselves and the native population. For example, focusing upon four different immigrant groups, Van C. Tran and colleagues put together an interesting data set from surveys conducted in 2008, 2010 and 2012. Because the data were aggregated, parents and their offspring cannot be directly compared. However, their data show that the relative educational rankings of groups of people in the first and second generation continue to be highly correlated, with the second generation consistently displaying upward mobility.

Not all immigrants, even those migrating from the poorest nations in the global South to the wealthiest nations in the global North, enter the destination nation with educational or occupational deficits relative to the native population. As discussed in Chapter 2, many immigrants are positively selected with respect to education, occupation, or the like. This was also the pattern followed by the groups studied by Tran and his colleagues. These findings, presented in Table 6.1, include educational figures for people from the same sending countries who did not migrate. Comparing this set of non-migrant figures (column one) to those of the first generation who did migrate (column two) shows the self-selection of the migrants with respect to advanced education.[10]

Table 6.1 Education Across Generations

Ethnic Group	Percentage Who Are College Graduates or More		
	Non-Migrants in Sending Country	First Generation in U.S.	Second Generation in U.S.
Nigerian	12	64	74
Chinese	4	53	61
Armenian	25	35	58
Cuban	14	24	41

Examining the figures in Table 6.1 shows that migrants from all of the sending countries included in the study were highly self-selected with respect to education. The percentage of college graduates who moved to the U.S. far exceeded the percentage of college graduates in the origin nation's non-migrating population. (Similar findings were discussed at length in Chapter 2.) Further, the second generation of co-ethnics apparently benefited from the selectivity of the first generation as reflected by the positive relationship between the educational rankings of each ethnic group's first and second generation. Examining column two in relation to column three shows that the greater the percentage of college graduates in the first generation of an ethnic group, the greater the percentage in the second generation.

Given that parents' educational level is a strong predictor of offspring's educational attainments, it is not surprising to observe this inter-generational relationship. We would, of course, like to know whether the relationship is confined to emigrants to the U.S. Relevant data were presented by van de Werfhorst and Heath from a study which included ten destination nations and a large, diverse group of sending countries. The destinations included the U.S. and Canada, plus eight Western European nations including France, England, Sweden, Belgium, etc. The investigators examined the relationship between the educational level of immigrants and the educational aspirations and attainments of their offspring. For the offspring, they relied upon three indicators: completion of upper secondary education, tests scores and pursuit of academic or vocational school tracks.[11] (The choice of an academic track was viewed as indicating higher academic aspirations.)

The data indicated that the offspring of positively selected (i.e. higher in education) immigrants tended to score higher on all three indicators, with the strongest effect upon offspring choosing academic versus vocational tracks and the weakest effect upon completion of secondary school. In other words, the children of relatively more educated immigrants were highly likely to incorporate their parent's high aspirations but did not consistently match those aspirations with attainments.

The "Immigrant Optimism Paradox"

High educational aspirations among immigrants' offspring have been observed in a number of studies involving diverse ethnic groups in different nations. Sometimes the educational attainments of the second generation have matched aspirations, but sometimes, as in the van de Werfhorst and Heath study described above, aspirations have outstripped attainments. This discrepancy has been labeled the "immigrant optimism paradox," and has been explained by the tendency for many first-generation immigrants to be positively selected educationally (and occupationally). The value they place upon education is transmitted to their offspring, but neither the parents nor their children necessarily have a realistic view of how to assess the children's educational prospects in their new nation.[12] They lack information and as a result they tend to underestimate the structural barriers that their children, as immigrant minorities, face in schools. Box 6.1 describes the difficulties in school that a group of adolescents born in North Korea faced when their families moved to South Korea.

Box 6.1 Educational Frustration and Suicide in South Korea

Despite facing a death penalty if they are captured, over the past few decades a small, but steady, stream of defectors from North Korea has crossed the border into South Korea. Economic and political motivations predominate as South Korea is a substantially wealthier and more democratic nation. It also has a more modern educational system and higher overall levels of educational attainment. North Koreans' incomes have increased with the amount of time they have lived in South Korea, but they continue to lag substantially behind that of the natives.[13] The adolescent children of these emigres, born in North Korea and now attending school in South Korea (G 1.5s) face educational expectations with which they are poorly equipped to deal as a result of their backgrounds in North Korea.

In order to examine how adolescents were emotionally impacted by their educational performance, Choi and Kim analyzed a large national sample of students in South Korea's middle and high schools (7th through 12th grade). Of most relevance here, the survey asked students their place of birth and how they would subjectively assess their own academic performance. (The investigators also obtained students' actual grades.) In addition, the survey included a number of questions focusing upon self-destructive behavior including suicidal ideas and plans and whether the student had actually attempted to commit suicide in the past.

The investigators found that the more students were unhappy with their academic performance, the greater was the likelihood that they had thought about and attempted suicide. (Variations in their actual grades did not have this effect.) The researchers concluded that when these adolescent children of emigres believed that they were performing poorly in school, regardless of their actual grades, that their disappointment in themselves led to low self-esteem and high stress, and that self-destructive ideas, plans and actions were the consequence.[14]

After analyzing a large Swedish data set, Per Engzell concluded that positively selected immigrants' children were especially likely to have high expectations, but not the means to fulfill them. To explain what he termed an "aspiration squeeze," Engzell noted that immigrants typically leave nations with lower overall levels of education than the nations to which they move. For these migrants to have had a relatively high educational standing in their origin nations would have required less education than their children would need, in the destination nations, to emulate their parents relative standing. The immigrant parents may want their offspring to be considered similarly well-educated, but not fully appreciate what that would now require.[15]

On the other hand, for the offspring of immigrant parents whose cohorts in the origin nation had very limited education or occupational earnings, even modest accomplishments in the destination nation can represent a degree of intergenerational mobility, and be a source of satisfaction. The children of working-class Mexican immigrants in prospering U.S. cities, for example, may rather easily surpass their parents' education and income, and regard themselves as very successful even if their attainments are relatively modest by U.S. standards. To illustrate, Lutz and Abdelhady interviewed a sample of Mexican immigrants' offspring in Dallas, Texas during a period in which the city's economy was growing rapidly. They found that for the children of the second generation to be educationally mobile a high school diploma was sufficient, and that they were considered successful occupationally if they were able to find jobs that simply paid them enough to buy some consumer goods and help to support other family members.[16]

Place Effects

In order further to clarify the effects of immigrant parents' educational (or occupational) selectivity, van de Werfhorst and Heath proposed that selectivity actually has two operating components: who is most likely to migrate and where do more educated migrants choose to move. It can be difficult, they noted, to specify how much of the effects associated with immigrant selectivity are due to the parents' educational status and how much is due to features of the places they choose to move.[17] The then booming economy of Dallas, for example, made it a helpful destination for the Mexican immigrants.

We begin this discussion by again turning to the historical study of immigrant passengers sailing to the U.S. Catron found that where in the U.S. immigrants settled had an important effect upon the occupational success of men in both the first and second generations. Those who were situated in the Northeast, for example, fared better overall than those who settled in the Midwest. It was probably the diversified economies of the large cities that were located in the Northeast – Boston, New York, Philadelphia, etc. – that provided more occupational opportunities both to the immigrant fathers and their sons, enabling them to become increasingly integrated.[18]

A number of other studies conducted in other nations have similarly reported large place effects upon immigrants' labor market integration. To illustrate, in England, the UK government has taken indices of local areas' economic deficiencies and combined them into a deprivation index that includes such variables as the immediate neighborhood's average wage levels, education and unemployment. An interdisciplinary group of researchers examined the labor force integration of new migrants to England in relation to their local area's overall deprivation index and the index's individual indices. They found that even after statistically controlling for numerous other determinants of wages, the recent migrants' earnings were higher when they lived in less deprived local areas. They also experienced less unemployment. The investigators concluded that the areas in which new migrants initially settled often provided limited opportunities for labor force advancement, which can result in segmented assimilation. Thus, the occupational integration of immigrants or their offspring may over time be highly dependent upon their secondary migration into less deprived local areas.[19]

Goodwin-White has reported similar results based upon analyses of U.S. census data. The most relevant finding that came out of this research was that immigrants who remained in their initial location, if that area contained a large immigrant population, often benefitted from a secondary move. The relative earnings advantages from an internal move were most pronounced for women and for immigrants with limited education.

The latter were especially likely to become trapped in low-paying ethnic enterprises when they remained in their initial location.[20]

As the preceding studies imply, ethnic concentrations are a strong correlate of place effects. Ballarino and Panichella noted that new immigrants often settle initially in areas that already house large numbers of their co-ethnics. For their first jobs, they are dependent upon this ethnic network which often means employment in a secondary labor market: part-time, high turnover jobs that pay poorly, for example, cleaning stores owned by co-ethnics. As a result, they found that in their sample of male immigrants that there was little occupational integration for the first generation in a number of European nations that had dense ethnic networks. The earnings disadvantage tended to continue into the second generation unless the offspring achieved a level of education comparable to natives. When they did, the earnings gap between them and natives disappeared.[21] The investigators did not examine internal mobility, but it might be expected that better-educated offspring would be more likely to leave the ethnically dense areas in which their parents settled.

Gender and Motive

Gender is a potentially consequential variable that has frequently been excluded from previous studies. Prior research has often only considered male migrants because the data providers only included males or because women's name changes with marriage made it more difficult for researchers to track them and their children over time. A second frequently overlooked variable concerns the people's major reason for migrating. Immigrants for whom the primary motive is economic might be expected to fare better with respect to occupational or earnings advancement than those who left for other reasons, such as political persecution or family reunification.

One recent study examined both gender and motive, separately and in conjunction with each other. Maskileyson, Semyonov and Davidov obtained a large sample of first- and second-generation immigrants to Switzerland from a National Health Survey. They compared income gains and losses of immigrants, male and female, in comparison to natives across both the first and second generations. The results indicated that those people who migrated primarily in search of economic opportunity were the most successful. In fact, many male economic migrants were able to earn more than their Swiss counterparts. It would be reasonable to assume, though the investigators did not examine it, that these economic migrants tended to be positively self-selected with respect to occupation and related variables. Furthermore, the offspring of these male economic migrants also tended to outperform their Swiss counterparts. In contrast, first-generation male migrants whose primary motivations were either political or familial earned considerably less than Swiss natives with the same qualifications, and their offspring did not close the gap.[22]

Females who migrated in search of economic opportunity, like their male counterparts, fared better than female migrants with other (i.e. non-economic) primary motivations. The first-generation female immigrants nevertheless lagged behind their Swiss counterparts economically and over the span of their own careers most of them were able only to partially close the gap. However, the earnings of children of all female migrants, regardless of their mothers' major motive for moving, caught up with comparable natives in the second generation, again indicating integration on this dimension.

Race, Skin tone and Gender: The New Immigrant Survey

The final conditional variable we will consider with respect to socioeconomic integration is the race/skin tone of immigrants and we will also consider this variable in conjunction with gender. While the darkness of people's skin is only one potential racial marker, in many nations it has historically been the dominant signifier.[23] A major source of data for studies of skin tone came from a New Immigrant Survey (NIS) conducted in 2003. It questioned a large sample of immigrants who were being granted permanent residence in the U.S. and as part of the survey interviewers were instructed to assess the immigrants'(and their spouse's) skin tone. For this assessment, they referred to a set of colors arranged from lighter to darker and associated with scores of 0 (lightest) to 10 (darkest). This scale, developed by Massey and Martin, proved to be reasonably precise and reliable.[24] The interviewers also asked immigrants about their occupations both prior to moving and in the U.S. In the years since NIS was conducted, the data set has been widely utilized by researchers to study the correlation between skin tone and socioeconomic integration.

In one of the studies most relevant to our current interest, JooHee Han examined the occupations of the immigrants being given permanent residence at three points in time: (1) immediately before they emigrated (2) upon first arriving in the U.S. and (3) current. The difference between (1) and (2) disclosed the initial effect of emigrating to the U.S. while the difference between (2) and (3) showed whether mobility occurred after arriving. If (3) was higher than (2) it indicated upward mobility, i.e. integration; but if (3) was lower than (2) it indicated downward mobility, i.e. segmented assimilation.[25]

Han found that upon arrival, Hispanic and Asian immigrants tended generally to experience upward mobility, though those with darker skin tone did not move up as much as those with lighter skin. Blacks overall moved downward initially, and those with darker skin tones moved down by the largest amounts. He interpreted this finding as being consistent with prior studies that suggested an association between segmented assimilation and dark skin tone. The heightened downward mobility, Han speculated, may have led darker immigrants to redefine the meaning of their color in the cultural stratification system in the U.S. He also found from comparing (2) to (3) that the dark skin penalty did not diminish over time. It was an obstacle that the dark-skinned migrants could not surmount, preventing occupational integration.

Working also from the NIS data set, Joni Hersch took a sample of the spouses of immigrants who were receiving legal status. Not all of them were immigrants, themselves, and this produced a sample of only married persons, and it included more females than males. However, despite the sample's distortions, her findings closely mirrored Han's. Specifically, dark skin was found to continue to suppress the spouses' occupational earnings, and the magnitude of difference in earnings between dark and light skin respondents was nearly identical to the differences among immigrants as reported by Han.[26]

When the same NIS data are examined specifically by gender some distinctions emerge. Cervantes and Kim found that darker skin had a negative effect upon immigrant's likelihood of finding employment, at least initially, among all three racial groups (Asians, Hispanics and Blacks), and especially among Asians. However, this effect was limited to the men in the sample. Within each racial group, the darkness of women's skin tone did not adversely affect their likelihood of finding employment in the U.S. The investigators concluded that stratification based upon color was gendered because the negative effect of color was linked only to males.[27] (Hersch's study of spouses similarly found that the earnings disadvantage of dark skin was more pronounced for males than for females.[28])

Time and Place Generalizations

The first issue that must be addressed before findings based upon the NIS data can reasonably be generalized concerns the time span. Most of the people being granted permanent residence had been in the U.S. for between six months and three years. So the mobility measure that compared (2) to (3) covered a relatively brief period in their working lives. It is not known from these data whether they managed to integrate further over a longer time span.

A unique dataset, enabling analysis of an extended time period, was compiled by Villarreal and Tamborini. They were able to link respondents from a large national survey to their individual tax records. From the survey, they obtained information about respondents' immigration history, race-ethnicity, education and other demographic variables. From tax records, they gathered information about individuals' earnings in the U.S. over a period of 20 years. The investigators assumed that convergence between the earnings of minority immigrants and native whites indicated integration or assimilation. By contrast, if ethnic or racial minorities lagged behind, but converged with minority natives of the same race or ethnicity, that would indicate segmented assimilation.[29]

The study's findings were consistent with both types of assimilation. Specifically, over a period of 20 years, white and Asian immigrants largely closed the earnings gap with native whites, indicating assimilation; Black and Hispanic immigrants largely did not. However, Black immigrants earned the same as Black natives within 20 years of arrival and Hispanic immigrants earned only 10% less than Hispanic natives during the same time period, both findings consistent with segmented assimilation. (They also found that the age at which people emigrated was a very important variable. The earlier in their working lives that they moved to the U.S., the greater was their earnings growth. In fact, the effect of age of migration upon earnings often exceeded the effect of race-ethnicity.)

There is also a second issue to be dealt with before the NIS findings are generalized, and it concerns the possibility that the dark skin penalty observed in the U.S. is tied to American culture. Is it also found in other societies? Some data to consider come from a study conducted in 2015 in Mexico which covered several thousand households. The sample did not focus upon immigrants, but the intergenerational results have clear implications for the second generation, and the question of the endurance of a dark skin disadvantage. One part of the questionnaire asked for information about all the adults in the household concerning employment, education and income; and their parent's income and education when the respondents were 14 years old. A comparison of the two yielded a measure of intergenerational mobility. The interviewers were also given skin color palettes of varying darkness on a scale of 0 (lightest) to 11 (darkest), and instructed to rate each respondent in a way that closely resembled the NIS procedure.[30]

The results showed that offspring in the lighter skin categories experienced the greatest degree of upward mobility. Regardless of their parents' socioeconomic standing when they were age14, people with lighter skin ranked 20 percentiles higher in the Mexican wealth distribution than people with the darkest skin. These findings closely resemble the results of a number of other studies focusing upon skin tone and ethnic mobility that were conducted in several different Latin American nations.[31]

Spatial Integration

The degree to which migrants and their offspring, who are part of a distinctive ethnic or racial group, are physically separated from others, and particularly from the native population, has long been a major indicator of the group's social integration. Both theoretical and empirical work in this area, primarily in Sociology and Geography, has been historically influenced by what has come to be known as the Chicago School.

The Chicago School

A theory of spatial separation and integration of immigrants and their offspring was a major component of the writings of Robert Park and Ernest Burgess which provided the initial foundations of "modern" urban sociology during the early decades of the 20th century. Based upon their observations of patterns of movement in the city of Chicago, they proposed immigrants initially moved, in concentrated numbers, into ethnic ghettos that were just outside of the center of the city. That was where the factories that employed them were located. Because Chicago was their natural observatory and they were professors at the University of Chicago, the theoretical perspectives and methods of Park, Burgess and their colleagues in sociology and geography were labeled, "the Chicago School."[32]

The Chicago School's writings contended that, over time, immigrants and their offspring assimilated and were able to move up economically. The typical accompaniment to economic mobility was movement out of the segregated ethnic concentrations into which immigrant groups initially moved. Specifically, they moved further out from the central city to where the more desirable residential neighborhoods were located. More desirable meant better housing stocks and higher socioeconomic status residents. Thus, integration was viewed as running along two parallel paths: economic and geographic. Moving up economically also entailed moving out and up, geographically.

The research carried out during the early decades of the 20th century in Chicago and in other cities that were major immigrant destinations generally reported findings that supported the parallel paths contention. By the second generation, people in most ethnic groups had been socio-economically mobile and left inner-city ghettos to be replaced by newer arrivals, and a succession continued: Newly arriving Italian immigrants replaced earlier arriving Irish immigrants who moved up and out, and then Polish immigrants replaced the Italians who moved up and out, and so on. However, for racial minorities, and the Black population in particular, what Park and Burgess termed "natural" processes of mobility and succession were often blocked. Many remained in isolated and segregated central city ghettos.[33]

New Immigration Patterns

During the last half-century immigrants' settlement patterns have changed markedly from the model described by the Chicago School. One major change has entailed many immigrants being attracted to a different type of destination: smaller towns and cities, and locations either at the fringe or outside of any metropolitan area. In the U.S. many of these new immigrant destination sites were located in rural areas of the midwest and south. The growth of various industries in these areas, such as meatpacking and automobile assembly, led to huge increases in the demand for labor, and companies actively courted immigrants to fill the positions.[34] These areas typically lacked any history of ethnic or racial concentrations. However, once fledgling ethnic communities were established they tended to grow, as their social networks led to self-sustaining flows from the same origins (previously introduced as cumulative causation).

This change in destination locations has been especially pronounced in the U.S., but also found in parts of Europe, though some of the settlement dynamics have been different. In Greece, for example, the government has followed "dispersal immigration policies" which have involved placing large numbers of refugees and asylum seekers in state-run facilities. Most of these facilities have been located at the edge of urban centers, in areas that were no longer being actively used.[35]

There has also been a marked compositional change in the immigrants, specifically involving large numbers of non-European, non-white immigrants from parts of Africa and Asia. This change in immigrant origins has also occurred in many destination nations, but the change has been most dramatic in a number of European nations. Given these differences in the destination locations and composition of immigrants, a great deal of recent research has focused upon whether the spatial integration of newcomers still follows the earlier historical pattern.[36]

One highly relevant study was conducted by two geographers in Sweden. Vogiazides and Chihaya utilized a database that contained every (known) international migrant between the ages of 25 and 55 that arrived in Sweden in 2003. This included over 15,000 people whose socioeconomic positions, housing and neighborhood economic conditions were updated annually, until 2012. The investigators used a sequence analysis to study the residential trajectories of this immigrant pool over the nine-year span of the study.[37]

The over-riding pattern they found was residential stability: over 80% of all immigrants remained in neighborhoods of the same socioeconomic status as their initial location. Non-European migrants, from Africa in particular, were especially likely to remain in deprived neighborhoods over the entire time period. There was also a small number of immigrants who experienced downward neighborhood mobility, going from middle-income to deprived residential areas. The investigators described this pattern as "spatial counter-assimilation," though it also entails segmented assimilation.

Only about 12% of all immigrants moved up to a higher-standing neighborhood during the nine-year period, going from deprived to middle-income or affluent neighborhoods. Upward residential mobility was associated with attaining higher socioeconomic status, in support of the parallel paths thesis of the Chicago School. However, the percentage of immigrants who moved up residentially and socioeconomically was probably less than would have once been expected by the Chicago School analysts, though it is possible that the time span of the Swedish study was too truncated for the pattern to emerge.

A small increase in all of the immigrants' spatial integration, with non-European immigrants lagging, was also reported in a much longer-term study in France.[38] Two researchers put together a data set from six French population censuses conducted between 1968 and 2007. They focused upon geographical areas containing about 2500 people that were demarcated by major streets, railroad lines or the like. However, they only included these small census tracts when they were located in urban areas of 50,000 or more because immigrants in France were largely concentrated in these large urban areas. To measure segregation they calculated Indexes of Dissimilarity, described in Box 6.2.

Box 6.2 The Index of Dissimilarity

The most widely used measure of the spatial separation of groups is the Index of Dissimilarity. Originally called the Duncan Index – the names of its developers—it is used extensively to measure the degree to which immigrants (or income groups, or racial-ethnic minorities) are geographically separated from each other, or from a group that does not share their distinctive quality, for example, native-born.[39]

Most applications of the Index begin with the percentage of each group to be compared that lives in a geographical area, such as a census track or a neighborhood. Based upon pairwise comparisons, it expresses the percentage of one group that would have to move to another area for the two groups to share the same geographical distribution. Index values range from 0 (no movement necessary because there is total integration) to 100 (complete segregation). These extreme values are virtually never obtained though; rather, intermediate scores are typical. Table 6.2 presents a sample of the native-immigrant Index values in a 2016 sample of European nations. To illustrate the interpretation of these values: the difference between Poland (34) and Ireland (8) means that immigrants in Poland were more than four times more separated from natives than they were in Ireland.

Table 6.2 Native-Immigrant Dissimilarity Indexes for Selected European Countries[40]

Country	Index
Belgium	29
Greece	13
Ireland	8
Italy	18
Poland	34
Spain	22
All Europe Ave.	20

The investigators found that in France between 1968 and 2007 there was an increase in the overall number of immigrants, and of non-European immigrants (from Africa and Asia in particular). The proportion of all immigrants found to be living in certain census tracts also increased so that many immigrants were living in ethnically varied tracts. The greatest concentrations of immigrants involved people from Africa and Asia. They tended to have the highest indexes of dissimilarity, and most of the tracts with the highest indexes were located in highly segregated communities in the Paris region. Over the 40-year span of the study the investigators found that there were consistent, but small, decreases in the index of dissimilarity. Immigrants became spatially a little more integrated over time, though the immigrants from Africa and Asia lagged behind the European immigrants in this respect.

Most of these studies analyzed spatial integration only among the first-generation immigrants because the datasets did not permit the actual identification of individuals which would be necessary to pair generations. These studies have cross-sectional data showing changes in the overall composition of neighborhoods, census tracts or other micro geographical units, but lack identifying information regarding the individuals or families who live there. On the other hand, when studies have been able to obtain intergenerational data they have often lacked detailed information about the geographical areas so they have had to rely upon measures of spatial integration other than the Index of Dissimilarity. In an analysis of immigrants in France, for example, McAvay relied upon residence in public housing and home ownership as indicators of integration. The findings showed that home ownership disparities between natives and immigrants decreased with successive generations, indicating integration, though immigrants from Africa lagged behind other immigrants. The African immigrants also had the greatest likelihood of remaining in public housing – indicating a lack of integration – and that did not decline very much in the second generation. These differences persisted net of socioeconomic variation; that is. even after people's socioeconomic conditions were statistically held constant.[41]

One conclusion that follows from the studies in France, Sweden, and elsewhere is that how quickly immigrants become spatially integrated may be highly dependent upon the composition of the immigrants, themselves. The more non-European their origins, the slower the integration. A comparison of immigrants' Index values in 27 European nations further reinforces this contention. In 25 of the 27 nations, immigrants from non-European countries (mostly in Africa and Asia) were more segregated from natives than those with European origins. And some of the differences were very pronounced. In five of the 27 nations, the Index values of non-European immigrants were more than twice as large as those for European immigrants.[42]

Intermarriage

If one were to arrange indicators of immigrant groups' social integration in a ranked hierarchy, rates of intermarriage with natives would be at, or at least very close to, the apex. That high placement is due to the fact that for marriages to occur between a native and an immigrant it is probably necessary for the immigrant's group to already be integrated along several dimensions. To begin, intermarriage pre-supposes that the immigrant group is not highly segregated otherwise it would be difficult for the close contacts with natives that are typically necessary before people select a spouse. In addition, given the tendency for people to marry others whose socioeconomic and other characteristics are similar to their own (homogamy), high rates of intermarriage imply that the immigrant group's socioeconomic status has converged with that of the native population. Socioeconomic convergence and an absence of segregation would also typically be associated with less cultural prejudice against the immigrant group.[43]

It has often been difficult, however, for researchers to identify when intermarriage is the consequence of integration and when it is an antecedent. For example, socioeconomic mobility can lead to increased likelihood of marriage to a native, but at the same time, marriage to a native can also lead to an immigrant's socioeconomic mobility. Interpretation of research findings is often confounded because a typical survey or census provides data at a single point in time. So, if researchers find a correlation involving intermarriage as one of the variables it can be difficult to be certain of the direction of the relationship because it is unclear which came first. Complicating matters further, some datasets fail to show how the date of an immigrant's marriage corresponds to the date of emigration. It is not easy, then, to tell whether the immigrant married before or after emigrating. We will be sensitive to these considerations in the following literature review.

Intermarriage is a complex phenomenon and it is influenced by a number of variables other than a group's social integration. To begin, groups have varying preferences for endogamy, that is, marriage within the group; and the sanctions for violating endogamy in selecting a mate are highly variable. In addition, because most marriages involve a male and a female, an unbalanced sex ratio within the migrant or native population can be a constraint against endogamy. For example, a surplus of males to females in the group can push males to marry persons outside of the group – exogamy. In addition, some nations have laws prohibiting exogamy of certain types, and religious proscriptions on exogamy are stronger in some groups than others. All of these variables can be thought of as exerting constraints on a nation's marriage market, thereby affecting the rate of intermarriage.

Marriage Markets

A marriage market can be conceptualized as being somewhat analogous to a financial market in that both provide platforms where people come together and the value of what they bring to the market is determined by supply and demand. Rather than buying and selling financial instruments, however, a marriage market involves people's expectations and the way men and women meet those expectations. To illustrate, if many men are looking for women who possess certain personal or social characteristics, and those characteristics are in short supply, then women with those qualities will be more highly valued in the marriage market. That will put them in a position to expect more in return from a potential mate.[44] For some people, though, their race, religion, or the like largely excludes them from entering certain marriage markets.

In many cases a marriage market is very local; people are meeting and mating within a town or city, and perhaps only in a small section of a town or city. At the other extreme, the market is global as people belong to social circles that cut across several nations. There is also increased interpersonal connectivity through social media that is not tied to a locale and can therefore free people from reliance upon one particular place.[45] While these conditions enable people to negotiate and arrange marriages across great distances, most marriages still involve people making choices in a more local marriage market.

The integration of an immigrant group, with respect to intermarriage, is indicated by how its members fare in a local marriage market. At the low end, the immigrants' race, religion, or other characteristics greatly disadvantage them in the local market, forcing them to marry only among themselves or else to "import" spouses from their country of origin. At the high end of integration, members of the immigrant group select spouses in the market without constraints, and are much more likely to marry natives.

Linguistic and Cultural Proximity

As described in Chapter 4, a nation whose language and culture are similar to one's own makes that nation a more attractive destination, and the degree of similarity is associated with more rapid socioeconomic integration. It would not be surprising, therefore, if there was also a higher rate of intermarriage between immigrants and natives when their language and culture were more alike because of the enhanced ability of immigrants to enter the larger marriage market. Studies have typically reported the expected result with respect to language and culture, though there is reason to suspect that this relationship has been exaggerated in some of the past studies.

In Switzerland, two investigators took data from a 2013 survey that included over 10,000 Swiss residents and provided information about their age, education and other social characteristics. It also identified whether each was a native Swiss, an immigrant with an annual or permanent residence permit, or a foreign citizen who had been living in the country for at least one year. The survey also provided detailed information about the timing of marriages and migrations making it possible to specify whether any immigrant's marriage occurred pre- or post-migration.[46]

The results indicated that the highest rate of inter-marriage between Swiss natives and immigrants occurred when the immigrant came from culturally similar, neighboring nations: Germany, France, etc. The lowest rate of intermarriage involved natives and culturally more distant immigrants from Southern and Eastern Europe: Italy, Yugoslavia, etc. In a supplementary analysis, the researchers found that the relative size of immigrant groups and the degree to which their sex ratios were balanced did not alter the ranking of groups with regard to the likelihood of an exogamous marriage to a native. Thus, it was apparently sociocultural similarities or differences rather than opportunity that accounted for the findings. The investigators also reported that the younger the cohort of native-born Swiss, the greater their likelihood of intermarrying, especially to a spouse from a culturally similar nation. This might indicate, they noted, a greater willingness of young people to accept some differences in values and lifestyles compared to less culturally permissive older generations.

Analysis of intermarriages in a more diverse sample of seven European nations – both Eastern and Western – reported findings that were congruent with the Swiss study. Within the Western European nations, including Switzerland, immigrants from culturally similar Western European nations had the highest rates of intermarriage among each other and with natives. The investigators surmised that this pattern was due to specific similarities in partner choice criteria in these countries of origin and destination. By contrast, immigrants from Eastern Europe or from non-European nations tended to have high rates of endogamous marriage, with few marriages occurring between them and either Western European natives or Western European immigrants.[47]

The offspring of immigrants in the seven European nations all tended to have higher inter-marriage rates than their first-generation parents, though the increases varied somewhat among immigrant groups and across nations. The most pronounced inter-generational decline in endogamous marriages tended to occur among the Eastern European and non-European populations in Western European nations. A separate study, examining only the UK, similarly reported than first-generation non-European immigrants had especially high rates of endogamous marriages and the likelihood of endogamous marriages declined markedly between the first and second generations.[48]

In almost all of the studies, the culturally more different immigrants from outside Western Europe also tended to have less formal education and be in lower earnings occupations than the Western European immigrants or natives. As a result, it can be difficult to specify how much the different rates of intermarriage were due to cultural rather than socioeconomic considerations. In order to examine their relative effects, an interdisciplinary team of social scientists in Spain conducted in-depth interviews with a sample of immigrants. They selected 58 individuals who were in exogamous marriages to a Spanish-born person and 36 who were in endogamous marriages where both spouses emigrated from the same nation. The investigators matched the individuals in both marital groups on education, age, religion, etc. so that the endogamous marriage sample could be viewed as a control group. They found that the immigrants in exogamous marriages (i.e. with natives) had higher language proficiency than their matched counterparts in endogamous marriages. This difference was especially pronounced among females and did not seem to rely upon any corresponding socioeconomic differences.[49]

From the lengthy interviews, the investigators reached the familiar conclusion that language proficiency increased the probability of an exogamous marriage. A number of immigrants in exogamous marriages stated that they were proficient in the native language before they met their spouses, and they reported that this fluency was a variable that put them on a path leading to marriage with a native. However, there were also a number of intermarried respondents who expressed the belief that their language proficiency was the *result* of having married a native. In addition to the native-speaking spouse, it brought them into their spouse's circle of native speakers. In other words, intermarriage preceded fluency. So, while it is clear that language fluency and intermarriage are connected, and that language fluency does lead to intermarriage, one must be cautious in interpreting cross-sectional studies that cannot temporally order the variables in their dataset because such studies may overstate the causal role of language fluency.

In the U.S., intermarriages follow a pattern similar to that described in Western European nations, even though the most prevalent origins of immigrants to the U.S. are different from those moving to Western Europe. The two dominant panethnic groups in the U.S. are Hispanic (consisting of migrants from Mexico, Colombia, etc.) and Asian (consisting of immigrants from China, India, etc.) An exhaustive overview of their marriage patterns was provided by Daniel Lichter and a team of sociologists who obtained information about more than 85,000 different-sex couples who had married in the preceding year (which was post-emigrating in all cases).[50]

Exogamous marriages to natives were found in both panethnic groups of immigrants, but especially among Hispanics, to be positively related to their English language facility. Marriage to a native was also related, in both groups, to the length of time they had been in the U.S. Over one-half of all marriages to a native involved an immigrant who had been in the country for more than 10 years which the investigators assumed was indicative of cultural assimilation. They also found that the "color line" that historically separated black and white natives in the U.S. marriage market operated similarly among immigrants. Specifically, white immigrants were far more likely to marry natives (mostly white) than black immigrants who were in turn found to have very high rates of endogamous marriages.

The relative absence of intermarriages between natives and some groups of immigrants suggests the existence of a marriage market that is racially or ethnically segregated. Black immigrants in the U.S., Eastern European and non-European immigrants in Western Europe are among the groups whose ability to select mates is constrained in this market, and most analysts interpret their endogamous marriage patterns as indicating segmented assimilation.

Marital Dissolution

In the Swiss study of cultural differences in marriage partners, the investigators also studied the rates at which marriages were terminated and found that, overall, exogamous (i.e. native-immigrant) marriages had a higher rate of dissolution than endogamous marriages. And the probability of a mixed marriage ending in divorce was greatest when it involved a Swiss native and a spouse from a culturally more disparate nation.

Other investigators have studied separation and divorce in Germany, Belgium, Estonia and elsewhere and reported congruent results: the likelihood of marital dissolution was higher in mixed (native-immigrant) marriages than in endogamous marriages between natives or between immigrants from the same country. After reviewing the studies, Kulu and Gonzalez-Ferrer offered several explanations for why there are similar patterns across many nations. When people from different backgrounds marry, they began, it is likely that they hold a number of different values and norms. This increases the likelihood of misunderstandings and conflicts between the partners. In addition, by having crossed social boundaries the partners in a mixed marriage may receive less support from their spouse's social (including familial) networks.[51]

When there are cultural differences there are also likely to be other differences between the spouses: in education, age, etc. If not taken into account, these differences could inflate the effects attributed to cultural dissimilarity. All of the studies of marital terminations have not been able to control all, or even most, of the potentially relevant contaminating variables. However, where studies have controlled for the effects of some of the most salient variables, they have reported that the effect of exogamy is reduced, but that mixed native-immigrant marriages continue to exhibit a significantly higher probability of dissolution.[52]

In conclusion, not only does cultural (and linguistic) dissimilarity between immigrants and natives lead to fewer marriages between them, but when such marriages do occur, crossing cultural boundaries, they also appear to result in less enduring marriages.

Marital Opportunities

At the micro level, marriages are the result of individuals making choices based upon some combination of personal and social attributes that they find attractive in a future spouse.[53] A shared nationality is often part of that complex of desired attributes. However, the mate selection process also occurs within a macro context in which the demographic structure creates varying opportunities for certain types of matches to happen.

The size of an immigrant's nationality group can present either opportunities for, or constraints against, endogamous marriages, including marriages between immigrants and natives whose families previously came from the same origin nation. In the U.S., for example, the single largest national origin of immigrants has, in recent decades, been Mexico. This creates greater marriage market opportunities for this nationality group which is largely responsible for the fact that in the U.S. first-generation immigrants from Mexico have the highest probability of marrying native-born coethnics.[54]

In most societies, most of the time, the ratio of males to females is approximately equal, exerting few limits upon people's opportunities to find a "suitable" spouse. However, war, gender-specific infanticide and other conditions can alter the "normal" sex ratio and result in increased intermarriages. Immediately after World War II, for example, there were an estimated seven million more women than men in Germany. This imbalance had a number of consequences: more non-marital births, a decline in endogamous marriages and an increase in German women's exogamous marriages to American, British and other occupying soldiers and administrators.[55]

In addition to population size and the overall sex ratio, if a generally desired attribute is distributed differently among men and women in either the immigrant group or the native population this imbalance can constrain endogamous marriages. For example, if within the native population, people prefer a spouse within a certain age range, but there are fewer women than men in that age range within the group, it may push native men into exogamous marriages with immigrants or the offspring of immigrants.

Education and Gender

Around the turn of this century, in a number of Western nations, the educational attainments of women caught up to, and in some cases surpassed, those of males. Given people's general tendency to select a mate who shares their social characteristics – homogamy – this educational imbalance might be expected to lead more women to marrying down with respect to education and place a marketplace premium upon males with advanced education.[56] A review of the recent research follows.

The increase in diverse migration into Spain during the past few decades has made the nation an interesting one in which to study intermarriage and gendered educational imbalance. In 2007, a National Immigrant Survey (NIS) was conducted and it included over 15,000 individuals living in Spain who were born outside the country. The timing of the survey corresponded with a rapid increase in the nation's in-migration and it has proved to be a useful dataset for research in intermarriage in Spain. In one study, a group of demographers linked NIS data with a Marriage Register that contained information about all marriages in Spain. They used the Register to examine native intermarriages, and they supplemented their subject pool with a sample of immigrants from NIS. The sample included those who were between the ages of 16 and 55 years and had spent at least one year in Spain before they married, so the temporal connection between migration and marriage was clear. For every immigrant who subsequently married, they classified the marriage as either endogamous – involving a spouse from the same country of origin – or exogamous – involving a Spanish-born spouse. All other alternatives were ignored. For the natives, all marriages were classified as either endogamous – to another native – or exogamous – to any immigrant.[57]

In the Spanish marriage market, the investigators found that educational levels were a key variable in influencing marriage patterns. Native men who had less than secondary education (and also tended to be in low-skilled occupations) faced a shortage of potential native partners because many women were seeking better-educated men. The less educated native men had a high rate of entering into exogamous marriages with women who were not natives (i.e. immigrants from diverse nations). Exogamous marriages in which both partners had less than secondary education were also common. Immigrant men with higher education had an advantage in this marriage market and for them the probability of an exogamous marriage to a native increased directly with their level of education. Among immigrant women, however, their level of education was irrelevant to intermarriage propensities.

A marriage market premium upon education has also been reported in the U.S. The previously introduced study by Lichter and associates found that both Asian and Hispanic immigrants were much more likely to marry natives, either white or coethnics, if the immigrants were college educated. Unlike Spain, however, in the U.S. marriage to a native was strongly associated with a college degree for both foreign-born men and women.[58]

Asian Americans

A different study focused in more detail upon Asian American marriage patterns. Qian and Qian reported that marriages among Asian Americans that cut across generations (especially the first and second generations) increased between 1994 and 2015. Intermarriage with whites was largely confined to highly educated second- and third-generation Asian Americans. The investigators described educational levels as leading to highly divergent paths within this group. The more highly educated Asian Americans became more integrated in workplaces and in residential areas, giving them more contact with whites and therefore more opportunities to intermarry. The racial identities among Asian Americans also correlated with levels of education and probabilities of intermarriage: The more educated thought of themselves as white and did not view marriage to whites as being interracial. These patterns are illustrated in Box 6.3.

Box 6.3   Asian American-White Intermarriage

Jay Caspian King, an Asian American writer, has pointed out that the "Asian American" label was initially presented as a political term by student activists in the 1960s. It was not offered by Asian Americans and it only resonates, he claimed, with upwardly mobile professionals who enter mostly white, middle-class spaces, and find it a convenient term to describe themselves. In claiming a multi-racial identity (i.e. Asian and American), they do not feel as though they are rejecting their Asian background, but rather that they are taking a step toward integrating based upon their assumption that "American equals white." For those who are less educated and less affluent, the Asian-American label has little meaning.

The 20 million people who fall into the Asian American category come from more than a dozen different nations and are a highly polarized group. They tend to be either poor and remain largely with co-ethnics or else they become "assimilation machines." King observed that he regularly comes across assimilated coethnic men venting about how one of their white neighbors mistook them for a delivery man, without realizing they were a doctor, a lawyer or a hedge fund manager. What mostly offended them, he thinks, is being mistaken for being poor – hence non-white. The assimilated upper-middle-class Asian Americans want to be as white as possible, and that includes marriage to a white spouse.[59]

Sociologist Jennifer Lee has written that it is important to remember that racial borders in the U.S., as in most nations, are open to social definitions. They are not biologically fixed but are open to negotiation and ultimately rely upon social constructions. Correspondingly, many Asian-white intermarried couples do not conceive of their union as being interracial. Only a marriage that crossed the black-white color line would qualify as being interracial, as they think about their place, and the meaning of race, in America.[60]

Assimilability as a Criterion

Around 1900, Canada and the U.S. – which were already large immigrant destinations – were among the very first nations to adopt immigration policies in which the potential assimilability of people was an explicit criterion for admission to the country. Canada initially excluded members of what the government referred to as an "unsuitable" race, but later changed the wording to focus on the traditional customs of people which would "probably" prevent them from being readily assimilated. The overt emphasis, in other words, shifted from race to culture. At roughly the same time, the U.S. instituted English literacy tests as a proxy for race. Offered in the name of encouraging assimilation, these tests were designed to exclude immigrants considered less desirable, Chinese in particular. Latin American nations, including Brazil, Cuba and Mexico, soon followed, enacting similar criteria and procedures which presumably indicated any group's potential assimilability.[61]

Around the turn of this century, as Western European nations became more sought-after immigrant destinations, many of these nations instituted pre-arrival integration tests, modeled after those that had been in use in the Americas for the past 100 years. The Netherlands was the first of this group to adopt the criteria, but they were soon followed by Germany, France and elsewhere. Fluency in the native language is typically a major part of the admission tests and they often also attempt to appraise the applicant's knowledge and acceptance of a nation's customs and laws. Germany, for example, asked, "Can you become German?" [62]

These tests are now widely used in Western European nations not only to screen potential immigrants but to decide which immigrants living in the country will be granted permanent residence and naturalized citizenship. The consequences of an immigrant's refusal to participate or failure to pass the tests can vary from reduction in benefits, for welfare recipients, to revocation of visas.

It is assumed that utilizing tests and mandatory instruction to require that newcomers learn about their new nation will improve immigrants' integration; but do they? To answer this question, Michael Neureiter analyzed a large sample of immigrants from 15 European nations. More specifically, he obtained survey data concerning the immigrants' self-reported employment, satisfaction with their earnings, their involvement with social organizations and political participation. He correlated these measures of integration with their nation's mandatory testing scores. The results indicated that immigrants in countries with higher overall scores reported higher levels of employment and greater satisfaction with their financial situation. The investigator attributed this relationship to the immigrants' greater success in meeting language requirements which enabled them to be successful in the workplace. However, immigrants in nations with higher test scores did not seem to be more socially or politically integrated.[63] So, more stringent testing increased only economic integration, and that was primarily due to the language component of the test.

At least in large part, one of the objectives of the Western European nations' screening is to deter Muslims, and when they have been admitted their integration has frequently lagged behind that of other immigrant groups across many Western nations. That difference is apparently due to two factors: (1) the resistance of Muslims to adopting Western customs with respect to dress, gender roles, etc. and (2) the tendency of natives to avoid Muslims so the absence of cross-group social ties has limited their ability to integrate. Both of these forces are illustrated in Box 6.4 which describes the experiences of a group of Palestinian women who moved to Iceland.

Box 6.4 Palestinian Women in Iceland[64]

A group of about 30 women and young children, Palestinian refugees, were resettled in a small town in Iceland. For them it was a dramatic transition. The climate and environment were very different from the place they left. There was also no Muslim community in the town and no one spoke their language. Nevertheless, the government assumed the women would soon be integrated by which the government meant that they would become economically self-sufficient. More than three years after arriving in Iceland, however, all of the women were living solely upon welfare benefits, and had hardly assimilated in terms of adopting Iceland's language and culture.

From the women's perspective, the attitudes of the natives were an important reason for their continued separation from the community. Several of the women had experienced overt hostility: local children spitting on them, grabbing their hijabs, making obscene gestures. More subtly, the women felt that locals looked at them disapprovingly. One of the Palestinian women described the reproachful look she saw in their faces and how she responded: "You can see it … I do not care … I do not feel they deserve I have to look or think about them."[65]

At the same time, the women intentionally built symbolic barriers to separate themselves and their children from the local people and their culture. Some prohibited their school children from speaking Icelandic in their homes out of fear that their children would forget their native language. They acknowledged some things about Iceland that they liked, such as its relative gender equality. This was new to them. However, the women emphasized that they would only marry a fellow Muslim and that with respect to raising their children in gender-appropriate ways, the most important thing to them was to maintain "the Islamic way of life."

Years after many European and North American nations had enacted integration requirements for immigrants to enter and/or become citizens, the government of Australia tried to follow suit. Initially proposed in 2017, and modified over the next two years, it would have tested immigrants' knowledge of, and commitment to, Australian laws and values. The bill passed the lower House in 2017, but failed in the Senate, and after several additional tries it was dropped. Some lawmakers wanted such a test to control immigration and to appease anti-immigration public opinion.[66]

While it has been widely assumed that mandatory testing would increase public support for immigration, the assumption had gone largely unexamined until Political Scientists Alarian and Neureiter designed a survey to address the issue. It was administered online to a sample of 1651 British adults whose demographic features appeared to be representative of the larger population. The survey began by describing a possible immigration test, and some of the British respondents were told it included a language requirement, some of the respondents were told it had a civic requirement, and some were told it contained both. The nature of the test was found not to matter, though. Regardless of the conditions presented to respondents, they tended to want to limit immigration. When the respondents were also presented with information about the national origins of the immigrants who would supposedly be tested, they expressed a strong preference for European rather than Middle Eastern immigrants; but regardless of the immigrants' origins, the possibility of integration requirements continued to have no appreciable effect on the public's acceptance of immigration.[67]

Transnationalism

Being connected to the society in which one lives is important at many levels. Psychologically, a feeling of belonging is important to people's sense of well-being. For the society, people's connectedness and their sense of belonging is likely to translate into more social participation, civic engagement and better citizenship. With the immigrant population in many nations increasing greatly in size, the study of social integration will almost certainly continue to be a very important topic, both to migration researchers and to the people who legislate social policy.

In the future, though, it will probably be increasingly necessary to modify some traditional conceptions of integration by according transnationalism a more salient role. Social media and modern transportation greatly facilitate the ability of people to connect to people and institutions in different nations. In other words, for many migrants becoming integrated in a destination nation does not have to mean severing ties in, or rejecting the values of, their origin nation because they are able to lead what has been termed dual lives.

Institutions that cut across origin and destination nations also facilitate dual connectedness. For example, Manglos-Weber has examined how religions can play this role in a study of native Ghanians in Accra and Ghanian migrants living in Chicago. From her extensive interviews and observations, she concluded that a global charismatic church based in Ghana created a sense of community among the migrants in Chicago while simultaneously connecting them to the church and its members still in Ghana.[68] To illustrate further, Mutambasere has described how migrants from Zimbabwe who were living in the U.K. formed an organization to work with NGOs in Zimbabwe. The founding members were predominantly middle class and largely assimilated to life in the U.K. However, because of their continuing commitment to Zimbabwe they formed an organization that was designed to shape their origin nation's economic development, human rights, etc.[69]

Not only can migrants keep one foot in each society, but the more firmly they plant their foot in the destination nation the stronger may remain their tie to the origin nation. An analysis of various refugee groups in the Netherlands, for example, found an overall tendency for migrants' economic integration in the Netherlands to be associated with more transnational activities, remittances in particular. The positive association between destination integration and continued origin involvement is termed, "resource dependent transnationalism." It was supported by the Netherlands study (and elsewhere) at the expense of an earlier "reactive transnationalism" hypothesis. The earlier view expected that it was a lack of integration in the destination nation that would lead people to compensate for what was missing in their lives by maintaining greater involvement in their origin nation.[70]

Finally, consider that the dual connectedness described by a number of transnationalism analysts implies that migrants' lives and identities are impacted only by events that occur in their origin and destination nations. However, Tahseen Shams contends that it would be better to conceptualize immigrants being in a tripartite arrangement which introduces how "elsewhere" – nations that are neither their origin nor destination – affects immigrants' activities and identities. For example, she shows how terrorist attacks by Muslims in Europe shape the lives of Muslims living in the U.S. despite the fact that they have no direct connection to the European actors or events. Thus, in the modern world, Shams concluded, transnationalism is best conceptualized on a global scale.[71]

Notes

1. This cultural aspect of integration has historically been referred to as acculturation, and at one time it was the subject of extensive study by anthropologists and sociologists. Today, its analysis is largely confined to psychology where it is integral to an active research program. See David L. Sam and John W. Berry, *The Cambridge Handbook of Acculturation Psychology*. Cambridge University, 2018.
2. See, for example, Richard Alba and Nancy Foner, *Strangers No More*. Princeton University, 2015.
3. Alastair Ager and Alison Strang, "Understanding integration." *Journal of Refugee Studies*, 21, 2008. For further discussion of the dimensions, also see the corresponding chapters in, National Academies of Sciences, Engineering and Medicine, *The Integration of Immigrants into American Society*. National Academies Press, 2015.
4. For a succinct presentation of his views, see Willem Schinkel, "Against 'immigrant integration'." *Comparative Migration Studies*, 31, 2018.
5. See the symposium, "Beyond the melting pot," in *City and Community*, 2, 2019.
6. See, for example, Alejandro Portes and Ruben G. Rumbaut, *Legacies*. University of California, 2001.
7. For a discussion of how second-generation Muslim groups have frequently failed to assimilate into the mainstream in France, see Lucas G. Drouhot, "Cracks in the melting pot?" *American Journal of Sociology*, 126, 2021.
8. Portes and Rubin, op.cit.. See also, Yu Xie and Emily Greenman, "The social context of assimilation." *Social Science Research*, 40, 2011.
9. Peter Catron, "The melting-pot problem?" *Social Forces*, 99. 2020.
10. Van C. Tran, et al., "Hyper-selectivity, racial mobility, and the remaking of race." *The Russell Sage Foundation Journal of the Social Sciences*, 4, 2018.
11. Herman G. van de Werfhorst and Anthony Heath, "Selectivity of migration and the educational disadvantages of second-generation immigrants." *European Journal of Population*, 35, 2019.
12. For a relevant study of students in secondary schools in Madrid, Spain, see Hector Cebolla-Boado, et al., "It is all about 'hope'." *Ethnic and Racial Studies*, 1, 2020. See also Zerrin Salikutluk *Immigrants' Aspiration Paradox*. Mannheim Centre Working Paper, n.d.
13. For further discussion of the recent history of the two Koreas, see Theodore Jun Yoo, *The Koreans*. University of California, 2020.
14. Sungjoo Choi and Keuntaw Kim, "We don't belong here." *International Migration*, 58, 2020.
15. Per Engzell, "Aspiration squeeze." *Sociology of Education*, 23, 2018.
16. Amy Lutz and Dalia Abdelhady, "Working-class children of Mexican immigrants in Dallas, Texas." *City and Community*, 19, 2020.
17. Van de Werfhorst and Heath, op.cit.
18. Catron, op.cit.
19. Ken Clark, et al., "Local deprivation and the labour market integration of new migrants to England." *Journal of Ethnic and Migration Studies*, 45, 2019.
20. Jamie Goodwin-White, "The shaping of selection." *Population, Space and Place*, 24, 2018.
21. Gabriele Ballarino and Nazareno Panichella, "The occupational integration of male migrants in Western European countries." *International Migration*, 53, 2015.
22. Dina Maskileyson, Moshe Semyonov and Eldad Davidov, "Economic integration of first- and second-generation immigrants in the Swiss labour market." *Population, |Space and Place*, 1, 2021.
23. For further discussion, see Nina G. Jablonski, "Skin color and race." *Physical Anthropology*, 175, 2020. See also, Angela R. Dizon and Edward E. Telles, "Skin color and colorism." *Annual Review of Sociology*, 43, 2017.
24. Douglas S. Massey and Jennifer A. Martin, *The NIS Skin Color Scale*. 2003.
25. JooHee Han, "Does "Skin tone matter?" *Demography*, 57, 2020.
26. Joni Hersch, "The persistence of skin color disadvantage for immigrants." *Social Science Research*, 1, 2011.

27 Andrea Gomez Cervantes and ChangHwan Kim, "Gendered Color Lines." Paper presented at the annual meeting of the *American Sociological Association*, August, 2015.
28 Hersch, op.cit.
29 Andres Villarreal and Christopher Tamborini, "Immigrant economic assimilation." *American Sociological Review*, 83, 2018.
30 Raymundo M Campos-Vazquez and Eduardo M Medina-Cortina, "Skin color and social mobility." *Demography*, 56, 2019.
31 For a summary of relevant research, see Edward Telles, *Pigmentocracies*. University of North Carolina, 2014.
32 Robert E. Park and Ernest W. Burgess, *The City*. University of Chicago, 1982. (Originally published in 1925.)
33 See Douglas E. Massey and Magaly Sanchez R., *Blocked Boundaries*. Russell Sage Foundation, 2012.
34 See, for example, the description of how a meatpacking company enticed immigrants to move to a small, rural town in the Midwest. Faranak Miraftab, *Global Heartland*. Indiana University, 2016.
35 For further discussion of these facilties, see Pinelopi Vergov, "Living with difference." *Urban Studies*, 56, 2019.
36 For an overview of the recent research, see Chenoa A. Flippen and Dylan Farrell-Bryan, "New destinations and the changing geography of immigrant incorporation." *Annual Review of Sociology*, 47, 2021.
37 Louisa Vogiazides and Guilherme Kenji Chihaya, "Migrants' long-term residential trajectories in Sweden." *Housing Studies*, 35, 2020.
38 Jean-Louis Pan Ke Shon and Gregory Verdugo, "Forty years of immigrant segregation in France." *Urban Studies*, 52, 2015.
39 Otis D. Duncan and Beverly Duncan, "A methodological analysis of segregation indexes." *American Sociological Review*, 20, 1955.
40 Adapted from Daniel T. Lichter, Domenico Parisi and Shrinkidhi Ambinakudige, "The spatial integration of immigrants in Europe." *Population Research and Policy Review*, 39, 2020.., op.cit.
41 Haley McAvay, "Immigrants' spatial incorporation in housing and neighbourhoods." *Population*, 73, 2018. Similarly, in Amsterdam, non-European immigrants were found to be most segregated from Dutch natives across all income and educational levels. William R. Boterman, Sako Musterd and Dorien Manting, "Multiple dimensions of residential segregation." *Urban Geography*, 42, 2021.
42 Lichter, et al., op.cit.
43 For further discussion of the relationship between intermarriage and other indicators of social integration, see Sayaka O. Torngren, et al., "Toward building a conceptual framework on intermarriage." *Ethnicities*, 16, 2016.
44 For further discussion, see June Carbone and Naomi Cahn, *Marriage Markets*, Oxford University, 2014.
45 For further discussion of local and global mate selection, see Daniel T. Lichter and Zhenchao Qian, "The Study of Assortive Mating." In *The Springer Series on Demographic Methods and Population Analysis*, 47, 2018.
46 Gina Potarca and Laura Bernardi, "Mixed marriages in Switzerland." *Demographic Research*, 38, 2018.
47 Tina Hannemann, et al., "Co-ethnic marriage versus intermarriage." *Demographic Research*, 38, 2018.
48 Hill Kulu and Tina Hannemann, "Mixed marriage among immigrants and their descendants in the United Kingdom." *Population Studies*, 73, 2019.
49 This bi-directional relationship was reported by Dan Rodriguez-Garcia, "Contesting the nexus between intermarriage and integration." *ANNALS of the American Academy of Political and Social Science*, 662, 2015.
50 Daniel T. Lichter, Zhenchao Qian and Dmitri Tumin, "Whom do immigrants marry?" *ANNALS of the American Academy of Political and Social Science*, 662, 2015.
51 Hill Kulu and Amparo Gonzalez-Ferrer, "Family dynamics among immigrants and their descendants in Europe." *European Journal of Population*, 20, 2014.
52 *Ibid*.
53 The exception, of course, is when marriages are arranged; but even here, the individuals involve frequently retain a degree of choice.
54 Daniel T. Lichter, et al., "Whom do immigrants marry?" *op.cit*.

55 For further discussion, see Elizabeth D. Heineman, *What Difference Does a Husband Make?* University of California, 2003; and Dirk Bethmann and Michael Kvasnicka, "World War II, missing men and out of wedlock children." *The Economic Journal*, 23, 2012.
56 See the review of relevant theories in, Jan Van Bavel, "Partner choice and partner markets." In Norbert F. Schneider and Michaela Kreyenfeld (Eds), *Research Handbook on the Sociology of the Family*. Edward Elgar, 2021.
57 Amparo Gonzalez-Ferrer, et al., "Mixed marriages between immigrants and natives in Spain." *Demographic Research*, 39, 2018.
58 Lichter, et al., op.cit.
59 Jay Caspian King, *The Loneliest Americans*, Crown, 2021.
60 Jennifer Lee, "From undesirable to marriageable." *ANNALS of the American Academy of Political and Social Science*, 662, 2015. Whiteness appears to be similarly open to social construction in Canada, at least with the Jewish population. See Tamir Arviv, "Stepbrothers from the Middle East." *Social & Cultural Geography*, 19, 2018.
61 For an historical review, see David S. FitzGerald, et al., "Can you become one of us?" *Journal of Ethnic and Migration Studies*, 1, 2017.
62 Ibid.
63 Michael Neureiter, "Evaluating the effects of immigrant integration policies in Western Europe." *Journal of Ethnic and Migration Studies*, 45, 2019.
64 The following description is based upon, Eria S. Kristjansdottir and Unnur Dis Skaptadottir, "I'll always be a refugee." *Journal of Immigrant & Refugee Studies*, 17, 2018.
65 Ibid., p 396.
66 Heli Askola, "Copying Europe?" *International Migration Review*, 55, 2021.
67 Hannah M. Alarian and Michael Neureiter, "Values or origin?" *Journal of Ethnic and Migration Studies*, 47, 2021.
68 Nicolette D. Manglos-Weber, *Joining the Choir*. Oxford University, 2018.
69 Thabani Golden Muambasere, "Diaspora citizenship in practice." *Journal of Ethnic and Migration Studies*, 47, 2021.
70 See Linda Bakker, et al., "In exile and in touch." *Comparative Migration Studies*, 2, 2014.
71 Tahseen Shams, *Here, There, and Elsewhere*. Stanford University, 2020.

7 Migrant Settlements

This chapter describes the types of places in which migrants initially settle after arriving in a destination nation. Some refugees have the most limited choices. As previously defined, international refugees are people who flee across a national boundary. The driver can be economic or environmental, and often it is armed conflict within their origin nation that causes people to run across a border in search of safety. Very large numbers of people are often involved in a very brief period of time. For example, just for three weeks in 2022, an estimated three million people fled from Ukraine following Russia's invasion. Over one-half of them initially crossed the border into Poland.[1]

Some refugees who are forced to leave in a hurry are fortunate enough to have family or friends in another nation that are willing to take them in, or find accommodations for them. Some refugees have sufficient means to obtain housing on their own in another nation. However, a large percentage of refugees have no choice but to settle, at least temporarily, in the refugee camps that the destination nation provides.

Migrants who are not refugees ordinarily have more freedom to select a place to settle in a destination nation, though they often face economic constraints and/or their nationality, race or religion might limit where they can reside in the destination nation. Ghettos are sometimes the only possibility and, as we shall note, refugee camps and ghettos share a number of features in common. Enclaves are another alternative, and while ghettos and enclaves also share some commonalities, there are also some marked differences in their typical geographical locations, the homogeneity of residents' socioeconomic status, and the degree to which the community has control over local institutions, such as schools, charitable organizations, and so on. For the more well-off or better-connected migrants, there is the possibility of moving directly to an ethnoburb: a suburban community dominated by their co-ethnics.

In the following pages, we will describe the dimensions along which these types of settlements differ, and note the social, geographical, cultural and economic features that distinguish each type. We will also examine the consequences of migrants' initial settlement type for their long-term social and economic integration.

Refugee Camps

Refugee camps are ordinarily built in response to a crisis in a neighboring nation that leads to a large influx of migrants. As individuals and families attempt to escape an untenable situation, host nations tend to erect settlements to accommodate them, usually assuming it will be temporary, but it frequently turns out to last many years. The camps are sometimes run by the local government, but the U.N., the Red Cross, and other

DOI: 10.4324/9781003158400-7

non-government organizations are often involved as well. The smallest of the camps usually hold only a few thousand people, but the largest – such as the Kakuma camp in Kenya, established in 1992 – held nearly 200,000 refugees as late as 2019. Most of the people in Kakuma and in Kenya's other large camps came from South Sudan or Somalia and the immediate precursors to them leaving their homes were civil wars.[2]

Migrants seeking refuge in a camp are usually detained initially outside of the camp in a holding facility where their requests for asylum are processed. There are often long lines outside of these centers where hungry, often ill, people, with only the clothes on their backs, may have to wait for months for their refugee status and asylum claims to be approved. Some may be turned away, and forced to return to a chaotic situation. Some may be routed to still other sites in the nation. Thousands of people fleeing from civil war in Myanmar, for example, have sought asylum in Thailand, and most have been settled in camps, but some of the Kayan, a small ethnic minority from eastern Myanmar, were moved into bamboo shacks in special villages because Thai officials thought they could be a tourist attraction.

The Kayan women wear long, decorated and very distinctive neck rings. Tour companies set up trips for Thais and tourists from China to visit the villages with the Kayan women on display as the attractions. The women earn a very small amount of money from the tour companies and by setting up stalls to sell cheaper versions of their traditional neck rings. Critics have called these villages, "ethnic theme parks."[3] Most of the Kenyans placed in these villages remained in them for years because they had no official documents which made them unable to go anywhere else. Further, without such paperwork they could not even apply for asylum in a third country. While most were not very pleased with their lives in the villages many thought it might still be better than living in the main Myanmar refugee camp with tens of thousands of crowded people.

Those refugees who are approved for admission to a camp are transferred to the facility itself and go through an intake process that resembles a prison or the military. New arrivals are typically given a health screening, registered and fingerprinted, then assigned to a space. It may be in a tent or a prefabricated hut, or they may be given materials with which to construct their own shelter. Physical conditions in most camps tend to be harsh, at best: access to water for drinking or washing is usually limited, food is rationed and sanitation facilities are usually very primitive. Medical care also tends to be very limited and inadequate, as illustrated in Box 7.1.

Box 7.1 Treating Patients in a Greece Refugee Camp

The Moria refugee camp on a Greek island was initially constructed to house about 3,000 inhabitants, but by 2020 it was home to more than 20,000 refugees. In early 2020, a London-based physician, Annie Chapman, volunteered to spend three weeks in the camp treating sick or injured refugees. Each day she recounted her observations in a diary, and when she returned to London she wrote an article describing the deprivation and suffering she encountered.

Every day refugees waited for hours in the dark and cold for the clinic to open. Patients could only enter with police papers that contained their name and number. Some came with infected wounds, made worse by their minimal access to clean water in the camp. Many were suffering from flu-like symptoms that spread rapidly in the over-crowded camp. And then there were the refugees struggling with psychiatric issues. Some were traumatized by events that occurred as they made their way to the camp or after they arrived. Some, women and children especially, had been the victims of sexual violence in the camp. Dr. Chapman described how they cried and screamed, but to her consternation there was little the clinic was equipped to do for them. "When we send them back to their tents," she wrote, "I feel ashamed."[4]

The camp had only limited electricity, so the staff had to carry out their patient consultations with battery-operated lights. They could not even treat those with the most serious illnesses or injuries. In those cases, Dr. Chapman would beg for an ambulance to take them to a hospital outside of the camp. Sometimes one came, and if everyone was fortunate it would pull up to the clinic so the staff did not have to carry patients, in the dark and freezing cold, from the clinic to the camp's entrance.

The administrators of a refugee camp usually provide some type of limited schooling for youngsters, stores that dispense groceries and medicine, and banking facilities where residents of the camp can receive funds from outside relatives. In some larger camps the residents have also created their own markets inside the camp, but more typically they are totally dependent upon the facilities provided by the administrators of the camp.

In most cases, the residents of the camp are not free to leave it. Again, like prisoners, they are confined to a place by fences and guards. Many of the distinguishing features of refugee camps are shared by prisons, as previously noted, but also by some ghettos in that they all fall at the low end on a voluntary residence continuum and a high end on an imposed institutions continuum. These similarities have led some theorists to elaborate on the similarities among refugee camps, prisons and ghettos.[5]

Ghettos

In the social sciences, much of the research on, and analysis of, ghettos traces its beginnings to the writings of Louis Wirth. He was a University of Chicago-trained sociologist and an influential part of the early Chicago School. His dissertation, which was published in book form in 1928, was entitled, *The Ghetto*.[6] In this work he focused upon Jewish ghettos, in Europe and the United States, but he also noted similarities between them and the ghettos of other racial and ethnic groups. Of most importance, Wirth laid out some basic features of all ghettos that provided starting points for later analysts, especially during the first half of the 20th century.

Wirth began by tracing Jewish ghettos back to distinctive settlements in several European towns in the Middle Ages. They formed, in his view, mostly by the desires of people who shared religious precepts and rituals to be together so that they could support communal institutions. At the same time, Wirth noted that Jewish populations were sometimes ordered into ghettos by people in power and that even when Jews "voluntarily" formed ghettos it was at least partially because they feared having routinely to deal with non-Jews. They physically separated themselves in order to escape hostilities. By virtue of their separation, regardless of how voluntary it was, relations between Jews and non-Jews historically tended to be limited, formal, and impersonal. Neither group was inclined to trust the other nor did they desire to be socially friendly.

Within the ghetto, by contrast, relationships among Jews tended to be extensive and highly personal. In fact, intimate relationships, such as marriage, were strictly confined to the in-group (i.e. endogamous) as demanded by religious teaching and social norms. When a person from the community nevertheless selected a spouse from outside the community, the married couple was ordinarily banished, that is, forced to live outside of the ghetto. Thus, in every respect, it was a closed community. However, Wirth noted that when, through education or commerce, external contact between Jews and non-Jews increased, more universal values tended to replace the ghetto's traditional values, and intermarriage increased. The eventual result of such assimilation, he concluded, could be the end of the ghetto, and in the early 20th century, Wirth thought there were some formerly insular Jewish communities close to disappearing in this manner.

In the United States, and in Chicago, in particular, Wirth described the largely voluntary formation of Jewish ghettos that both resembled and differed from their European counterparts. One big difference was in their proximity to other similarly segregated groups. The Jews were one of several immigrant groups that succeeded each other in forming dense settlements in the inner city. The immigrant waves began with Germans and Irish, and as they moved out they were displaced by Jews who, in turn were displaced by Poles and Italians, and they were later succeeded by African Americans. One could observe the transformations on an almost daily basis as Lutheran churches became synagogues and then African M.E. churches. At many points during the process, different ethnic and racial groups lived side by side. The boundaries among them were maintained in these dense, inner-city neighborhoods, according to Wirth, by the fact that they generally detested and distrusted each other. What they all shared in common was poverty status, but this common economic position did not create an overarching bond among them. When Jews (or others) attained a degree of economic success they wanted to escape from their inner-city ghettos. Moving up socially meant moving out geographically.

For a couple of decades after the publication of Wirth's book, American Jewish settlements were the prototype of the ghetto in much of the scholarly literature of the then dominant Chicago School. At the same time, however, the researchers in this group (and others) also studied the ghettos being formed by immigrant Italians, Poles, and others. They examined each of the separate communities in detail and also described how they were geographically distributed across the city. Robert Park, a senior colleague of Wirth's, depicted the constellation of ethnic ghettos in Chicago during this period as resembling, "a mosaic of little worlds that touch but do not interpenetrate."[7]

In sum, for roughly the first half of the 20th century, the key defining features of a ghetto included: its relative ethnic or racial homogeneity; its separateness, meaning interactions between people living inside of the ghetto and outside of it were very limited; the distinctive institutions and facilities it offered to residents, including places of worship, restaurants, food stores, etc. and an emphasis upon the attractive pull of the ghetto combined with a recognition that decisions to live within it were not entirely unconstrained.

The last of the above defining characteristics was of particular significance in Mitchell Duneier's historical analysis of the concept of a ghetto. Many of the Chicago School pioneers and their followers, Duneier noted, viewed the northern urban ghettos merely as "way stations" for newcomers who would assimilate to modern urban life and move up and out. These segregated communities of initial residence for immigrants were theorized to be largely the result of voluntary and natural forces and they were viewed as serving as useful and temporary places of residence. It was not necessary, therefore, to be overly critical of segregated ghettos nor to formulate policies intended to eliminate them.[8]

During the second half of the 20th century, there was a dramatic change in the way the social sciences in the U.S. viewed ghettos. The first change was in whose settlements were considered the prototype of ghettos, and in this respect non-whites replaced Jews. One reason for this substitution was the Nazi's enforced encampment of Jews in Germany, Poland, and elsewhere in occupied Europe before and during World War II. Hitler justified these actions in part by arguing that he was just putting Jews back in the ghettos where they had been for centuries. However, it was prison-like qualities that predominated in the ghettos Hitler designed, and they lacked any of the attractions that had characterized Jewish ghettos in the past. No one would have voluntarily chosen to live in them especially because they usually turned out to be stops not on the way to upward mobility but to Nazi death camps.[9]

At the same time that Hitler changed the meaning of Jewish ghettos, there were large migrations of non-white populations, moving within nations (e.g. African Americans from the rural south to the industrial north in the United States) and between nations (e.g., from the Caribbean to the United Kingdom). Most of these migrants had limited formal educations and were relatively unskilled; but, the growing number of factory jobs that were becoming available in industrializing cities offered comparatively good wages for workers who entered factories without skills. The factory wages enabled stable, working-class communities to grow, but then the factory jobs began to disappear – de-industrialization – and they were not replaced by comparable jobs that the inner city residents could fill. Unemployment rates increased, entire communities became impoverished and dependent upon government assistance for housing, food, etc.

The difficulty of finding employment in these cities was especially pronounced for African American males without high-school diplomas. Studies report that many had no expectation of ever finding work. As a result, they had little basis for resisting "street culture," which encouraged segmented assimilation: for example, engaging in reckless behavior that further jeopardizes their chances of being upwardly mobile. Their pessimistic assessment of their future included a belief that they were very unlikely ever to have a stable marriage, so sexual relations were separated from marital plans and the communities tended to have high rates of non-marital births. The poor, single mothers often lacked the means to control their youngsters which contributed to a cycle of school dropouts, drugs, gangs and crime.[10]

Danger so suffuses everyday ghetto life that it creates an oppressive climate of fear that, along with the poverty of the area, results in widespread institutional withdrawal. Hospitals and public health facilities minimize their community involvement or move out of the area; public schools, libraries and youth clubs lack facilities and limit their functions. So just when there was the most pronounced need for assistance – because of the large number of single-parent families living in poverty – that help and support was not available.

In order to control crime in these areas, local governments have tended to rely heavily upon incarceration. A combination of vigilant policing, authoritarian courts, and expanded prisons, according to Loic Wacquant, were specifically designed to control, by "warehousing." This resulted in a highly disproportionate number of young, unemployed black males being in prisons so even if a traditional marriage following pregnancy was supported by ghetto norms, there would be too few males available as long-term partners.[11]

Summary

From the preceding discussion, we can identify five principal characteristics that are now typically associated with a contemporary U.S. ghetto. The prototype from which these characteristics are deduced is the African American ghetto found near the center of many U.S. cities between roughly the 1960s and the present.

1. They occupy a distinct geographical space that is recognized as such both by the occupants and by outsiders, and also tend to be both physically and socially isolated from the rest of the city in which they are located.
2. The occupants share a distinctive attribute – race – that is held in low regard in the society (stigmatized) and subject to negative stereotyping.
3. The ownership or control over most retail establishments, housing and local institutions lies outside of the community (e.g. absentee business ownership, government-run housing, etc.)
4. The relationship between residents and the external political system (municipal or state) is punitive and exploitative, maintaining the marginalized status of residents.
5. They tend to live in deteriorated private housing or crowded public housing in neighborhoods with high rates of crime and violence that offer few amenities. People remain in such places not because of any attachment, but because they have nowhere else to go.

In the U.S. there have been many immigrant settlements that have largely met all the ghetto criteria as described above. To illustrate, in 1986, a large groups of Cambodian refugees were resettled in the Bronx section of New York City where they were largely isolated from the communities around them. It was initially envisioned as a temporary arrangement. but decades later many of the first-generation immigrants and their off-spring remained unemployed, in dilapidated housing, in an economically impoverished, blighted inn-city neighborhood. The poverty and violence that characterized the community along with its relatively homogeneous ethnic-racial makeup led researcher EricTang to label it a "hyperghetto"[12]

Ghettos in European Cities

Outside of the U.S. until recently, the immigrant communities that appeared to most closely resemble American ghettos were in some of the suburbs of Paris ("banlieues"). They were formerly manufacturing centers in which factory jobs attracted large numbers of immigrants from Morocco, Algiers and other parts of Northern and Sub-Saharan Africa. However, de-industrialization had the familiar consequence of leading to high unemployment and the communities became impoverished. Wacquant described them as having a number of ghetto-like conditions, including deteriorated public housing, stigmatized minorities and high rates of poverty; but, he also argued that the French housing projects were less isolated than their American counterparts – here he focused upon the south side of Chicago – and that they were less disadvantaged by policies of the larger political system. He also stated that the problems of crime and poverty were less pronounced in the suburbs of Paris than in the Chicago (or other United States) ghettos. Wacquant concluded that it was incorrect to equate the worst parts of the banlius with American ghettos. However, some analysts have argued that both the prototypical

Chicago ghetto and the Paris banlieus have been changing, and growing more alike. Most notable, perhaps, has been the rising levels of unemployment, crime and social marginality in parts of the French suburbs, making them increasingly like U.S. ghettos.[13]

During the late 20th century social scientists around the world wrote so much about the American ghettos that some analysts believe that European researchers were overly influenced by the concept and imagery. As a result, researchers may have been predisposed to view poor communities in European cities as ghettos, even though many of the distinguishing features of ghettos were lacking.[14] Following the immigrant surge into Europe during the early decades of this century, however, the more recently formed immigrant communities in many European cities do seem to qualify as ghettos.

In Madrid, Spain, for example, San Cristobal is a geographically isolated area in which over one-half of the residents are either first or second-generation immigrants, largely having come from Morocco and other non-European nations. Due to factory closings, the community is characterized by high unemployment and young people dropping out of school at high rates. The major way in which this community appears to differ from the prototypical American ghetto is that there is less everyday violence in San Cristobal. Nevertheless, as in recent American ghettos, and unlike the historical ghettos described by Wirth, except for those who have to live there, "it is a place no one would go to."[15]

According to researchers and officials in Denmark, the growth of ghettos in that country has been pronounced. Beginning in 2010, Denmark has compiled an annual "ghetto list." In 2020 there were 29 communities on the official list. The criteria for a community's inclusion are the familiar characteristics by which ghettos are now usually defined. Over one-half of the residents must be first or second-generation immigrants. Most of those now in Denmark left Lebanon, Pakistan, and other non-European, Muslim nations so they share a distinctive attribute that tends to be stigmatized in their new nation. Other criteria for determining whether a community is placed on the ghetto list in Denmark include high rates of: school drop-outs, unemployment and crime. Denmark's criteria show the obvious influence of descriptions of ghettos in the U.S.

Dispersal Policies

As the number of officially designated ghettos has grown in Denmark, the government has concluded that the ghettos should be eliminated by demolishing the public housing in which many residents have been living. The government not only wants to knock down many of the public housing units and replace them with private housing but to bar people with low incomes from living in the new buildings.[16] The objective, of course, is dispersal.

The assumption that usually underlies government attempts to disperse immigrants is that it will hasten integration. Theoretically, breaking up an immigrant concentration could have this effect in two ways: (1) the ghetto neighborhood is likely to offer residents only limited opportunities. They may do better if forced to live elsewhere, and (2) living with fellow immigrants may discourage learning the host nation's language and cultural skills which, as we have noted in prior chapters, is negatively related to integration.

For a number of years, Sweden has tried to disperse immigrants from the places in which they first permanently settled if these neighborhoods were dominated by co-ethnics. To examine the consequences of this government policy, a group of social scientists examined all the immigrants from Iraq, Iran and Somalia who entered Sweden between 1995 and 2004. From a number of administrative registers they obtained data on their port of entry, and followed them until 2014, noting their incomes, education, etc. The final sample included over 25,000 immigrants who were between 25 and 59 years after the 10-year follow-up.[17]

The analysis initially indicated that immigrants from the nations listed above who settled in neighborhoods with high concentrations of co-ethnics were less likely to be employed a decade after they arrived. When the investigators dug deeper into the data, though, they discovered that the negative effect of co-ethnic concentrations was entirely due to the female refugees. It was only women who were strongly impacted. These immigrant women, particularly those with children, were presumably more subjected to neighborhood social pressures, and when traditional patriarchal norms predominated, the result was fewer women being employed outside of the household. However, the degree to which women's labor force participation was adversely impacted by the size of the co-ethnic concentration depended upon neighborhood patterns. Specifically, the higher the rate at which co-ethnics were employed in the neighborhood, the less were female employment prospects reduced by the co-ethnic concentration. In other words, it was in concentrations of traditional immigrants that over the years had lower overall employment rates than women who were newcomers were especially likely to not be employed.

The above finding with respect to employment – that ethnic concentrations, per se, have little effect – has been reported in a number of other realms as well. For example, in a study of refugees in Sweden's larger cities, the size of the ethnic concentration in which they settled was found, in and of itself, not to affect the likelihood of immigrants voting. Rather, their political participation depended upon the degree of political participation that had been occurring among previously settled co-ethnics.[18]

The take-away from this body of research is that the integration of immigrants that most nations seek is not necessarily retarded by their living in communities with concentrated numbers of co-ethnics. It is the predominant behavioral patterns among co-ethnics rather than their size that is most consequential. It therefore follows that to promote integration governments should not pursue blanket dispersal policies, but rather focus upon routing newcomers away from those concentrated ethnic communities in which immigrant integration has not been occurring.

Enclaves

The existence of concentrated numbers of people of the same race or nationality is one of the principal criterion for designating a neighborhood either a ghetto or an enclave. Deciding which classification better describes a specific place can, as a result, sometimes be problematic. However, there are a number of other features that can be utilized to distinguish between an enclave and a ghetto.

The difference between them that has most frequently been cited in the literature involves where ghettos and enclaves are placed along an attractiveness-to-residents continuum. At the high end of this continuum a community forms and remains by the choice of residents because it has qualities that they find appealing; it is where they choose to live. At the low end, residents are relegated to a place because external prejudices cut them off from more desirable alternatives or because they cannot afford to live elsewhere. They are not there by choice. Enclaves and ghettos can be mixed in this respect, that is, all of their residents are neither entirely voluntary nor entirely constrained. However, enclaves are, by definition, closer to the apex of the continuum while ghettos are closer to the base.[19]

A major reason for the relative attractiveness of an enclave is the presence of grocery and clothing stores, pharmacies, restaurants and bakeries, funeral parlors, hair salons and so on that serve the specialized needs of the immigrant community. Many of these establishments tend to be owned and/or managed by local co-ethnics who understand the unique preferences of the residents. In a typical ghetto, by contrast, there are usually few establishments that cater to the specialized needs of residents, and few that are locally owned. Most of the grocery stores, pharmacies, and so on that are found in ghettos tend to be parts of national chains that are headquartered in distant cities, and the products they offer are mostly the same everywhere. The absence of facilities tending to the immigrant community's specialized needs is one of the reasons that most residents of a ghetto find it an unattractive place to live.

It would be difficult to overestimate the importance of such local businesses to the daily lives of enclave residents. If, for example, the immigrants are Muslims it would only be in an enclave (and not in a ghetto) that they would be able to follow traditional Muslim practices in arranging marriages, observing religious rites, properly burying the dead, etc. People with the necessary technical skills and facilities would be difficult to find in a ghetto. The way co-ethnic establishments meet the specialized needs of an immigrant community is illustrated by the role of grocery stores in a Chinese enclave in the suburbs of Toronto, as described in Box 7.2.

Box 7.2   Grocery Stores in Toronto's Chinese Enclave

On the northern edge of Toronto there are several large concentrations of immigrants from Mainland China and Hong Kong. Across several towns recent figures estimate that there were an estimated total of 140,000 ethnic Chinese residents, and in some of the communities the Chinese comprised approximately 50% of the population. As defined by Statistics Canada, the largest group were economic migrants, and the smallest group were refugees.[20]

Throughout these communities, there are a large number of strip malls that are typically anchored by a supermarket that caters to Chinese shoppers. These small clusters of stores also typically contain Chinese restaurants serving authentic Chinese dishes, banks with tellers that speak with customers in Cantonese and Mandarin, and so on. The parking signs are in Chinese as is much of the lettering in store windows, giving these strip malls an immediately visible ethnic identity. The communities contain both Chinese and "mainstream" shopping venues, but the Chinese make their purchases mostly in the stores with co-ethnics that specifically cater to them.

Geographer Lucian Lo interviewed a sample of 800 local residents, asking them where they shopped, how and why. Focusing upon supermarkets, she found that among the Chinese residents adherence to cultural traditions strongly influenced their consumption patterns. For example, many shopped at the Foody Mart which offered shelves of salted duck eggs, live fish in tanks (to be considered fresh by the Chinese, they must be alive) and poultry intact with head and feet (as preferred by the Chinese). While the Chinese shoppers moved their carts through the isles, Shanghai pop played over the store's speakers. Lo concluded that the Chinese supermarkets in the enclave were the place that Chinese residents could buy the proper ingredients to prepare their meals and feel comfortable doing it.[21]

Many of the residents of an enclave work at diverse jobs under highly variable conditions in the enclave. They are local store owners, managers and employees. Some are self-employed with most of their clients living in the enclave. Some work at a variety of jobs outside of the enclave. As a result, there tends to be substantial income differences among residents of an enclave while the residents of a ghetto tend to be uniformly poor. The Cuban enclave in Miami, for example, was formed by three distinctly different waves of migrants from Cuba. The earliest group to leave was largely comprised of professionals and business owners, most of whom were able to bring financial assets with them. The third group was poorly educated and uniformly poor. The immigrants in the second wave were intermediate. The immigrants in the first group accessed start-up capital and opened a variety of businesses, many of which served the local Cuban community, and the latter arriving groups provided abundant labor.[22]

Entrepreneurship is found in both ghettos and enclaves, but the existence of more assets and stronger ethnic bonding in enclaves results in entrepreneurship taking a different form. At the lowest level of entrepreneurship, according to Portes and Martinez, independent workers are part of the informal economy and primarily work outside of the enclave. They are street vendors selling contraband, men seeking casual day work as laborers and women who were willing to work as maids to clean the homes of middle-class families. Their work is usually "off the books" so they lack any legal safeguards, and they are primarily interacting with people from outside of their ethnic community making it easier for them to be cheated and exploited. The informal and temporary nature of their employment has been termed "precarious labor" and it also entails shifting of the risks from employer to employee.[23] If they are injured on the job, for example, they bear the costs of medical treatment.

Immigrant entrepreneurship carried out within an enclave, by contrast, relies upon more cohesive ethnic networks. Here co-ethnics provide start-up capital based upon trust to entrepreneurs who could not get credit from mainstream banks. To illustrate, Portes and Martinez point to the economic growth of the Cuban enclave in Miami which was based largely upon ethnic solidarity between lenders and recipients, and the successful start-up of Chinese garment firms in Northern Italy which was similarly dependent upon ethnic solidarity.

Leave or Stay?

There is a long history of research into whether immigrants are economically better off in the long run if they remain in the enclave or seek their fortunes outside of it. A number of early studies concluded that enclaves often acted as "traps" in which co-ethnics provided initial employment to new immigrants, but it was in jobs that offered very limited mobility opportunities. Immigrants would, presumably, be better off if they left the enclave.

A unique program enacted during the early 20th century provided a group of geographers with an opportunity to assess the costs or benefits of remaining in an enclave. A relocation program, in 1910, provided funds to 39,000 poor Jewish households in New York City enclaves. The funds were used to relocate them to several highly integrated neighborhoods around the country. Historical documents enabled the researchers to mimic an experimental design because they provided data on the occupation and income of those who moved and their original neighbors who did not move. The investigators matched the two groups in 1910 and then compared their incomes in 1920. Those who left the enclave in 1910 had more income than those who remained, even if they later returned, and the income differences were still greater among those who left and did not return. Further, 30 years later (i.e. in 1940) the sons of the program participants who were relocated were found to earn more than the sons from comparable households that did not relocate. Finally, those that relocated in 1910 were less likely to marry Jewish spouses. The investigators concluded that leaving an ethnic enclave facilitated economic advancement and assimilation into the broader society.[24]

A recent trend, in several nations, has involved migrants initially moving to new, historically atypical, locations. In these new destinations, as introduced in Chapter 6, they are geographically separated from their larger co-ethnic communities, and tend to be in places that historically received few migrants; for example, rural areas. However, in some cases economic ties have been forged between workers living in the enclave and businesses established in the new destinations. These situations provide another lens with which to compare the monetary differences between working in and out of an enclave.

An international team of social scientists described how the linkages between rural businesses and co-ethnic workers from an urban enclave can be maintained. They focused specifically upon Chinatown in New York City, which like its counterparts in other major cities, has been a traditional settlement location for Chinese immigrants. It has also been the primary locus of employment for new migrants, at least initially. In recent years, a number of Chinese entrepreneurs have moved to areas far outside of the city and opened restaurants. Their clientele is mostly non-Chinese and they hire some local employees, but for most of their help they rely upon co-ethnics who commute from Chinatown. Dozens of specialized employment agencies and bus companies have been established in Chinatown to connect immigrant workers living in the enclave with jobs in the Chinese restaurants located outside of the city. The workers who leave Chinatown to commute to these restaurant jobs appear to do better economically than those who continue to live and work in Chinatown's restaurants. Chefs, for example, are paid over 10% more in the distant locations than their city counterparts.[25]

While most of the research indicates that migrants benefit from seeking employment outside of the enclave, there is some recent research focusing upon immigrant entrepreneurship which suggests that remaining in the enclave can be economically beneficial. The difference in conclusions is at least in part probably due to the fact that economic activities in enclaves have more recently tended to involve transnational business linkages between firms in original and destination nations. Examples include import-export enterprises, specialized travel agencies, and so on. These linkages have benefitted co-ethnics who remained in the enclave. However, as that type of activity increases, enclaves are transformed into ethnoburbs, which are discussed at length in the following section.

Tourism

There is sometimes an additional source of income coming into enclaves in the form of tourism expenditures. Unlike ghettos, enclaves often become tourist attractions, creating employment opportunities for residents and support for local establishments. Enclaves are frequently interesting to outsiders because the people and places they contain look different than mainstream communities. The residents often look and dress differently and the commercial centers tend to be comprised of small, non-chain, family-owned stores, and restaurants. This sets them apart from typical communities dominated by the same big-box retailers (e.g., Walmart) and the same fast food restaurant chains.

Building upon their uniqueness, many cities actively market enclaves as exotic and authentic components of a tourist's experiences. Examples of such promotions include the Arab Quarter in Paris, the Caribbean enclave in Brixton (London) and Chinatown in New York. Tourist expenditures help to support enclave restaurants, bakeries, souvenir shops, and so on. However, there is a downside to a community being promoted as a tourist attraction. Decisions concerning where to invest in the community may be likely to be selected according to their probability of generating a tourism-related return rather than according to their potential contribution to the lives of residents. Elementary schools that are currently in use, for example, are not typically included in the agendas of tourists while historical theaters usually are included. As a result, theaters may be more likely to attract investment than schools, though most residents would probably not share those priorities.[26]

Associated with tourism there is also a breaking down of a community's separation from the rest of a metropolitan area. To promote tourism, a city may improve access roads connecting the enclave to the rest of the city or add mass transit stops convenient to an enclave. Its attractions can then lead tourists and other city residents to become frequent visitors. This lack of separation between an enclave and the rest of the city in which it is located stands in marked contrast to the social and physical isolation of ghettos, which is one of their most distinguishing features.

Summary

In sum, while ghettos and enclaves are both dominated by a single ethnic or racial group, we have identified a number of ways in which enclaves can be differentiated from ghettos. The major distinctions include the following:

1 Although both are segregated communities, the segregation of an enclave is based more upon its attractiveness to a particular group of people while the segregation of a ghetto is more involuntary. (Note in this respect, the Jewish ghetto described by Wirth would be closer to what we now describe as an enclave.)
2 The income of residents in an enclave tends to be highly variable compared to the more homogeneously poor residents of a ghetto.
3 Enclaves often become tourist attractions while ghettos rarely do, and when enclaves become tourist attractions they usually become better connected to the city of which they are apart while ghettos tend to be socially and physically isolated.

It is also important to recognize that the above-noted differences are sometimes matters of degree rather than categorical; for example, some enclaves can be almost as isolated as a typical ghetto. Further, the distinction between these two types of communities is not necessarily fixed permanently. In some case a community can move from being more enclave-like to being more ghetto-like, and vice versa.[27]

Becoming Cross-National

By the end of the 20th century, a number of immigrants in ethnic enclaves in destination nations established business relations with co-ethnics in their origin nation. One factor responsible for the increase in these small companies was the widespread tendency for immigrants to be entrepreneurial. In Britain and Ireland, for example, studies have found immigrants to be substantially more likely to start businesses than native-born people. Second are the assets that accrue to immigrants that can be essential for the survival of cross-national start-ups, but do not require capital which many immigrants lack. Specifically, sharing an ethnic identity generates trust and reduces uncertainty in cross-nation negotiations while also improving access to local markets. These assets based upon shared ethnicity may also help to keep large corporations from competing in these markets.[28]

One of the most significant differences between an enclave and an ethnoburb – our next topic – is the extent of cross-national business activities begun in the enclave that serves the local ethnic market by linking it to ethnically-oriented goods and services from the origin nation. When this type of business activity reaches a certain level, a community is designated to be an ethnoburb rather than an enclave, as far as this criterion is concerned.

Ethnoburbs

Ethnoburbs are a more recently developed classification for communities, initially indebted largely to a series of articles and books by Wei Li.[29] The major model of an ethnoburb in her research was the concentration of ethnic Chinese in suburban Los Angeles, the San Gabriel Valley, and the city of Monterey Park, in particular. From Li's research, Monterey Park became the prototype of how an ethnoburb can form, and later in this chapter we will briefly describe its historical development. However, it is important to note that while a great deal of ethnoburb research has focused upon Chinese immigrants (especially from Hong Kong and Taiwan) – because they have been the group most likely to form this type of settlement – other Asian groups as well as some non-Asian groups are also living in communities that largely fit the ethnoburb model. These studies have also been conducted in U.S. states other than California, and in the suburbs of cities in Canada, New Zealand, and elsewhere.[30]

One major limitation to where ethnoburbs can form lies in the nature of a city's peripheral areas. To be suburban in this context implies that the peripheral location consists of newer, higher status and low-density construction, and it is in such suburbs that ethnoburbs are situated. However, defined in that way, the areas outside of Beijing, for example, would not qualify as suburban. It would also not fit many of the banlieues outside of Paris, as previously described. Where such suburbs do not exist neither, by definition, could ethnoburbs, although a neighborhood could resemble an ethnoburb in other respects.

In order to further differentiate between ethnic enclaves and ethnoburbs, Christina Tan employed diverse methods in a study of neighborhoods in suburban Los Angeles, partially overlapping the area studied by Li. It contained communities that Tan (and many residents) considered to be either enclaves or ethnoburbs. She obtained demographic data on their ethnic composition, population density and socioeconomic status. She also interviewed a sample of people from the neighborhoods, asking them to describe and evaluate the different neighborhoods in the study area. Two of the variables that best distinguished between ethnoburbs and enclaves were population density (it was lower among ethnoburbs) and socioeconomic status (which was higher in ethnoburbs). These are the differences that would be expected.

Because of its convenience, a number of respondents said they would remain in their enclave or would move back to it if they had left after they retired. Living in the suburbs, the alternative, they said would routinely require a lot of driving; but in the enclave food, clothing, all basic services are "just a bus away." Other informants, however, looked down on the relative poverty of the enclave, stating "It's not a great place for kids." And others explained that if you wanted your mother and other family members to be able to live with you, then you needed a sizeable house and you could not get that in the smaller, inner-city housing of an enclave.[31]

The features that Li and others have emphasized in distinguishing an ethnoburb from other types of communities, in addition to their suburban location, include a significant concentration of one ethnic group, often Chinese, and the simultaneous presence of substantial numbers of other ethnic groups. In Monterey Park, there were three major groups. There were the Anglos who moved there first, when the town had been a more typical homogeneously white suburban community. Many of them reacted with anger to the influx of Chinese residents and their conspicuous restaurants and businesses. A third group in the community was Hispanic, from Mexico and other Central American nations. They too initially resented the Chinese "invasion," though they later formed a coalition with the Chinese in opposition to the Anglos. The ethnic diversity that typically characterizes an ethnoburb is illustrated in some of Melbourne's suburbs, described in Box 7.3.

Box 7.3 Diversity in Melbourne's Suburbs

In the northern suburbs of Melbourne, since the last decades of the 20th century, there has been a substantial in-migration of affluent and well-educated immigrants. Many of the migrants came from Hong Kong and other Asian nations, but their origin nations were highly diverse. The influx of ethnic Chinese has led to the growth of Melbourne's traditional Chinatown, located in the central city, and it has also directly increased the population of several suburban communities that are now comprised of high-status migrants from China and a number of other nations. Observers have described them as, "super-diverse ethnoburbs."[32]

Because Chinese restaurants, groceries, boutiques, etc. are conspicuous in the suburban shopping areas, the neighborhoods seem to many non-Chinese residents to be predominantly Chinese, and they disapprove. They fear that the Chinese population may completely dominate their neighborhood, both economically and politically. Many of the long-term residents of these neighborhoods express nostalgia for the old days when the local stores were Australian and not Chinese-owned. In fact, ethnic Chinese usually comprise less than one-quarter of any neighborhood's population. Especially to non-Asians, however, there is a tendency to view immigrants from Japan, Korea, and other Asian nations as Chinese which has the effect of attributing an exaggerated Chinese presence to these places.

Despite inflated perceptions of Chinese domination, the highly diverse residents of these suburban neighborhoods tend to be multi-cultural in their outlooks and tastes. For example, many non-Chinese prefer to eat traditional Chinese foods, in traditional Chinese restaurants; and much of the help in these establishments is not Chinese. Unlike the economic organization of enclaves, ethnic solidarity is less important to the success of these suburban Melbourne businesses.[33]

Los Angeles and Monterey Park

The Chinese population in the Los Angeles area was originally concentrated in an inner-city area known as Chinatown. Settlement in the community began in the late 19th century and its population grew into the early 20th century. While the original Chinatown had some enclave-like features (for example, it offered a variety of specialized goods and services specifically for co-ethnics), it largely resembled a ghetto because people moved to the community mostly in reaction to the anti-Chinese hostility expressed by the surrounding white population and the community was comprised almost entirely of relatively poor residents. The primary tie between the residents of Chinatown and their homelands involved correspondence with family and a small amount of family-related travel. There were very few business connections.

When a large part of the Chinese population in Los Angeles lived in Chinatown, the area that later became the City of Monterey Park (it was incorporated in 1916) was still a sparsely settled agricultural area. It grew slowly, initially viewed by its developers as a potentially high-end community, partially because its hilly landscape resembled Beverly Hills, a wealthy suburb with high-end shopping located just east of the city of Los Angeles. By the end of World War II, however, it had become a typical, middle-class suburban town, almost all white, with fewer than ten Chinese residents.

During the 1970s and 1980s, the movement of Chinese from various parts of Los Angeles to Monterey Park increased, and there was a very large influx of international migrants, especially from Taiwan to the Los Angeles area, including Monterey Park. This led to one of the city's nicknames "Little Taipei." (Taipei is the capital of Taiwan.) During the 1970s, as relations between the United States and the People's Republic of China (PRC) were normalized, many wealthy families in Taiwan feared that their country would be reclaimed by the PRC. This fear prompted a capital and migrant outflow from Taiwan to the United States, with the Los Angeles area the favored destination of both capital and immigrants. They were joined by an exodus from the PRC, and their combined presence had a dramatic effect upon Monterey Park as well as the greater Los Angeles area: airlines added numerous nonstop flights from Los Angeles to Taipei and Beijing; the PRC opened a consulate general office in Los Angeles to promote trade and cultural exchanges; the number of Chinese-owned banks proliferated; and greater Los Angeles became the U.S. metropolitan area with the largest concentration of Chinese-owned firms. Two of the hilly sections of Monterey Park became favored locations for all of the ethnically Chinese migrants, both from other parts of Los Angeles and abroad. This led to the city's other nickname, "the Chinese Beverly Hills," and that was one of the ways it became widely known, both in the Los Angeles area and abroad.[34]

Cross-National Enterprise

Many of the international migrants, from Taiwan and from Hong Kong, were entrepreneurs who wanted to open businesses in Monterey Park, and they came with the resources to purchase homes and start local businesses. Using the capital they brought from China or could get from Chinese-owned banks in the Los Angeles area, new arrivals from Taiwan and Hong Kong established import-export business that tied their local community to the places the immigrants had left. They also built malls and condominiums, developed commercial strips and opened travel agencies specializing in connecting parts of China with Los Angeles and Monterey Park.

Historically, immigrants tended to settle in the center of cities, then with assimilation and economic attainment, many experienced social and geographical mobility, moving to suburban areas. Those who left Los Angeles' Chinatown for Monterey Park fit this model. In most ethnoburbs, this historical type of migration has been combined with a second pattern that features transnational movement directly to the suburban area. The Taiwanese migrants to Monterey Park followed this form, and they were the ones primarily responsible for establishing economic ties to their homeland.

These changes in the destination locations of emigres have been widespread, and are one of the main reasons for the increase in ethnoburbs. To illustrate further, in Chicago, Polish enclaves formed in the city since the turn of the 20th century. They were among the ethnic neighborhoods described by researchers in the Chicago School. These communities were predominantly comprised of Poles, and these immigrants typically lacked much formal education and worked at low-paying, unskilled jobs. Many worked in the meat processing plants that were tied to Chicago's stockyards. Over time, many of them and their offspring moved up and out. More recently, however, thousands of people have left Poland and emigrated directly to suburban areas north of Chicago. Many of them are entrepreneurs and professionals, with economic ties to Poland. And like other ethnoburbs, the communities into which they are now moving contain a mix of other racial and ethnic groups, in addition to the Polish concentration.[35]

The direct movement of migrants to the fringes of metropolitan areas has also involved small numbers of people not connected to a migrant stream. These small clusters of migrants have become parts of diverse suburban communities that at first glance could appear to be ethnoburbs. However, they are lacking two of the major features that define ethnoburbs. Specifically, no one ethnic group predominates in the local mix nor are there local businesses, operated by members of an ethnic group that have transnational ties to co-ethnic enterprises in the homeland. Illustrative of these suburban towns is Almere.

Located 30 km east of Amsterdam, Almere is a satellite suburb that in recent years has attracted migrants from Portugal, the U.S., Germany, and other nations. It has been selected by a growing number of young immigrants because of its relatively affordable housing (especially when compared to Amsterdam). It is a community in which a lot of residents value its diversity and display a cosmopolitan outlook which Tzaninis argues has been viewed, erroneously, by urban theorists as confined to city dwellers. However, despite its suburban location and ethnically heterogeneous population, Almere lacks a dominant ethnic group and transnational enterprises that are necessary for a community's designation as an ethnoburb.[36]

Comparing Settlement Types

There are a number of apparent similarities between ethnoburbs and enclaves, especially in comparison to ghettos. Living in either an enclave or ethnoburb tends to be based upon attraction more than external constraints while living in ghettos usually involves a lack of choice. The income of residents in both enclaves and ethnoburbs also exceeds that of ghetto residents, but the average income in ethnoburbs tends to be higher than in enclaves. In addition, both enclaves and ethnoburbs are typically more connected to the urban area of which they are a part in contrast to ghettos which tend to be more isolated.

While enclaves and ethnoburbs share some similarities in relation to ghettos, there are some clear differences between them. Enclaves can be located anywhere, in a city or its periphery, but ethnoburbs are confined to suburban areas and they are less likely than enclaves to become tourist attractions. Ethnoburbs also tend to be less segregated, less homogeneous communities. Finally, there is an important distinction that entails the amount of transnational economic activity that is conducted. It is much higher in an ethnoburb than in an enclave.

The strong ties that business people in an ethnoburb establish with counterparts in their nation of origin can expand their notion of "home," to encompass both here – their current place and there – their former place. This bilocal conception of home can lead to estrangement, however, according to Waldinger. Other people in their current place of residence may find their attachment to their former nation to be disconcerting, especially if relations between the two nations are strained by international events. At the same time, having emigrated certainly sets them apart from their former cohorts who remained. These people with bilocal conceptions of home may, as a result, be in a marginal position in which they do not fully fit in anywhere, except with each other.[37]

Notes

1 Patricia Cohen, "Europe Braces For High Costs of Refugee Aid." *The New York Times*, March 16, 2022, p A1.
2 UNCHR, *Global Report 2020*. 15 June, 2021.
3 Hannah Beech, "Tradition becomes tourism." The New York Times, December 15, 2020, p A7.
4 Annie Chapman, "A doctor's story." *The Guardian*, February 9, 2020.
5 For further discussion of the overlap between refugee camps and ghettos, see Andrew M. Jefferson, Simon Turner and Steffen Jensen, "Introduction," in Simon Turner and Steffen Jensen (Eds), *Reflections on Life in Ghettos, Camps and Prisons*. Routledge, 2020.
6 Louis Wirth, *The Ghetto*. University of Chicago, 1928.
7 Robert E. Park, "The City." In Robert E. Park and Ernest W. Burgess (Eds), *The City*. University of Chicago, 1984. (Initially published in 1925.)
8 Mitchell Durneier, *The Ghetto*. Farrar, Straus, and Giroux, 2016. For further discussion of the long-term history of the term, see also, Daniel B. Schwartz, *Ghetto*. Harvard University, 2019.
9 Durneier, op cit.
10 Especially relevant are two books by William J. Wilson: *The Truly Disadvantaged*, University of Chicago, 1990 and *When Work Disappears*, Vintage, 1997. See also, Harold Wolman, et al., *Coping With Adversity*. Cornell University, 2017.
11 Loic Wacquant, *Punishing the Poor*. Duke University, 2009.
12 Eric Tang, *Unsettled*. Temple University, 2015.
13 See for example, Ernesto Castaneda, "Places of Stigma." (Chapter 7) In Ray Hutchinson and Bruce D. Haynes (Eds), *The Ghetto*. Westview, 2012.
14 H. Julia Eksner, "Revisiting the 'Ghetto'." *Social Anthropology*, 21, 2013.
15 Cecilia Eseverri Mayer, "A Spanish ghetto?" *Migraciones Internacionales*, 9, 2017, p 2.
16 Ellen Barry and Martin S. Sorensen, "In Denmark, Harsh New Laws for Immigrant 'Ghettos.'" *The New York Times*, July 1, 2018; and Fergus O'Sullivan, "How Denmark's 'ghetto list' is ripping apparent migrant communities." *The Guardian*, March 11, 2020.
17 Roger Andersson, Sako Musterd and George Galster, "Port-of-entry neighborhood and its effects on the economic success of refugees in Sweden." *International Migration Review*, 53, 2019.
18 Henrik Andersson, et.al., "Effect of settlement into ethnic enclaves on immigrant voter turnout." *The Journal of Politics*, 84, 2022.
19 For an early and influential statement of this difference, see Peter Marcuse, "The Enclave, The Citadel and The Ghetto." *Urban Affairs Review*, 33, 1997. For a more recent application of the perspective, see Raphael Susewind, "Muslims in Indian Cities." *Environment and Planning* A, 49, 2017.
20 These figures are from, Xuanxiao Wang, *Suburban Chinatowns in Canada*. School of Urban Planning, McGill University, 2019.
21 Lucia Lo, "The Role of Ethnicity in the Geography of Consumption." *Urban Geography*, 30, 2009. Description of the Foody Market is from, Sadiya Arsari, "Everybody fits in." *The Guardian*, September 4, 2018.

22 For further discussion, see Silvia Pedraza-Bailey, "Cuba's Exiles." *International Migration Review*, 19, 1985; and Alejandro Portes and Aaron Puhrmann, "A bifurcated enclave." *Cuban Studies*, 43, 2015.
23 Alejandro Portes and Brandon P. Martinez, "They are not all the same." *Journal of Ethnic and Migration Studies*, 46, 2020. They describe a hierarchy of entrepreneurship and relate it to differences in the strength of co-ethnic bonds. They do not utilize a ghetto-enclave distinction, but such a distinction is very congruent with their theory. The term precarious labor is associated with Arne Kalleberg, *Precarious Lives*, Polity, 2018.
24 Ron Abramitzky, Leah Boustan and Dylan Connor, *Leaving the Enclave*. Working Paper 20-031, Stanford Institute for Economic Policy Research, July, 2020.
25 Zai Liang, et.al., "From Chinatown to every town." *Social Forces*, 97, 2018.
26 For further discussion of ethnic tourism, see Jarkko Saarinen and Sandra Wall-Reinius, "Enclaves in tourism." *Tourism Geographies*, 21, 2019.
27 These changes are discussed in, Mark Abrahamson, *Globalizing Cities*. Routledge, 2020.
28 Large corporations may also be deterred by the low-profit margins that are often associated with these markets. For further discussion, see Osa-Godwin Osaghae and Thomas M. Cooney, "Exploring the relationship between immigrant enclave theory and transnational diaspora entrepreneurial opportunity formation." *Journal of Ethnic and Migration Studies*, 46, 2020.
29 Wei Li, *Ethnoburb*. University of Hawaii, 2009.
30 See, for example, Daniel Fittante, "The Armenians of Glendale." *City & Society*, 30, 2018; and Noriko Matsumoto, *Beyond the City and the Bridge*. Rutgers University, 2018.
31 LingLing Gao-Miles, "Beyond the ethnic enclave." *City & Society*, 29, 2017.
32 Shilpi Tewari and David Beynon, "The rise of the super-diverse 'ethnoburbs.'" *The Conversation*, February 5, 2018.
33 Gao-Miles, op.cit.
34 Li, op.cit.
35 Jason Schneider, "From urban enclave to ethnoburb." *Iowa Journal of Cultural Studies*, 15, 2014.
36 See Yannis Tzaninis, "Cosmopolitanism beyond the city." *Urban Geography*, 41, 2020.
37 See the discussion in, Roger Waldinger, *The Cross-Border Connection*. Harvard University, 2015.

8 Immigrants' Contributions and Natives' Perceptions

During the past decade there has been a marked increase, in many nations, in the number of prominent politicians whose policy positions have prominently featured a negative stance toward immigrants and immigration, in general. They have advocated strict limitations and fanned fears of cultural degeneration, rampant crime and economic calamity if the "hordes" of immigrants are permitted to continue to "invade." The appeals to their potential supporters have combined hostility to foreigners – xenophobia – with a devotion and loyalty solely to their nation – nationalism – and a tendency to attribute negative qualities to members of other racial-ethnic groups – racism. Much of the mass media has often explicitly or implicitly supported xenophobia, nationalism and racism by presenting negative accounts of immigrants' behavior that would justify closing national borders.[1]

It would be a mistake, however, to infer that xenophobia, nationalism or racism first appeared in the 21st century. Fifty years ago there were popular nationalistic movements with racist undertones in Scotland, Ireland, Catalonia (in Spain), Quebec (in Canada), etc. In the U.S., as early as in 1750, Benjamin Franklin publicly expressed concern that foreigners were "overwhelming" American society, and in the 19th century an American political party (the Know Nothings) promoted ethnic hatred as their centerpiece and wanted to deport all of the "foreign beggars."[2]

In contemporary Britain, sociologist Sivamohan Valluvan has described how populist nationalism, and its attendant outlooks, has been increasing, strongly resembling developments in Russia, the U.S. and elsewhere. The driving force behind this nationalism, he asserted, is race, white nationalism, in particular. It is the centerpiece that marginalizes all non-white groups. On the political left is an identification with the white working class that was impoverished by de-industrialization. On the political right is a nostalgic look back to when Britain was a white nation, largely without foreigners. The common strand in both political positions is race.[3] While Valluvan focused upon Britain, his conclusions could largely apply also to the contemporary U.S. and other nations as well.[4]

Misperceptions About Immigrants

The treatment of immigrants in their everyday lives, by native neighbors, police and other government officials, clerks in stores, and so on depends largely upon how the immigrants are viewed, that is, the personal and social characteristics that are attributed to them as a group. These views also shape government policies concerning the granting of visas, integration programs, deportation policies, etc. The accuracy of people's attributions

DOI: 10.4324/9781003158400-8

is therefore important, but a number of studies have raised questions about their veracity. We will review a wide range of these studies in the following pages.

Fear of Crime

One of the threats most commonly associated with xenophobia is a fear of crime. When immigrants are accused of committing crimes their status as immigrants, especially if they are undocumented, is typically highlighted in the media. This can help lead the public to believe that immigration is associated with increased crime, and justify their fear of opening their nation's borders to foreigners.

In Chile, for example, the foreign-born population (largely from Venezuela) roughly doubled between 2010 and 2020. A group of social scientists examined crime-related news in Chile's television and newspapers, and found that there was a highly disproportionate amount of coverage of immigrant-perpetrated homicides in relation to their actual involvement in murders. The investigators also found that the media coverage led to heightened security concerns, especially in municipalities with strong media presence. The frightened population increased their expenditures on home security systems, and the years in which Chile had the largest immigration increases were the years in which such expenditures most increased. However, when the investigators examined annual rates of immigration and annual crime rates (as indicated by victimization surveys), they found no relationship at all. They concluded that any correlation between immigration and crime in Chile was illusory, but that increased migration clearly did trigger public apprehension.[5]

A number of studies on immigration and crime have been conducted in European nations, including the UK, Switzerland and Germany. There have been some exceptions, but for the most part these studies have reported no increases in violent crime, that is, crimes against persons such as assault and murder; but they have sometimes reported small increases in property crimes (e.g. burglary) – which have been attributed to immigrants' slow economic integration.[6] There has been some uncertainty about how to interpret this apparent increase in some nations because almost all of the studies have relied exclusively upon "official" crime records. These data compile figures on the number of people who were arrested and then successfully prosecuted. The uncertainty arises because the people whose actions create these data – the police decisions to arrest, the judges' guilty verdicts, etc. – may be influenced by stereotyping and prejudice.[7]

Continuing the focus upon property offenses, Andresen and Ha present Canadian data that show the complexity of the immigration-crime relationship. Focusing upon census tracts in Vancouver, they obtained data on immigrant populations (mostly ethnic Chinese) and police-recorded data, that is property crimes reported to the police. In all, they had figures on one-half dozen types of property crimes: residential burglary, theft of a vehicle, etc. For each census tract they also had descriptive information on residents' incomes, types of housing, etc. They found some tendency for immigration and property crimes to be positively related in Vancouver's census tracts. However, the positive relationship was confined to certain types of property crimes and the relationship between immigration and all types of property crimes varied in relation to differences in census tracts' housing and socioeconomic characteristics.[8] So, while there was an overall tendency for immigration to be associated with increased property crime, the relationship was conditional and complex.

In the U.S., a number of studies have examined the possible link between immigration (sometimes including undocumented immigration) and crime. None of the studies have reported a very strong relationship, either positive or negative, between them; but the results have not been completely consistent, and methodological differences among the studies have made their findings difficult to compare. To be specific, there has been variation among studies in whether investigators take into account: features of the communities in which immigrants live (its SES, overall crime rate, etc.); the composition of the immigrant group studied (its age and sex distributions, etc.); the migration motives of immigrants in the study (economic, family reunification, etc.).[9] This listing includes just a few of the considerations that could substantially alter the results of any research project.

After noting a number of methodological differences among studies and reviewing the literature, Ousey and Kubrin have offered the tentative conclusion that the relationship between immigration and crime in the U.S. is very weak, and tends to be negative, meaning that geographical units with larger immigrant populations actually tend to have slightly lower overall crime rates.[10] One of the relatively few studies to include detailed information on the status of immigrants has also reported findings congruent with this tentative conclusion. Michael Light and associates had complete data on the immigrant status of everyone arrested in the state of Texas between 2012 and 2018. They found that undocumented immigrants had lower arrest records for all types of crime than either documented immigrants or native-born U.S. citizens. And most of the differences were large. For example, compared to undocumented immigrants, the native-born citizens were twice as likely to be arrested for violent crimes.[11] Given that undocumented immigrants would not only face criminal charges in the U.S., but face deportation as well, it is perhaps not surprising that they would be less inclined to commit crimes. The consequences of a conviction for an "aggravated felony" are described in Box 8.1.

Box 8.1   Consequences of Criminal Convictions for Noncitizens

An aggrevated felony is a legal category containing a number of individual offenses, many of which would be considered relatively minor especially in relation to the implications of the category's title. It was initially defined by the U.S. Congress in 1988 to include the serious offenses of murder and trafficking of drugs or weapons. Over the years, however, additional crimes were added to the list and it expanded to encompass over 30 offenses, including failure to appear in court, filing a false tax return, and other relatively minor crimes. If noncitizens are convicted of any crimes in the aggravated felony category they are subject to immediate deportation, and they are without any legal protections; for example, they can be deported without a removal hearing in immigration court.[12]

If noncitizens convicted of an aggravated felony are imprisoned rather than deported, federal authorities are required to detain them after their release from prison. After their release they are ineligible to apply for asylum or other forms of relief that could delay or prevent their deportation, even if they are being returned to a nation in which their safety is imperiled. Finally, after they are deported they are permanently inadmissible to the U.S. If they nevertheless are able to reenter illegally, and are apprehended at any time, they are subject to being imprisoned for up to 20 years.

In sum, the findings concerning the relationship between immigration and crime are complex and inconsistent. It seems reasonable tentatively to conclude that no increase in violent crime has been associated with increased immigration. Some increases in property crime have sometimes been associated with increased immigration, likely due to immigrants of low socioeconomic standing; but decreases in property crime have also been reported, and sometimes there is no relationship at all.[13]

Crime in Sanctuary Cities

A small number of cities (and sometimes larger geo-political entities) have instituted what is termed, "sanctuary policies." Precisely what such a designation includes is variable, but it typically entails two sets of actions. First, it involves enacting helpful local policies such as issuing driver's licenses to immigrants, documented or not, training court personnel on the immigration consequences of convictions, etc. Second, it involves policies or resolutions concerning the locale's limited cooperation with federal authorities charged with enforcing immigration laws. This often includes restrictions on the ability of local police to enforce federal immigration laws, limiting the access of federal officials to immigrants in detention in local jails, etc. This second set of policies, focusing upon the relationship between local and federal officials is often regarded as the centerpiece of sanctuary policies.[14]

There are estimates of the number of cities and larger geo-political entities that have instituted sanctuary policies. A 2020 survey of the largest 95 cities in Europe reported that there were 28 sanctuary cities in this grouping.[15] In the U.S., a 2018 survey estimated that there were nearly 200 sanctuary cities, counties or states, but unlike the European estimate, this figure was not derived solely from a sample of large entities so some of the U.S. sanctuary cities were very small.[16] The places included in these surveys also differed substantially from each other in the number of sanctuary policies that they implemented; varying from as little as one, to more than one dozen.

Sanctuary policies are strongly associated with cosmopolitan outlooks which regard all people, including documented and undocumented immigrants, as citizens of the world and thereby entitled to fundamental rights regardless of where they happen to be living. However, critics contend that by imposing restraints on the police, cities or other geo-political entities with sanctuary policies in place will experience higher rates of crime.

A number of studies have reported no association between rates of crime (both property and violent) and sanctuary policies. To reach this conclusion, research has generally compared overall crime rates in cities or counties that have some sanctuary policies in place to areas without such policies.[17] Their conclusions are somewhat weakened, however, by a lack of controls in their research designs. The cities or counties being compared may differ from each other in a number of other ways that may affect crime rates, but these potentially confounding variables have not usually been adequately controlled.

By contrast, an especially thorough analysis of the relationship between crime in sanctuary versus non-sanctuary locales was reported by Gonzales, Collingwood and El-Khatib. They obtained data for all types of crime in 55 U.S. cities that passed sanctuary policies and compared the cities' crime rates the year before such policies were implemented with the rates the year following. If sanctuary policies led to increased crime, then the rate would be higher the year after. The investigators found that in some cities the rates went up a little, in some they went down a little, and in a number they stayed the same. There was no overall pattern which led to the conclusion that a sanctuary policy does not lead to more crime.[18]

As a second test, the investigators carefully matched the 55 sanctuary cities with a sample of non-sanctuary cities that were the same with respect to: population size, racial distribution, income, education, etc. This was designed to prevent variables that could be related both to a city's crime rates and its likelihood of implementing sanctuary policies from affecting the study's results. When they compared crime rates in the matched cities, the investigators found no differences between the two pairs. They concluded, again, that sanctuary policies in cities had no positive or negative impact on cities' rates of crime.

Welfare Benefits

In public debates in many countries in the global north people express fear that immigrants will be more likely than natives to be dependent upon welfare benefits. To conservative critics, in particular, their "freeloading" will jeopardize the benefits of the citizenry who were originally intended to be the beneficiaries. The central question that researchers have addressed is whether immigrants rely upon welfare more than natives.

There are a number of potentially confounding variables that are related to how much immigrants and natives are seen to benefit from welfare, and studies have not typically been able to take all of these variables into account. The potentially most important of these confounding variables include: immigrants' demographic composition (e.g. age and sex distribution, education and income levels); types of welfare benefits examined in the research (e.g. old-age, unemployment, dependent children); the generosity of destination nations' different types of benefits; the destination nation(s) included in the sample. To illustrate how these variables can confound an analysis consider the potential effect of a compositional variable such as educational level. If immigrants have less formal education than natives they may, as a result, have a higher propensity to apply for certain types of welfare assistance. A higher level of education would have the opposite effect.

There have been a number of studies addressing the welfare question conducted in both Europe and the U.S. By a small margin, the studies appear to suggest that immigrants tend to rely upon welfare less than natives, but the results have been mixed.[19] The primary cause of the variation in findings seems to be discrepancies in how the studies were conducted. One recent U.S. study attempted to take most of the potentially confounding variables into account, and in so doing helped to clarify why some of the differences in past findings occurred. The study covered a lengthy time period – 1995 to 2018 – which enabled the investigators also to note how macroeconomic fluctuations impacted immigrant and native welfare use.[20]

The investigators found that there was an elevated utilization by immigrants, compared to natives, of a variety of safety net programs. However, when they statistically adjusted the characteristics of immigrants to match those of natives, the differences went in the opposite direction; that is, with the same characteristics, immigrants would have relied less upon welfare than natives. (The higher proportion of immigrants with high school degrees or less was particularly relevant here.) They also found that immigrants were more sensitive than natives to periods of recession, so studies that were conducted during economic downturns in the U.S. (e.g. 2008–9) would have been more likely to find higher welfare use among immigrants.

Another study that attempted to take a number of potentially confounding variables into account was conducted by Igor Jakubiak, a demographer in Warsaw. Included in his sample were 17 European nations, each of which was analyzed separately, and data on immigrants' origin nations. Jakubiak also had extensive information regarding the composition of immigrant groups, including educational attainment, marital status, age, etc. Note that with this data set he was able, in his analyses, to take into account most of the potentially confounding variables.[21]

The overall conclusion that best fit all of the data was that immigrants were less likely than natives to rely upon welfare, and that when they did, they tended to receive lower benefits. This was the pattern in 13 of the 17 nations included in the sample. However, there were no differences between immigrants from EU nations and natives in three of the nations and in one – France – the immigrants received more welfare benefits than natives, especially when they were from non-EU nations. Most of the differences in welfare participation rates between immigrants from EU nations and natives were due to differences in their characteristics (age in particular) so if there had been no compositional differences their reliance on welfare would have been the same in both groups. There was one limited set of conditions in which immigrant reliance upon welfare did exceed that of natives in most of the 17 nations. When old-age benefits were excluded from the analysis – a type of welfare the non-EU immigrants did not often qualify for – then the non-EU immigrants in most of the nations relied more on welfare than EU immigrants or natives.

In sum, welfare dependence is seen to vary in relation to a number of highly specific variables including immigrants' country of origin, age and other compositional variables, destination nation and types of welfare benefits. That variability could certainly account for many of the differences in the results reported by previous studies. Nevertheless, transcending these variations is the over-riding generalization that differences between immigrants and natives in welfare reliance are small, but that where there are differences, immigrants probably tend to be less welfare reliant than natives.

Economic Impact: Low-Skill Workers

Critics of lenient immigration policies contend that an influx of immigrants will lead to increased competition for jobs, resulting in lower wages and/or fewer jobs for natives. Because most migration flows are dominated by low-skill workers – farm laborers, construction workers, domestic help, etc. – the immigration-fueled job and wage losses would be expected to be most acute among low-skill native workers. On the other hand, a large percentage of the less skilled migrants take jobs that are widely perceived to be dangerous, difficult or unpleasant. These are jobs that natives typically shun. If not for the migrants the fruit would simply not be picked, households would have to get by without domestic help, and so on; and there would be no loss of native employment or wages because natives are not interested in these jobs.

One recent and extensive study in the U.S. examined the wages of a large sample of full-time, private sector workers aged 25 to 65. Covering the time period between 1990 and 2015, investigators Lin and Weiss calculated the proportion of foreign-born persons in each state who could be classified as either low-skilled (because they had no more than high school education) or high-skilled (because they had completed at least some college).[22]

Their analysis found that an increased number of low-skilled immigrants in a state was associated with a small wage loss for low-skill, low-wage natives. The negative effect, the investigators surmised, was due either to an over-supply of labor because both natives and immigrants were seeking the same kind of work, or because that competition with immigrants squeezed natives into less competitive sectors of the economy where they suppressed wages in these areas. Similar results, that is, an influx of low-skill migrants leads to wage reductions for low-skill natives, have also been reported in studies in Mexico and Canada,[23] and in several Asian nations.[24]

It is also worth noting that in the U.S. study, increased numbers of foreign-born, low-skill workers were especially likely to increase competition for jobs among immigrants themselves, and the wages of low-skill immigrants were suppressed by the competition more than that of low-skill natives. Other studies conducted both in the U.S. and in several European nations also found that the strongest suppressing effect of low-skill immigrants was upon the wages of other immigrants like themselves.[25]

On the other hand, an influx of low-skill immigrants has been shown, in a number of nations, to have a positive effect on the wages of high-skill natives. The most frequently offered explanation for this effect stresses the complementary contributions that low-skill immigrants are able to make, and how they enhance the productivity of high-skill workers. For example, studies in Italy and the U.S. have found that low-skill immigrants provided household services, such as childcare and housekeeping. They lowered the cost of these services, enabling high-skill female workers to increase their workplace hours and productivity.[26] (Were these gains perhaps at the expense of native household workers?)

In addition, there are a number of studies that suggest a positive effect of low-skill immigrants on nations' economies. Especially when a nation's fertility rates are low and there is strong demand for labor that natives cannot adequately supply, an influx of low-skill migrants can lead to diverse benefits as well as overall economic growth (e.g. increased GDP).[27] New Zealand's seasonal worker program, originally introduced in Chapter 2, provides an interesting illustration of the potential benefits.

During the busy agricultural season, New Zealand admits a number of low-skill workers from nations in the global south. They are brought in to help meet the demand for agricultural labor that natives either cannot or will not meet. Some years this seasonal influx has displaced some native New Zealand workers from farms and orchards that were growing kiwi, grape and other products. However, there is some evidence that the added immigrant labor enabled farms to expand, later increasing the total number of jobs that were available in the agricultural field to both immigrants and natives. The immigrants' labor also led to improved grape harvests which later created more low-skill jobs in New Zealand's wine industry.[28]

Economic Impact: High-Skill Workers

Across many nations of the global north there has been an excess of demand over the supply of high-skill workers. Governments have responded by modifying their immigration policies to encourage more in-migration of qualified people. In Germany, to illustrate, officials stated in 2021 that they would like to recruit 400,000 skilled immigrants every year: from college professors to electricians. In order to facilitate that inflow, nations have lowered barriers to entry for high-skill workers, reduced immigration paperwork and promised permanent status to those who wanted it. Some have even offered subsidized housing and salary inducements.[29]

The implicit assumptions behind these recruitment efforts are that high-skill workers will make large contributions to a nation's economy and, because there is an acute shortage of such workers, an influx of high-skill immigrants will not adversely impact high-skill natives. The data supports their position. For example, the Lin and Weiss study in the U.S. found with respect to high-skill immigrants that an influx did not suppress the wages of high-skill natives. In fact, an increased number of either high or low-skill immigrants resulted in substantial wage gains for high-skill natives. In addition, while low-skill immigration led to depressed wages for low-skill natives, high-skill immigration led to wage gains for the low-skill natives, but their gains were smaller than those that accrued to high-skill natives. The wage increases that were associated with high-skill immigration may be due to the foreign capital that some bring with them or to their entrepreneurial contributions to a nation's economy, either of which produces income that could go to wage increases.[30]

The contributions of immigrant scientists, engineers and other researchers have been especially well researched. Primarily from studies in the U.S., but to a less extent from Germany and the U.K. as well, foreign-born PhD holders were found to have high rates of scientific publications, patenting of new ideas and the invention of breakthrough technologies. And they were found to be about twice as likely as natives to form new engineering and technology firms. Their innovations and entrepreneurship obviously have strong positive effects upon national economies.[31]

The recruitment of many highly skilled professionals often begins by attracting students to a nation's graduate programs. Foreign, or international, students comprise a large percentage of all students enrolled in the post-graduate programs of many of the leading destination nations. And the more advanced the academic program, the higher the typical percentage of foreign students. Specifically, in six of the eight leading destination nations, there was a higher percentage of foreign students in Doctoral than in Master's programs. From data collected between 2016 and 2018, Table 8.1 shows the percentage of all Master's and Doctoral graduate students who came from another country and are enrolled in academic programs in the nations with the largest numbers of international students.[32]

Foreign students make a number of contributions to the nations in which they receive academic training. To begin, especially in scientific fields, in many nations of the global north there is a shortage of native professors so foreign students increase the demand for foreign-trained faculty. After completing their degrees, many of these highly skilled students remain in the country in which they earned their degrees where they are then well-positioned to contribute to local economies and the nation's GDP.[33]

Table 8.1 Foreign Students in Graduate Programs

Nation	Total International Students (Rank)	% Foreign Students in Programs at	
		Master's Level	Doctoral Level
Australia	3	46	34
Canada	7	18	32
France	5*	13	40
Germany	5*	13	9
Japan	8	7	18
Russia	4	4	5
U.K.	2	36	43
U.S.	1	10	40

Note
* These nations are tied in number of foreign students enrolled.

In sum, immigration appears to have mixed consequences for natives in the labor force. Low-skill immigration suppresses the earnings of low-skill natives while both low and high-skill natives benefit from high-skill immigration. High-skill immigrants also make positive contributions to the host nation's economy.

Community Effects

Beginning in the last decades of the 20th century and continuing to the present, millions of refugees to the U.S. have been settling in smaller cities, suburban and rural areas. This represented a marked departure from historical patterns in which most immigrants settled in major urban centers, often in close proximity to co-ethnics and other immigrants. In these smaller towns, by contrast, the refugees are typically located in the midst of a native population from whom they are very different with respect to race, religion, language and dress. The initial reception of the refugees has been mixed, with some natives fearing that these different strangers will take their jobs and ruin their neighborhoods.

The small city of Missoula, Montana, for example, in 2016 became a resettlement destination for refugees from Congo, Iraq and Syria. Right before they arrived, over 100 people rallied outside Missoula's courthouse to protest. They carried signs with messages such as, "Refugees or Terrorists?" and "They rape, kill, destroy." During the summer of 2017 Lauren Fritzsche spent several months interviewing and observing the refugees, native residents and government officials. She and Lise Nelson later concluded that the Syrians, who were Muslims, were the primary targets of the native's distrust. One local native explained that the distrust was because they believed the Muslims did not understand American culture. "All they know is what they come from." Another resident focused upon their fear of Muslims. "There are things that I hear that frighten me about … this particular group of people … and I want to preserve my society."[34]

(There were also a lot of Missoula residents, who were more cosmopolitan and multicultural in their outlooks, who went out of their way to welcome the newcomers.)

In most of the small cities in which refugees have been settled, the newcomers have economically integrated. In Missoula, the refugees almost immediately began to develop business skills, selling homemade foods, such as injera (flatbread) and Iraqi baklava, at the local farmer's market. Over time, many of the small town immigrants have also politically integrated. In several small cities in mostly rural areas of Arkansas, for example, in 2020 the first Latino and the first Indian American were elected to their City Councils.[35] In order to provide a wider overview, geographer Pablo Bose interviewed over 250 mayors, resettlement officials and city managers in smaller U.S. cities and towns. He asked them to assess the effects of the immigrant influx. A sample of their responses is presented in Box 8.2.

Box 8.2 Refugees in Small Cities[36]

Of special concern to Bose was how refugees were adjusting to life in small cities and towns where they were typically marked as racially, religiously and/or ethnically very different from the native population. How did the refugees adjust to life in these places, and how did natives come to view them over time? One of the main themes that the officials he interviewed stressed concerned how the refugees had been drivers of urban renewal. With respect to housing, one informant offered an assessment that many others echoed.

> "Our recent refugees have ... had a lot of home purchases ... And they fix up these homes, they really fix up the whole street."

The newcomers typically moved into the worst parts of town, areas that had been loosing residents and had deteriorated. They helped to reverse the downward trend:

> "When the refugees first start coming, X avenue was pretty run down. But they moved into it and they really fixed it up."

Most of these smaller cities had been losing population and businesses, and were eager to attract newcomers, even if they were refugees. As one put it:

> "I don't care where we get people from ... Syria ... Africa ... Mexico ... We're losing people ... they're all moving out and I am afariad there'll be more empty houses and boarded up businesses ... I'll take who'll make my city look lived in again."

Businesses as well as people had left the areas into which the refugees settled. The newcomers were also viewed as having given these areas a commercial boost.

> "We have quite a few ethnic restaurants grocery stores, and ... other businesses ... We have increased the tax base, economically ... It's a big part of how we make the neighborhood ... which was kind of falling apart, come back to life."

To Change Misconceptions

The literature reviewed here has shown some consistent discrepancies between the characteristics popularly attributed to the immigrant population and their characteristics as described by carefully done research. And these incorrect perceptions have been associated with antagonism to immigrants. Some investigators have taken their research a step further and designed studies from which they could infer the conditions under which people's perceptions of immigrants could be changed. One specific issue that has received a lot of study concerns people's misconceptions about the size of the immigrant population.

Perceptions of Size

A pattern that has been observed in a number of nations is for an increased foreign inflow to be associated with increased hostility toward immigrants. This relationship is most pronounced in global north nations when the migrant inflow is from the global south (which is the dominant pattern). A number of social scientists including sociologist Christian Czymara have interpreted this relationship as due to various perceived threats, including the risk of increased crime, concern that there will be an economic cost of supporting refugees and the threat that foreigners pose to the continuation of traditional culture.

Using data from the European Social Survey, he examined hostility toward refugees across a large sample of European nations. The long-term differences among nations, which tended to be stable, did not explain more recent changes in nations' attitudes nearly as well as recent changes in the number of in-migrants to a nation. For example, the increased foreign-born population in Germany and Sweden was significantly associated with contemporaneous increases in those nations' hostility to foreigners, despite their historically relative openness to in-migrants.[37]

There is also a widespread tendency for natives to exaggerate the size of the foreign-born population in their nation, and to correspondingly exaggerate the threat they pose. This has led a number of social scientists to conduct experiments to see if they could alleviate those size misconceptions and thereby reduce hostility to immigrants. In the U.S., political scientist Daniel Hopkins and associates have found that providing subjects with accurate information about the size of the foreign-born population does lead them to reduce the magnitude of their size over-estimation; but it leads to only a trivial reduction in their unfavorable attitudes. Perhaps, the investigators concluded, people's negative attitudes are a cause rather than a consequence of their magnified perception of the size of the immigrant population.[38] In other words, it may be hostility to foreigners that leads people to over-estimate their size, and not vice versa. Correcting their size misconceptions would not, under these conditions, be expected to reduce their unfavorable attitudes.

Leading political figures in the U.S. and elsewhere have encouraged the public to believe that the size of immigrant groups is larger than it actually is, and therefore, poses a greater threat. The officials have advocated policies and regulations based more upon racism and nationalism than upon any empirical evidence. This has led some social scientists to argue that these immigration policies are "fact-free," as described in Box 8.3.

Box 8.3   The U.S.'s Fact-Free Immigration Policy

The Mexican Migration Project (MMP), introduced in Chapter 4, contains information concerning over 175,000 individuals from a sample of 170 representative Mexican communities. In addition to providing basic demographic characteristics, household heads describe migration histories for themselves and their spouses in detail. One primary purpose of MMP is to provide detailed and unbiased data on Mexico's documented and undocumented migration to the U.S. The reliability of its data has been attested to by a number of professional associations, and it has been used in hundreds of published migration studies.

MMP data are made available to everyone – and yet the directors of MMP have noted that U.S. immigration policy toward Mexico remains "disconnected from reality" and involves a "willful denial of facts and evidence."[39] They have offered a number of examples, including the following:

1   In 2018 then President Trump demanded millions of dollars to build a border wall to keep what he described as dramatically increased numbers of undocumented Mexicans from entering the country. In fact, however, MMP data indicated that between 2007 and 2018 more undocumented

Mexicans *left* the U.S. than arrived, and border apprehensions at this time were at their lowest level in nearly 50 years.
2   There was an enormous increase in funding for border patrols, but MMP data showed that it had no effect upon the number of undocumented Mexican who tried to cross the border or on the number who were apprehended at the border. The border patrol enhancements also had no effect upon the likelihood of undocumented migrants successfully crossing the border. Paradoxically, because it did make unauthorized border crossings more difficult, it led to a decline in rates of return migration, opposite to the policy's objectives.[40]

Changing Attitudes

At least with respect to native's exaggerated perceptions of the size of the immigrant population, the previously discussed Hopkins' study indicated that when people were presented with factual information that contradicted their perceptions that most people would adjust their incorrect perceptions accordingly. However, their antagonism to immigrants was hardly reduced by such specific factual adjustments. Should we then conclude that negative attitudes toward immigrants can hardly be changed by presenting people with factual information to correct their misconceptions?

A team of social scientists wondered whether the public's attitude toward immigration might change if people were presented not only with information to correct misconceptions about that population's size but also given information that accurately described other characteristics of the immigrant population. To begin, the investigators asked a sample of respondents how worried they were about immigration, assuming that to be very worried indicated a negative attitude toward immigrants. Next the investigators asked them to estimate various characteristics of the immigrant population, such as their unemployment and incarceration rates. Most of the study's subjects had exaggerated assumptions about these negative attributes.[41]

One group of subjects was given detailed, correct information about all of these immigrant characteristics, and the investigators found that these people updated their beliefs accordingly. Further, the changes in their perceptions had persisted to the last time that the respondents were re-questioned, one month later. Of special significance, these changes in perception were associated with the respondents' more positive views on immigration. A second set of subjects was given correct information about the size of immigrant groups, but not their other characteristics. The analysis of this set of respondents indicated, as in Hopkins' study, that correcting size misconceptions alone did not have much effect upon respondents attitude toward immigrants. So, it may be that many of people's assumptions must be simultaneously challenged for people's negative attitudes toward immigrants to change.

International sport has in recent years provided a highly visible realm in which many immigrants have excelled and that may be one area in which the racism, nationalism and xenophobia that produce hostility to immigrants can be reduced. A dramatic example is provided by the way the star Egyptian football (soccer) player on the Liverpool team has helped to break down negative stereotypes. It is discussed in Box 8.4.

> **Box 8.4 Egyptian Soccer Player in Liverpool Changes Attitudes**
>
> Mo Salah is an Egyptian and a Muslim who is also considered one of the best football players in the world. He is the star of the Liverpool team. After scoring a goal, which he often does, he regularly celebrates by dropping to his knees and touching his forehead to the ground in an Islamic prayer position. The predominantly British (and non-Muslim) fans in the Liverpool stadium have embraced Salah, both as a soccer player and as a Muslim. They regularly respond to Salah's mode of celebrating by chanting, "If he scores another few, then I'll be Muslim too."[42]
>
> Hate crimes, especially involving Muslim victims, had generally been increasing across the UK, Liverpool included, since the World Trade Center bombings in New York in 2001. After Salah signed with Liverpool FC in 2017, however, hate crimes in and around Liverpool declined by about 19% according to police reports. A group of political scientists further analyzed the police figures and reported that the decline in hate crimes was larger in Liverpool than in other areas of Britain. The investigators also conducted a survey in the Liverpool area and found that fans of the Liverpool team had reduced by one-half the number of anti-Muslim tweets that they posted. They also found that the soccer star had broken down the fans' previously held stereotypes of Muslims as "threatening" figures Perhaps most noteworthy, among fans of the team there was a significant increase in the proportion of people who believed that Islam was compatible with British values.[43]

Notes

1 For an overview, see Neeraj Kaushal, *Blaming Immigrants*. Columbia University, 2019.
2 For a history of xenophobia in the U.S., see Erika Lee, *America for Americans*. Basic Books, 2019.
3 Sivamohan Valluvan, *The Clamour of Nationalism*. Manchester University, 2019.
4 See the relevant essays in David C. Bretherton and Philip Kretsedemas (Eds), *Immigration Policy in an Age of Punishment*. Columbia University, 2018.
5 Nicolas Ajzenman, Patricio Dominguez and Raimundo Undurraga, "Immigration, Crime, and Crime (Mis)Perceptions." *IZA Discussion Paper Series*, January, 2021.
6 See the review of studies in Catalina Amuedo-Dorantes, Cynthia Bansak and Susan Pozo, "Refugee admissions and public safety." *International Migration Review*, 55, 2021.
7 For further discussion, see Arjen Leerkes, Ramiro Martinez and Pim Groeneveld, "Minority Paradoxes." *British Journal of Criminology*, 59, 2019.
8 Martin A. Andresen and Olivia K. Ha, "Spatially varying relationships between immigration measures and property crime types In Vancouver census tracts." *British Journal of Criminology*, 60. 2020.
9 For a discussion of these methodological differences, see Graham C. Ousey and Charis E. Kubrin, "Immigration and Crime." *Annual Review of Criminology*, 1, 2018; and Michael Clemens, et al., *Migration Is What You Make It*. Center for Global Development, May, 2018.
10 Ibid.
11 Michael T. Light, Jingying He and Jason P. Robey, "Comparing crime rates between undocumented immigrants, legal immigrants, and native-born US citizens in Texas." *Proceedings of the National Academy of Sciences*, December, 2020. On the positive side, this study had particularly complete data on immigrant status, however it was confined to the state of Texas, with its distinctive immigration profile.

12 American Immigration Council Fact Sheet, "Aggrevated Felonies: An Overview." March 16, 2021.
13 For a review of studies conducted in several nations with a focus upon how immigration policies affect crime, see Fransesco Fasani, et al., *Does Immigration Increase Crime?* Cambridge University, 2019.
14 For further discussion, see Loren Collingwood and Benjamin G. O'Brien, *Sanctuary Cities*. Oxford University, 2019.
15 David Kaufmann, et al., "Sanctuary Cities in Europe." *British Journal of Political Science*, (letter), June, 2021.
16 Center for Immigration Studies, "Sanctuary Cities." November, 2018.
17 There is a summary of this research in American Immigration Council, "Sanctuary Policies." October, 2020.
18 Benjamin Gonzalez O'Brien, Loren Collingwood and Stephen Omar El-Khatib, "The politics of refuge." *Urban Affairs Review*, 55, 2019.
19 For a review of studies in the U.S., see Tim O'Shea and Cristobal Ramon, "Immigrants and Public Benefits." *Bipartisan Policy Center*, November, 2018; for Europe, see Antonio Conte and Jacopo Mazza, Migrants and Welfare Dependency. *JRC Technical Reports*, 2019.
20 Xiaoning Huang, Keeraj Kaushal and Julia She-Huah Wang, "What explains the gap in welfare use among immigrants and natives?" *Population Research and Policy Review*, 40, 2021.
21 Igor Jakubiak, "Are Migrants Overrepresented Among Individual Welfare Beneficiaries?" *International Migration*, 58, 2020.
22 Ken-Hou Lin and Inbar Weiss, "Immigrants and the Wage Distribution in the United States." *Demography*, 56, 2020.
23 Abdurrahman Aydemir and George J. Borjas, "Cross-country variation in the impact of international migration." *Journal of the European Economic Association*, 5, 2007.
24 See the review in, Eric Fong and Kumiko Ahibuya, "Migration patterns in East and Southeast Asia." *Annual Review of Sociology*, 46, 2020. Annual.
25 Giovanni Peri, "Immigrants, productivity, and labor markets." *Journal of Economic Perspectives*, 30, 2016.
26 For a review of these studies, see Marie McAuliffe and Adrian Kitimbo, "Reflections on Migrant's Contributions." Chapter 5 in, *UN World Migration Report 2020*.
27 Ibid.
28 John Gibson and David McKenzie, "Development through Seasonal Worker Programs." In Robert E. Lucas (Ed), *International Handbook on Migration and Economic Development*. Edward Elgar, 2015.
29 Parag Khanna, *Move*. Scribner's, 2021.
30 Lin and Weiss, op.cit.
31 See Max Nathan, "Ethnic diversity and business performance." Environment and Planning A, 48, 2016; and McAuliffe and Kitimbo, op.cit.
32 Figures from, OECD, *2019 International Migration and Displacement Trends*.
33 Peri, op.cit.
34 Description of Missoula and quotations are from, Lauren Fritzsche and Lise Nelson, "Refugee resettlement, place, and the politics of Islamophobia." *Social & Cultural Geography*, 21, 2020.
35 Miriam Jordan, "Immigration Decline and Some Regions Sputter." *The New York Times*, August 11, 2021, p A16.
36 All of the following quotes are from, Pablo Shiladitya Bose, "Refugees and the transforming landscapes of small cities in the U.S." *Urban Geography*, 1, 2020.
37 Christian S. Czymara, "Attitudes toward refugees in contemporary Europe." *Social Forces*, 99, 2020.
38 Daniel J. Hopkins, John Sides, and Jack Citrin, "The Muted consequences of correct information about immigration." *The Journal of Politics*, 81, 2019.
39 Jorge Durand and Douglas S. Massey, "Debacles on the border." *ANNALS of the American Academy of Political and Social Science*, 684, 2019.
40 It had previously been common for undocumented Mexicans to cross the border surreptitiously, work for a period of time, return home, then repeat the cycle. But the pattern was interrupted by the cost and risk of returning to the U.S.
41 Alexis Grigorieff, Christopher Roth and Diego Ubfal, "Does information change attitudes toward immigrants?" *Demography*, 57, 2020.
42 Kate Whiting, "How Mo Salah may have reduced Islamophobia in Liverpool." *World Economic Forum*, June, 2019.
43 Ala' Alrababa'h, et al., "Can Exposure to Celebrities Reduce Prejudice?" *Stanford University Immigration Policy Lab,* Working Paper, 2019.

Glossary

American Community Survey (ACS)   Conducted annually by the U.S. Census Bureau, it provides extensive data on specific communities, and is used to describe the nation.
Arranged Marriage   Families or paid agencies select mates and set up marriages with the couple involved having varying influence over the decisions.
Chain Migration   A stream of migrants, comprised of families or friends, that share the same origin and destination.
Chain Multiplier   The increase in a nation's migrants due to family reunification policies that permit other family members to follow an initial immigrant.
Churning   When a migrant keeps changing one low-paying job for another.
Culture   Involves people's social institutions and their values, norms and technology. Their language is sometimes utilized as a specific indicator.
Cumulative Causation   The tendency for rates of emigration to continue in a self-sustaining process.
Emigrate   Refers to people who leave a country; the out-flow.
Enclaves   Community with a distinctive racial or ethnic composition whose specialized needs are served by co-ethnic-run establishments.
Endogamy   Marriages between persons from within the same group.
Ethnoburb   Suburban areas with diverse populations and one predominant ethnic-racial group that maintains cross-national business connections.
Exiles   Migrants who usually left their homelands for political or religious reasons with a continuing commitment to return. Also used to refer to migrants' separation from their home, as "in exile."
Exogamy   Marriages involving people from two different ethnic-racial groups.
Expatriate, *or Expat*   Very similar to exiles, and they typically retain citizenship in the nation they left.
Foreign Student   A non-citizen who is enrolled in formal degree program.
Ghettos   Communities with concentrated numbers of predominantly poor members of a minority group, usually with high rates of school drop-outs, non-marital births and crime.
Global North   Contains nations that are wealthy and, for the most part, politically stable. Most are in Europe and North America.
Global South   Contains nations that are poor and often politically unstable. Many were former colonies.

Homogamy People's tendency to marry others whose social characteristics are similar to their own.
Immigration Multiplier When citizens sponsor the in-migration of other family members, thereby increasing the total number of immigrants.
Immigrant Optimism Paradox The discrepancy between immigrants' aspirations and their likely attainments.
Index of Dissimilarity Measures segregation by calculating the percentage of one group that would have to move for two groups to have the same residential distribution.
Informal Economy Transactions involving low-earning workers, paid in cash, not recorded in official records.
International Labor Organization (ILO) A specialized agency of the UN that assembles data on migrant workers.
International Organization for Migration (IOM) An agency that compiles migration statistics and regulations and provides various services.
Internationally Mobile Student Anyone who moves to a different nation to pursue educational activities.
Macro Analysis Focuses upon large in scale social structures and processes, with little attention to individual agency.
Marriage Migration The movement of one spouse to the country of the other, when the other spouse is a citizen or legal resident.
Marriage of Convenience When the desire of a spouse to move to the other spouse's nation is an important motive in marrying.
Medical Tourism When people travel from their home country to seek medical care; it is typically combined with conventional tourist activities.
Meso Analysis Intermediate to macro and micro, it tends to focus upon individuals in relationship networks.
Mexican Migration Project (MMP) An ongoing survey in Mexican towns and cities that focuses upon out-migration to the U.S.
Micro Analysis Focuses upon individuals in small groups or in small geographical areas.
Migrants People who move to a country other than the one in which they usually resided, and remain for at least three months.
Migrant Workers People who are currently employed, or seeking employment, other than the one in which they hold citizenship.
New Immigrant Survey (NIS) Conducted in 2003, it rated the skin tone of U.S. immigrants and obtained data on their occupations.
Organization for Economic Cooperation and Development (OECD) A voluntary organization of 37 mostly economically advanced nations.
Purchasing Price Parity (PPP) The cost of a basic package of goods in relation to average hourly earnings.
Refugees Migrants who were in peril and were forced to flee the country in which they had been residing.
Reintegration The process of establishing new roles and relationships when migrants return to their origin nation.
Relative Deprivation Emphasizes that people evaluate their situations relative to that of others.

Remittances Funds sent by migrants back to family members in their origin nation.

Residual Method Estimates the undocumented population by subtracting the legally resident foreign-born in a nation from the nation's total foreign-born population.

Sanctuary Cities Provide benefits to and enact protections for undocumented immigrants living in their boundaries.

Segmented Assimilation When some members of an immigrant community integrate into a non-mainstream group, often resulting in little upward mobility.

Selective Assimilation When immigrants integrate in some aspects of the destination society while retaining commitments to some parts of their origin nation.

Selectivity Involves the way people who migrate self-select in terms of education, occupation, motivation, etc.

Sex Tourism When a sexual fling is expected to be part of the tourist experience. Also referred to as romance tourism.

Social Integration The degree to which an immigrant group's socioeconomic attainments converge with natives; their degree of spatial segregation; and their adoption of the nation's culture and language.

Socioeconomic Status (SES) People's standing in a social hierarchy, typically indicated by educational level and/or occupational status.

Stepwise Migration Describes the tendency for migrants to move to several different destination nations. (Also referred to as serial migration.)

Trafficking *(or Human Trafficking)* Recruiting and moving people when coercion or deception is involved.

Transnational Corporations (TNCs) Enterprises with facilities in countries other than the one in which they are headquartered.

Transnational Professionals Credentialed specialists who move often between projects in different nations.

Undocumented Migrants Migrants who lack legal status in their current country of residence. Also referred to as "irregular" migrants.

United Nations High Commissioner for Refugees *(UNCHR)* Collects data on, and provides emergency services for, refugees.

Xenophobia Hostility toward foreigners.

Index

Abdelhady, D. 124, 141n16
Abdurrahman, A. 175n23
Abel, G. 65, 67n54
Abrahamson, M. 161n27
Abramitzky, R. 161n24
Abreu, A. 35, 46n31
Aburn, A. 47n56
Adachi, N. 92n5
Adaptation 65–67
Adelman, R. 115n6
Adler, G. 21, 25n77
Adsera, A. 92n6; African-American 148–149
Agadjanian, V. 64, 69n53
Ager, A. 118, 141n3
Aggarwal, P. 69n57
Ahibuya, K. 175n24
Ahmed, S. 93n53
Ahrens, J. 93n33
Ajzenman, N. 174n5
Akay, A.O. 47n56
Alarian, H.M. 139, 143n67
Alba, R. 141n2
Albeck-Ripka, L. 116n26
Alpes, M.J. 116n40
Alrabab'h, A. 175n43
Ambinakudige, S. 142n40
American Community Survey 97–99
Aminuddin, M.F. 93n45
Amuedo-Dorantes, C. 174n6; and migration 2–4
Andersson, H. 160n18
Andersson, R. 160n17
Andresen, M. 163, 174n8
Apatinga, G.A. 93n38
Arcaya, M. 68n38
Armenta, A. 115n4, 117n64, 117n69
Arrendordo, J. 116n16
Arsari, S. 160n21
Arviv, T. 143n60
Asad, A.L. 117n17
Ashenfelter, O. 36–7, 47n36, 47n37
Askola, H. 143n66
aspirations 31–33, 44, 87–89
Atos, M. 69n56

Ayedemir, A. 175n23
Aysa-Lastra, M. 87, 93n37, 93n55

Bach, H. 23n22, 67n2
Back, L. 96, 115n5
Bakewell, O. 46n4, 92n23
Bakker, L. 143n70
Ballarino, G. 125, 141n21
Bansak, C. 174n6
Barry, E. 160n16
Beech, H. 160n3
Beine, M. 53, 67n18
Belanger, D. 24n66
Belot, M. 73, 74, 92n11
Berlemann, H. 68n19
Bernardi, L. 142n46
Bernzen, A. 68n46
Berry, J.W. 141n1
Beynon, D. 161n32
Bhai, M. 47n60
Biden, Joe 104–105
Bigwaard, G. 94n61
Bilsborrow, R. 68n27
Bloom, D.E. 34, 46n24
Borjas, G.J. 37, 47n38, 175n23
Borrelli, L.M. 117n73
Bose, P. S. 170, 175n36
Boterman, W.R. 142n41
Boustan, L. 161n24
Bowen, A. 47n57
Boyce, G.A. 117n75
Braun, B. 68n46
Bretherton, D.C. 174n4
Brettell, C. 24n66, 24n71, 82, 93n35
Brzozowski, J. 47n50
Burgess, E. 128, 142n32, 160n7

Caldwell, B.C. 117n76
Campbell, D.T. 39, 47n42
Campbell, I. 47n53
Campos-Vazquez, R. 142n30
Cao, S. 93n49
Capoferro, C. 98, 116n11

Index

Carbone, J. 142n44
Carling, J. 46n16, 92n23
Caron, L. 89–90, 94n68, 94n69
Carrillo, H. 76–77, 92n17
Castanada, H. 115n7
Castaneda, E. 160n13
Castle, S. 23n7, 23n8
Catron, P. 121, 124, 141n9, 141n18
Cattaneo, C. 54, 68n20, 68n29
Cebolla-Boada, H. 45, 47n62, 141n12
Ceccarelli, D. 92n15
Cervantes, A.G. 126–127, 142n27
chain migration 75–80
chain multiplier 78
Chapman, A. 145–146, 160n4
Charmes, J. 24n37
Chen, J.J. 67n13, 68n24, 68n26
Chicago School 128–129
Chihaya, G.H. 129, 142n37
Choi, C. 24n57
Choi, S. 123, 141n14
Christou, A. 90, 94n65
churning 99–100
Citrin, J. 175n38
civic conflict 64–65
Clark, K. 141n19
Clemens, M. 30, 33, 46n13, 46n29, 46n33
Clemons, M. 174n9
Clibborn, S. 23n25
Cohen, P. 160n1
Cohn, D. 116n13
Cohn, N. 142n44
Collingwood, L. 165, 175n14, 175n18
competition for jobs 167–170
Connor, D. 161n24
Connor, P. 115n8, 116n17, 116n18
Conte, A. 175n19
Cook, T.D. 39, 47n42
Cook-Martin, D. 115n3
Cooney, T.M. 161n28
Corrales, J. 46n6
Cortes, P. 93n44
Cosson, C. 69n59
Coulter, K. 116n32
Crawley, H. 82, 93n34
Creighton, M.J. 46n16
Crime rates 163–166
culture 70–75, 132–135
cumulative causation 41, 78–80
Current, G.B. 24n52
Curtis, K.J. 68n34
Czymara, C. 171n37

Dahir, A.L. 116n38
Dao, T.H. 33, 46n21
Davadson, R. 23n24
Davidoff, E. 125, 141n22

de Haas, H. 46n3
De Valk, H.A. 47n40
Deichmann, U. 68n28
DeJong, P.W. 37–38, 47n40
DeParle, J. 93n50
deportation 114–115
Desai, S. 115n6
Dettridge, M. 117n43
DeWaard, J. 68n34
dispersal policies 150–152
DisSkaptadottir, U. 143n64; distances between 73–74, 132–135
Dizon, A.R. 141n23
Docquler, F. 73, 92n2
Dominguez, P. 174n5; downward mobility 43–44
Dramski, P. 47n60
Drouhot, L.G. 141n7
Duncan, B. 142n39
Duncan, O.D. 142n39
Duneier, M. 147–148m
Durand, J. 92n24, 116n12, 175n39

Ederveen, S. 73–74, 92n9, 92n11
Eksner, H.J. 160n14
Elejalde-Ruiz, A. 47n57
El-Khatib, S.O. 165, 175n18
Emont, J. 93n51
enclaves 151–156
Engzell, P. 47n55, 123, 141n15
entrepreneurship 153–156
Entwisle, B. 54, 68n21, 90, 92n18, 94n64
Erdal, M.B. 87, 94n58
Erdel, M. 23n34
Ermisch, J. 93n28
Eroglu, S. 46n32
ethnoburbs 156–160
Eurenius, A.M. 46n18
Eurenius, A.M. 77–78, 92n19; European 149–150
exiles 12–13
expatriate 13

family migration 15–16
Farrell-Bryan, D. 142n36
Fasani, F. 175n13
fast-onset events 48–53
Feliciano, C. 39, 40, 47n45
Feng, E. 175n24
Fernandez, N.T. 24n69, 24n70, 24n72
Fernandez-Reino, M. 47n61
Ferriera, C.M. 46n25
Fink, D. 23n19
Fitzgerald, D.S. 143n61
Flahaux, M.L. 91, 96n70
Flippen, C.A. 142n36
Foner, N. 141n2

Fong, E. 93n39, 93n42
forced marriage 110; *see also* sexual exploitation
Ford, K. 69n52
foreign students 14–15, 169–170
Fritzsche, L. 175n34
Fullmeth, G. 93n43
Fussell, E. 59, 68n34, 68n36, 79, 92b22, 92n25

Galster, G. 160n17
Gao-Miles, L.L. 161n31, 161n33
Garcia, A.S. 24n47
Geiger, M. 24n43
Georgi, F. 24n43
ghettos 146–151, 155–156
Ghimire, D. 93n46
Gibson, J. 36, 42, 47n34, 47n54, 175n29
Gignoux, J. 68n40
Gillespie, B.J. 80, 93n29
Giralt, R.M. 93n32
Glaser, S.M. 64, 69n51
Glennon, R. 68n23
Global North 16, 24n61, 49, 53, 58–60, 82
Global South 16, 24n61, 49, 53–59, 82
globalization 1–4
Gonzales, D. 116n16
Gonzales-Ferrer, A. 142n51, 142n51, 142n59
Goodwin-White, J. 124, 141n20
Gorina, E. 64, 69n53
Graham, E. 93n40
Gray, C.L. 52, 67n16, 68n24, 68n27
Greenman, E. 141n8
Greve, A. 94n63
Grigorieff, A. 175n41
Groeneveld, G. 174n7
Guercini, S. 92n15
Guichard, L. 40, 47n49
Gutierrez, J. 67n2

Ha, O.K. 163n8
Haemmerli, G. 24n66
Hagan, J.M. 94n67, 94n71, 115n1
Hak, S. 116n27
Hall, M. 116n15
Hamilton, C. 24n68
Han, J.H. 126, 141n25
Han, X. 24n56
Hannemann, T. 142n47, 142n48
Harrington, B. 23n28
Hartmann, B. 67n6
Hartnett, L.A. 24n48
Haver, M.E. 68n35
Hayes, M. 25n80
Haynes, B.D. 160n13
He, J. 174n11
Healy, J. 23n18, 23n20, 23n21
Heath, A. 122, 124, 141n11, 141n17
Hedstrom, P. 46n10

Heineman, E.D. 143n55
Henderson, J.V. 68n28
Hendrix, C.S. 64n51
Henroth-Rothstein, A. 24n51
Hersch, J. 126–127, 141n26,141n28
Heslin, A. 67n10
high skill workers 6–7
Hobbs, A. 12, 24n46
Hofstede, G. 92n3
Hollified, J.F. 46n1
Holloway, S.R. 68n35
Holtgraves, T.M. 92n4
Hooper, K. 24n58
Hopkins, D. 172–173, 175n38
Huang, X. 175n20
Huennekens, J.M. 117n58
Hutchinson, R. 160n13

Icduygu, A. 116n39
Ichou, M. 47n55, 94n68
Ietto-Gillies, G. 23n3
immigrant generation defined 89–90
immigrant optimism paradox 44, 122–124
index of dissimilarity 129–131
intermarriage 131–137
international migrants defined 3
inverted U 32–33
Issar, S. 68n37

Jablonski, N.G. 141n23
Jakubiak, I. 166–167, 175n21
Jampaklay, A. 64, 69n52
Jang, H. 117n57
Jefferson, A.M. 160n5
Jenkins, C. 68n46
Jensen, S. 160n5; Jewish 146–148, 155
Jones, K. 82, 93n34
Jordan, M. 166n30, 116n31, 175n35
Jordan, M. 46n28, 46n29
Jung, H.K. 117n57

Kabo-bah, A. T. 68n43
Kakar, M.M. 117n54
Kalleberg, A. 161n23
Kang, S.J. 93n49
Kaplan, E. 116n33
Karabell, Z. 23n6
Karasaapan, O. 24n38
Kashima, Y. 92n4
Kashimo, E. 92n4
Kaufmann, D. 175n15
Kaushal, K. 174n1, 175n20
Kelly, M. 93n33
Kelman, I. 67n3
Khana, P. 175n29
Kidd, E. 92n4
Kim, C.H. 142n27

Kim, K. 123, 141n14
King, J.C. 143n59
King, R. 90, 94n65
Kitimbo, A. 175n26
Kitroeff, N. 68n30
Klineberg, E. 69n56
Kolbel, A. 23n9
Koslov, U. 69n56
Kramer-Mbula, E. 24n37
Kretschmer, D. 46n32
Kretsedemas, P. 174n4
Kreyenfeld, M. 143n56
Kristjansdottir, E.S. 143n64
Krogstad, J.M. 116n17
Kubrin, C.E. 164n8
Kulu, H. 135, 142n51
Kvasnicka, M. 143n55
Kwok-bun, C. 94n63

Laczko, F. 116n21; language as proxy 71–72
language, measures of 72
Launius, S. 117n75
Lee, E. 174n2
Lee, E. 46n15
Lee, H.K. 94n66
Lee, J. 137, 143n60
Leerkes, A. 174n7
Leghtas, I. 24n39
Levy, B.S. 69n50
Li, W. 156–157, 161n29, 161n34
Liang, Z. 161n25
Lichter, D.T. 137, 142n40, 142n42, 142n45, 142n50, 142n54
Lieberson, S. 39, 47n43
Light, I. 79–80, 93n27
Light, M. 164, 174n11
Lin, K-H. 167, 175n22, 175n30
Lindstrom, D.P. 47n51, 47n58
linguistic distance 74–75, 134
Liu, C.C. 46n11
Liu, M-M. 92n21
Lo, L. 152, 161n21
Logan, J. 59–60, 68n37
Long, K. 46n4
low skill workers 8
Lucas, R.E. 47n34, 175n28
Lucht, H. 68n42, 68n45
Lunt, N. 25n79
Lustgarten, A. 67n5, 67n6
Lutz, A. 124, 141n16

Mach, K. 64, 69n49
Mach, K.J. 69n49
Machen, J. 116n25
macro theories 26–19, 32–33, 46n1, 70
Madison, A. 22n2
Manglos-Weber, N.D. 140, 143n68

Manting, D. 142n41
Marcuse, P. 160n18
marriage markets 132, 136
marriage migration 16–18
Martin, J.A. 126, 141n24
Martinez, B.P. 161n23
Martinez, R. 174n7
Martinez-Aranda, M.G. 117n67
Marx, M. 46n11
Maskileyson, D. 125, 141n22
Massey, D. 41, 46n, 23n26, 79, 92n13, 92n22, 93n24, 98, 116n11, 126, 141n24, 142n33, 175n39
Matsumoto, N. 161n30
Mayer, C.E. 160n15
Mazza, J. 175n19
McAdam, J. 116n24
McAuliffe, M. 175n26
McAuliffe, M.I. 116n21, 126n41, 126n42
McAvay, H. 142n41
McDonald, J.S. 92n13
McDonald, L.D. 92n13
McKenzie, D. 175n28
McKenzie, D.M. 36, 47n34
McLeman, R. 68n33; measures of 70–71
Medina-Cortina, E. 142n30
melting pot 119
Menendez, M. 68n40
Mensa, C. 68n43
meso theories 34, 70
Mexican Migration Project 79, 98, 172–173
Meyer, F. 46n22
micro theories 29–31, 33, 70
Migali, S. 46n17
migrant selectivity 38–45; methodological issues 39–40; personality traits 44–45; socioeconomic status 40
migrant workers 4–6
migration stages 41
Mikai, I. 73, 92n8
Miraftab, F. 142n34
Mirdal, G.M. 93n57
Moinester, M. 117n63
Montenegro, C. 46n13
Moore, J.D. 92n1
Morad, M. 92n14
Mortey, E. 68n43
Mu, Z. 24n65
Muambasere, T.G. 143n69
Mueller, V. 52, 67n16, 68n24, 68n26
Mulder, C.H. 80, 93n29
Munshi 68n44
Musterd, S. 142n41, 160n17

Nathan, M. 175n31
NELM 34–35, 90
Nelson, L. 175n34

Neureiter, M. 138, 143n63, 143n67
New Immigrant Survey 126–127
Newland, K. 94n72
Nielsen, J. 117n74
Novo-Corti, I. 73, 92n8
Nurick, R. 116n27

Obeng, F.A. 93n38
Obokata, R. 68n33
O'Brien, B.G. 175n18
Oda, T. 68n35
Oeppen, C. 23n34
Omata, M. 94n59
Ormend, M. 25n78
Osaghae, O.G. 161n28
O'Shea, T. 175n19
Ousey, G.C. 164, 174n9

Paddock, R.C. 92n16
Palinkas, L.A. 67n11
Panichella, N. 125, 141n21
Parades-Orozco, G. 79, 93n26
Parisi, D. 142n40
Park, R.E. 128, 142n32, 160n7
Parker, S.W. 47n47
Parrenas, R. 111, 117n57
Parsons, C. 53, 67n18
Passel, J.S. 115n8, 116n13, 116n17, 116n18
Paul, A.M. 24n40, 81, 93n31
Pecoud, A. 24n43
Pedraza-Bailey, S. 161n22
Pellander, S. 24n64
Peltier, E. 67n9
Pena, R.P. 116n38
Penboom, B. 93n47
Peri, G. 54, 68n20, 175n25
Perkins, G. 47n46
Phillips, T. 46n7, 46n9
Piracha, M. 86, 93n54
Polavieja, J.G. 45, 47n61
Polek, E. 47n59
Ponce, A. 47n39
Portes, A. 120, 141n6, 141n8, 161n22, 161n23
Potarca, G. 142n46
Pozo, S. 174n6
Prazeras, L. 24n55
Pritchett, L. 46n13
proximate drivers 61–62
Puhrmann, A 161n22
purchasing price parity 35–36, 47n35
Purkayastha, B. 117n52, 117n56
push-pull theory 27, 70
Pytlikova, M. 74, 92n6, 92n12

Qian, Z. 137, 142n45

Raihan, S. 86, 93n53

Raker, E. 52, 60, 67n12, 68n38, 68n39
Ramirez, A.L. 47n51, 47n58
Ramon, C. 175n19
Ramos, M. 47n61
Randazzo, T. 86, 93n54
Rangel, C. 46n7, 46n9
Ravenstein, E. 46n2
refugees 8–11, 144–145, 170–171
relative deprivation 34–35
remittances 30, 84–87
Rendall, M.C. 47n47
residual method 97
return migration 87–91
Riosmena, F. 92n21
Robey, J.P. 174n11
Rogers, A. 24n60
Rosales, R. 115n4, 117n64
Roth, C. 175n41s
Rumbaut, R.G. 142n6

Saarinen, J. 161n26
Sacchetto, D. 92n14
Sachs, J.D. 22n1
Saguin, K. 94n73
Salaff, J.W. 94n63
Salah, M. 174
Salant, B. 24n58
Salikutluk, Z 141n12
Salzmann, Z. 92n5
Sam, D.L. 141n1
sanctuary cities 165–166
Schatral, S. 24n43
Schewel, K. 46n16
Schiller, N.G. 81, 93n30
Schinkel, W. 119, 141n4
Schneider, J. 161n35
Schneider, N.F. 143n56
Schwirtz, M. 24n41
Seabrooke, L. 23n28
Seagrave, M. 102, 116n23
segmented assimilation 120, 127
selectivity, *see* migrant selectivity
Semyonov, M. 125, 141n22
Sener, M.Y. 94n69
Serpa, S. 46n25
sexual exploitation 109–111
Shaeye, A. 92n10
Shams, T. 140, 143n71
Shibuya, K. 93n39, 93n42
Shon, J.L. 142n38
Singha, S. 96, 115n5
slow-onset events 48–53, 56, 61
smugglers 105–108
socioeconomic status and; integration 120–122; selectivity 122–124
Song, S. 95, 115n2
Sontag, K. 23n29

Sorensen, M.S. 169n16
Soysal, Y.N. 45, 47n62
Stark, O. 34, 46n24
Steinhardt, M.F. 68n19
step-wise migration 11, 80–82
Storeygard, A. 68n28
Stouffer, S.A. 46n30
Strang, A. 118, 141n3
Su, J.H. 115n6
Sultianti, D. 25n78
Susewind, R. 160n19
Switzer, D. 67n15

Tamborini, C. 127, 142n29
Tansel, A. 92n2
Tavaro, M.F. 23n30
Taylor, J.S. 24n67
Telles, E.E. 141n23, 142n31
ten Berge, J.M. 47n59
Tetteh, B.K. 67n14
Thomas, M.J. 80, 93n29
Todaro, M. 29–31, 46n12
Torngren, S.O. 142n43
tourism and; enclaves 154–155; medical treatment 21–22; migration 19–21, 154
trafficking 11–12, 107–111
Tran, V.C. 47n48, 121, 141n10
transnational corporations 1–2
transnational professionals 7–8
transnationalism 140–141
Tumin, D. 142n50
Turkewitz, J. 46n8
Turner, S. 160n5
Tzaninis, Y. 161n36

Ubfal, D. 175n41
Ueno, H. 117n65
Undurrago, R. 174n5

Valluvan, S. 174n3
van de Worfhorst, H.G. 122, 141n11, 141n17
van der Geest, K. 63n17, 68n47
Van Hear, N. 46n4

van Schendel, W. 68n22
VanLiempt, I. 93n33
VanOudenhoven 47n59
Vaughan, J. 24n59
Vaughn, J. 92n20, 117n58
Verdery, A. 68n21, 92n18
Verdugo, G. 142n38
Vergov, P. 142n35
Veronis, L. 68n33
Villarreal, A. 127, 142n29
visa overstays 111–113
Vogel, D. 101, 116n19
Vogiazides, L. 128, 142n37
Voigiazides, L. 142n37

Wagner, I. 23n32
Waldron, D. 117n60
Ward, Z. 89, 94n60
Warren, R. 99, 116n9, 116n14
Wassink, J.T. 94n67, 94n71, 115n1
Waters, M.C. 68n38
Weitzer, R. 117n55
welfare dependence 166–167
welfare magnet 37–38
Werfhorst, H.G. 122, 124, 141n11, 141n17
Wesselbaum, D. 58, 67n4, 67n31, 67n32
Williams, N. 68n21, 92n18
Wunch-Vincent, S. 24n37

xenophobia 162–163
Xu, Z. 68n37

Yeung, W.J. 24n65
Ylikoski, P. 46n10
Yeoh, B.H. 93n41
Yousaf, F.N. 117n52, 117n56
Yoo, T.J. 141n13

Zehn, Y. 92n10
Zelinsky, W. 32, 46n19
Zharkevich, I. 85–86, 93n52
Zimmerman, C. 38, 47n41
Zug, M. 24n63